The New Is
Not Yet Born

The New Is Not Yet Born

Conflict Resolution in Southern Africa

Thomas Ohlson
Stephen John Stedman

with Robert Davies

THE BROOKINGS INSTITUTION
Washington, D.C.

Library of Congress Cataloging-in-Publication data:
Ohlson, Thomas.
    The new is not yet born : conflict resolution in southern Africa / Thomas Ohlson,
    Stephen John Stedman, with Robert Davies.
       p. cm.
    Includes bibliographical references and index.
    ISBN 0-8157-6452-9 (alk. paper) — ISBN 0-8157-6451-0 (alk. paper : pbk.)
    1. Africa, Southern—Politics and government—1975– 2. South Africa—Politics and
    government—1989– 3. Nationalism—Africa, Southern. 4. Africa,
    Southern—Economic conditions—1975–
I. Stedman, Stephen John. II. Title
DT1165.O35   1994
968.06—dc20   93-51052
                                                     CIP

9 8 7 6 5 4 3 2 1

The paper used in this publication meets the minimum requirements of the American
National Standard for Information Sciences—Permanence of paper for Printed Library
Materials, ANSI Z39.48-1984

Set in Palatino

Composition by AlphaTechnologies/mps
Mechanicsville, Maryland

Printed by R.R. Donnelley and Sons Co.
Harrisonburg, Virginia

ⒷTHE BROOKINGS INSTITUTION

The Brookings Institution is an independent organization devoted to nonpartisan research, education, and publication in economics, government, foreign policy, and the social sciences generally. Its principal purposes are to aid in the development of sound public policies and to promote public understanding of issues of national importance.

The Institution was founded on December 8, 1927, to merge the activities of the Institute for Government Research, founded in 1916, the Institute of Economics, founded in 1922, and the Robert Brookings Graduate School of Economics and Government, founded in 1924.

The Board of Trustees is responsible for the general administration of the Institution, while the immediate direction of the policies, program, and staff is vested in the President, assisted by an advisory committee of the officers and staff. The by-laws of the Institution state: "It is the function of the Trustees to make possible the conduct of scientific research, and publication, under the most favorable conditions, and to safeguard the independence of the research staff in the pursuit of their studies and in the publication of the results of such studies. It is not a part of their function to determine, control, or influence the conduct of particular investigations or the conclusions reached."

The President bears final responsibility for the decision to publish a manuscript as a Brookings book. In reaching his judgment on the competence, accuracy, and objectivity of each study, the President is advised by the director of the appropriate research program and weighs the views of a panel of expert outside readers who report to him in confidence on the quality of the work. Publication of a work signifies that it is deemed a competent treatment worthy of public consideration but does not imply endorsement of conclusions or recommendations.

Foreword

Southern Africa's vast economic potential has been distorted if not lost for decades as a result of violent conflicts. As Thomas Ohlson, Stephen John Stedman, and Robert Davies detail in this book, the struggles of the peoples of the region for political and economic justice have prevented development. Although the precise nature of the new order in southern Africa remains uncertain, the authors evaluate both the difficult challenges ahead and the enormous capacities of the region.

This volume is part of the Brookings series on conflict resolution in Africa. The first volume, *Conflict Resolution in Africa*, edited by Francis M. Deng and I. William Zartman, included papers presented at an October 1989 research conference. As a result of that conference, Brookings commissioned several regional case studies to provide an empirical basis for understanding the complex and interlinked conflict issues on the continent. This book is the first of those case studies.

Recent changes in the world are abundantly clear in Southern Africa. Since our 1989 conference, Nelson Mandela went from prison to winning South Africa's first nonracial election, Zambia transferred power democratically, Namibia received its independence, and an agreement to end the conflict in Mozambique was negotiated. However, the tragic events that continue to unfold in Angola following a failed attempt to end conflict caution us that resolution is a process fraught with setbacks.

Thomas Ohlson is a research fellow at the Department for Peace and Conflict Research at the University of Uppsala. Previously, he headed a research program at the Centro de Estudos Africanos, Eduardo Mondlane University, in Maputo, Mozambique. He consults regularly on Southern Africa for the Swedish International Development Agency. Stephen John Stedman is an assistant professor of African studies and comparative politics at the Johns Hopkins University School of Advanced International Studies. In 1993 he was a Fulbright senior research fellow at the University of the Western Cape, South Africa. He was an official international observer of Angola's election in September 1992 and South Africa's election in April 1994. Robert Davies is codirector of the Centre for Southern African Studies at the University of the Western Cape. The authors are grateful to the staff and students of their respective universities for their encouragement and assistance.

This book is a collaborative product. The sequence of chapters, their overall content, and the general flow of the argument were jointly conceived and developed by the principal authors of the volume, Ohlson and Stedman. Together they drafted all the chapters. Robert Davies contributed ideas and sections for chapters 3 and 8. After the initial draft was completed in April 1993, Stedman rewrote the manuscript and brought it up to date.

The authors want to thank Francis M. Deng, Terrence P. Lyons, and Director John D. Steinbruner of the Brookings Foreign Policy Studies program for giving advice and support, and Gilbert Khadiagala, Donald Rothchild, and I. William Zartman for each reading a complete draft. They are grateful to Corinne Thomas and Margareta Eliason for their encouragement. They would also like to acknowledge their many colleagues and friends in Southern Africa, without whose practical experience, academic expertise, political insights, and friendship this book could not have been written. None are mentioned here, but none are forgotten. Donna Verdier edited the manuscript; Khalid Medani verified its factual content; Kirsten Soule prepared the manuscript for publication; and Max Franke provided the index.

This conflict resolution project was made possible by a grant from the Carnegie Corporation of New York. Other activities supporting the project were funded by the Rockefeller Foundation and the Rockefeller Brothers Fund. Brookings gratefully acknowledges this support.

The views expressed in this book are those of the authors and should not be ascribed to the people whose assistance is acknowledged, to the organizations that supported the project, or to the trustees, officers, or staff members of the Brookings Institution.

BRUCE K. MAC LAURY
President

June 1994
Washington, D.C.

Contents

Part 2: National Conflict in Southern Africa

Part 3: The Regional Question

Acronyms of Southern African Groups and Organizations

Aford	Alliance for Democracy
ANC	African National Congress
ASP	Afro Shirazi Party (merged with TANU into CCM)
AWB	Afrikaner Weerstandsbeweging (Afrikaner Resistance Movement)
AZAPO	Azanian People's Organization
BCP	Basutoland Congress Party
BDP	Botswana Democratic Party
BNP	Basotho National Party
BPP	Botswana People's Party
CCM	Chama cha Mapinduzi
CODESA	Convention for a Democratic South Africa
CONSAS	Constellation of Southern African States
COREMO	Comitê Revolucionário de Moçambique
COSAG	Concerned South Africans Group
COSAS	Congress of South African Students
COSATU	Congress of South African Trade Unions
FAPLA	Forças Armadas Populares de Libertação de Angola
FLEC	Front for the Liberation of the Enclave of Cabinda
FLS	Front Line States
FNLA	Frente Nacional de Libertação de Angola
FRELIMO	Frente de Libertação de Moçambique
IFP	Inkatha Freedom Party
MCP	Malawi Congress Party
MDM	Mass Democratic Movement
MMD	Mass Movement for Democracy
MNR	Mozambique National Resistance (original name of RENAMO)
NP	National Party

OAU	Organization for African Unity
PAC	Pan Africanist Congress of Azania
PF	Patriotic Front
PLAN	People's Liberation Army of Namibia
Pudemo	People's United Democratic Movement
RENAMO	Resistência Nacional Moçambicana (see MNR)
SACU	Southern African Customs Union
SADC	Southern African Development Community (see SADCC)
SADCC	Southern African Development Coordination Conference (now known as SADC)
SADF	South African Defence Force
SWAPO	South West African People's Organization
SWATF	South West African Territorial Forces
TANU	Tanganyika African National Union (merged with ASP into CCM)
UDF	United Democratic Front
UNAMO	União Africana de Moçambique Independente
UNIP	United National Independence Party
UNITA	União Nacional para a Independência Total de Angola
UPA	União das Populaçoes de Angola
ZANLA	Zimbabwe African National Liberation Army
ZANU	Zimbabwe African National Union
ZAPU	Zimbabwe African People's Union
ZIPRA	Zimbabwean People's Revolutionary Army

Chapter 1

Southern Africa's Interregnum

South African writers, using Antonio Gramsci's notion, often referred to the 1980s in their country as the "interregnum." As Gramsci put it, "The old is dying, and the new cannot be born; in this interregnum a great variety of morbid symptoms appear."[1] Nadine Gordimer, Andre Brink, Sipho Sepamla, and J. M. Coetzee, among others, described a country seemingly impervious to change yet teeming with contradictions and disparities that could ultimately lead to genocide. In 1990, however, the South African government unbanned the African National Congress (ANC) and the South African Communist Party, released Nelson Mandela from prison, and began to eliminate the legal trappings of apartheid. Optimism abounded throughout Southern Africa. A new South Africa, embodying all of that country's tremendous diversity and strengths, seemed on the verge of birth.

The gestation period has proved longer than optimists had hoped. By the end of 1993 the main parties to the conflict in South Africa, the ANC and the National Party (NP), had finally agreed on the outlines of a political settlement. The former antagonists established a transitional executive council that would steer the country to elections in April 1994. South African voters would then elect—for the first time on the basis of "one person, one vote"—an interim government of national unity and a constituent assembly. That assembly would write South Africa's new constitution constrained by a set of principles agreed to in advance, including a justiciable bill of rights, regional powers within a unitary state, and proportional representation in elections.

1. Antonio Gramsci, *Selections from the Prison Notebooks of Antonio Gramsci*, ed. and trans. Quintin Hoare and Geoffrey Nowell Smith (New York: International Publishers, 1971), p. 276.

1

But troubling questions persist. Will the convergence of the ANC and NP survive attacks from spoilers such as the ethnically driven Inkatha Freedom Party, whose leader, Mangosuthu Buthelezi, has threatened to plunge South Africa into civil war? Or from the white right wing, whose shadowy connections to the South African Defence Force and police could render the new South Africa stillborn? Will the interim government work to build a democratic society and an equitable economy to support its transition to democracy? Or will the new partners, in the words of one radical critic, "get married and give birth to a baby named neo-colonialism"?[2]

The four years since the historic events of February 1990 are best described as South Africa's second interregnum. This one differs from that of the 1980s in two important respects. People's expectations about and demands for change have grown, and profound uncertainty about what form change would take has raised the political stakes for all concerned. Those four years have seen impressive progress in negotiations, problem solving, and conflict resolution. But in the same period political violence has claimed more lives than in all of the turbulent 1980s. One province, Natal, teeters on the brink of civil war. Massacres of civilians lead to speculations about a "third force" based in the South African military and police which wants to undermine any peaceful transition.[3] As economic growth stalls and unemployment climbs to unprecedented levels, criminal violence—theft, rape, and murder—escalates. Economic crisis, rampant violence, and the slow pace of negotiations have led some blacks to demand nothing less than revolutionary transformation. White extremist groups threaten to sabotage any agreement that falls short of granting them a racial "homeland."

The metaphor of the interregnum also describes the larger region of Southern Africa.[4] For thirty years the region was the arena for a conflict

2. Benny Alexander, secretary general of the Pan Africanist Congress, quoted in "PAC Accuses ANC of Selling Out the Struggle," *Argus*, February 16, 1993.

3. *Massacre* in this book refers to an attack in which ten or more people are injured or killed. In Natal alone there were more than 120 such attacks between 1990 and 1992. See Antoinette Louw and Simon Bekker, "Conflict in the Natal Region: A Database Approach," in Simon Bekker, ed., *Capturing the Event: Conflict Trends in the Natal Region, 1986–1992* (Durban: Centre for Social and Development Studies, 1992), pp. 49–50.

4. Southern Africa comprises the Republic of South Africa and the member

that married three different, interlocking confrontations: the struggle for independence in Angola, Mozambique, Zimbabwe, and Namibia; the attempt by South Africa to maintain white supremacy at home; and the undeclared war waged by South Africa against Mozambique, Angola, and Zimbabwe when those states gained independence.

In one sense an old era has died. A peace accord brokered by the United States led to the withdrawal of South African and Cuban troops from Angola and the attainment of independence and majority rule in Namibia. Another settlement ended the Mozambican civil war; its former combatants now campaign for the right to rule their country through elections. In 1991 Frederick Chiluba ended the twenty-seven-year reign of Kenneth Kaunda as president of Zambia, which was then only the fourth country in Africa to witness a peaceful succession of ruler by way of the ballot box. In 1993 Lesotho successfully held elections; in Malawi a referendum resulted in the overwhelming rejection of its one-party state. Only Swaziland seems immune to the trend toward multiparty democracy.

Other changes also signal the end of an era. Eight Southern African countries have undertaken extensive economic liberalization through structural adjustment programs. New leaders govern, and they hold new assumptions about regional and national politics. For instance, in the 1970s Kenneth Kaunda of Zambia, Julius Nyerere of Tanzania, Seretse Khama of Botswana, and Samora Machel of Mozambique—all associated with the early struggle for independence—sought regional cooperation against South Africa. Since then two of those leaders have died, one has retired, and one was voted out of office. Their replacements are less enamored with regional solidarity and are more likely to emphasize narrowly construed national interests.

The triumphs of conflict resolution in Namibia and Zimbabwe, as well as the halting progress toward majority rule in South Africa, raise hopes that Southern Africa might break free from insecurity, militarization, and underdevelopment. Yet recent events raise doubts. Civil war resumed in Angola when UNITA (União Nacional para a Independência Total de Angola) refused to accept its defeat in elections supervised by the United Nations. Large-scale violence threatens to infect the

---

states of the Southern African Development Community, which are Angola, Botswana, Lesotho, Malawi, Mozambique, Namibia, Swaziland, Tanzania, Zambia, and Zimbabwe.

region as Mobutu Sese Seko attempts to cling to power in Zaire. And the precarious cease-fire in Mozambique has been violated repeatedly by one of its signatories, RENAMO (Resistência Nacional Moçambicana). Despite all the positive changes and enormous potential of Southern Africa, the economic and political difficulties facing the region could easily push it into chaos.

Conflict in Southern Africa has taken a heavy toll. Between 1980 and 1988 wars in Angola and Mozambique led to between 1.2 million and 1.9 million deaths; in Mozambique nearly 500,000 of these were children under the age of five. Some 7.5 million people in those two countries have been displaced.[5]

Alongside the cost of conflict in human lives are the more calculable economic costs. War-related damage to the economies of the region runs about $90 billion. Although the need for reconstruction is obvious, Southern African countries suffer from a crisis of economic productivity; unemployment and poverty are rampant throughout the area. Mozambique is the poorest country in the world—in 1992 the average Mozambican's standard of living was two-thirds that of the average Somalian.[6] Three countries in the region—Mozambique, Angola, and Malawi—demonstrate "extreme human suffering."[7]

Southern Africa also confronts a medical crisis. Diseases once considered controlled, such as yellow fever, typhoid, and tuberculosis, again

5. The lower figure for deaths in Angola and Mozambique comes from Phyllis Johnson and David Martin, *Apartheid Terrorism: The Destabilization Report*, report prepared for the Committee of Commonwealth Foreign Ministers on Southern Africa (London: James Currey, 1989), p. 45 (for Mozambique); and Andrew Meldrum, "Hungry to Vote," *Africa Report*, vol. 37 (November–December 1992), p. 27 (for Angola). The higher figure is derived from David Sogge, *Sustainable Peace: Angola's Recovery* (Harare: Southern Africa Research and Documentation Centre, 1992), p. 23; and Ernest Harsch and Roy Laishley, "Mozambique: Out of the Ruins of War," *Africa Recovery Briefing Paper*, no. 8 (May 1993), p. 13. Data on children's deaths in Mozambique are in United Nations and Economic Commission for Africa, *South African Destabilization: The Economic Costs of Frontline Resistance to Apartheid* (Addis Ababa: U.N. Department of Public Information, 1989), p. 3. The number of displaced persons is in Susanna Smith, *Front Line Africa: The Right to a Future* (Oxford: Oxfam, 1990), p. 49.

6. World Bank, *World Tables* (Johns Hopkins University Press, 1993), p. 3.

7. See *International Human Suffering Index* (Washington: Population Crisis Committee, 1992).

afflict the region, and in 1992 and 1993 cholera epidemics swept through Luanda, Lusaka, Harare, and Maputo. The spread of AIDS is especially alarming: 20 percent of Zimbabweans already carry the human immunodeficiency virus (HIV). Projections show a similar percentage of cases in South Africa by 2005; according to one estimate, more than 2.5 million Southern Africans will die from AIDS by that year.[8] Recurrent drought, attended by severe malnutrition and death, compounds the medical calamity. And when drought combines with war, as it has in Angola and Mozambique, millions of people face starvation.

A new Southern Africa depends on resolving Angola's long-lived civil war, reconstructing the war-damaged societies of the region, creating new institutions so that Southern Africans can manage conflicts without violence, and transforming South Africa—the region's dominant power—into a stable democracy. All this is a tall order indeed. But, with the end of minority rule in South Africa, the chance exists that the region can, for the first time, attain security for all its peoples.

PURPOSE OF THE BOOK

This book is the first in a series of case studies produced by the Brookings Institution on regional conflict and conflict resolution in Africa. In it we set out to identify the past, present, and possible future sources of conflict in Southern Africa; describe the political, socioeconomic, and security implications of conflict in the region; and evaluate institutions, organizations, and policies that might help reduce or resolve conflict and provide security for the peoples and countries of Southern Africa.

Three corresponding themes, which we return to throughout the book, emerged from our research. First, while South Africa and Southern Africa undergo tremendous changes, the effects of past conflict issues, partial resolutions of those issues, and prior methods of conflict resolution will impair the search for security in the region. Conflicts of the near and distant past have left both mental and structural legacies. Second, individual security, national security, and regional security are interdependent in Southern Africa. Conflict within countries in the region has great potential for spilling over into other countries; con-

---

8. See Alan Whiteside, "At Special Risk: AIDS in Southern Africa," *Indicator: South Africa*, vol. 10 (Summer 1992), pp. 66–72; and Mary Crewe, *AIDS in South Africa: The Myth and the Reality* (London: Penguin Books, 1992), pp. 66–67.

versely, conflicts between countries in the region can weaken the ability of states to resolve conflicts within their borders. Third, regional security in Southern Africa will demand a shift from ad hoc strategies of conflict resolution at the regional and national levels to the creation of institutions and organizations that will keep future conflict within bounds and resolve it without violence.

In exploring these themes we do not focus on the influence of extraregional actors and interests on the processes of conflict and conflict resolution. To be sure, international events and processes have played a key role in Southern Africa's history, and we credit them when credit is due. Likewise, international actions and policies can make a difference in building a more secure Southern Africa; we suggest such actions when appropriate. But we believe that the problems confronting Southern Africa can be solved only by the region's own people and leaders, for two practical reasons. First, international mediation or development assistance can perhaps lead to short-term agreements and policies, but long-term solutions hinge on Southern Africans' willingness to abide by them and on their creativity in forging institutions and organizations for security and development. Second, Southern Africa will most likely find an indifferent—if not hostile—international environment.

Change in Southern Africa takes place nested within processes of international change. The end of the cold war and the dissolution of the Soviet Union removed the superpower competition in Southern Africa, peeling away one layer of conflict that had been imposed on the region. The ending of the U.S.-USSR competition contributed to negotiated settlements in Angola and Namibia. Mikhail Gorbachev's pursuit of political liberalization in the Soviet Union, the National Party claimed, enabled the South African government to reorient its attitudes toward its opponents at home and in the region, freeing it to take the bold steps it did in February 1990.

On the other hand, the countries of Southern Africa now lack the leverage supplied by two rival blocs in the international system. The Eastern European countries that once supplied Southern Africa with aid, equipment, and assistance are now fellow supplicants to the world lending community. The demise of Soviet-style socialism forecloses one political, ideological, and economic model for the states of the region and narrows options for Southern African political elites.

Moreover, the end of the cold war and the tumult accompanying the breakup of the former Soviet Union provide a new focus for the United

States and Western Europe. If Southern Africa once found itself a pawn in the larger game between the United States and the USSR, it now may find itself not playing in the game at all.[9] Civil war rages on the borders of Europe, and the former communist regimes of Eastern Europe and the Soviet republics are destitute, pleading for help from already over-extended international aid organizations. In the words of one observer, "The East has become the South."[10] At the same time, economic recession in the United States has limited its willingness to increase the budgets of the World Bank, the International Monetary Fund (IMF), and the United Nations.[11]

Money is short, and Africa must compete for it. As countries there fall from the third world into the fourth and fifth worlds, international donors begin to practice triage. They may assist only those countries that show long-term potential for recovery or else help only countries such as Somalia where economic and political breakdown is complete. The United States, while it remains committed to providing aid and assistance to Africa in the short run, may abandon the effort. As one high-ranking American official told us, "In the short term we will continue to aid countries in Africa, especially those who make strides in democratization and economic reform. But the bottom line is that at some point soon these countries are going to have to show commercial viability."[12]

But Africa will not become commercially viable at "some point soon." Southern Africa, like the larger continent of which it is a part, is

---

9. James Goldgeier and Michael McFaul, "A Tale of Two Worlds: Core and Periphery in the Post–Cold War Era," *International Organization*, vol. 46 (Spring 1992), pp. 467–91.

10. Adam Przeworski, *Democracy and the Market: Political and Economic Reforms in Eastern Europe and Latin America* (Cambridge University Press, 1991), p. 191.

11. On the issue of American assistance to democracy in Africa, Carol Lancaster writes, "Financing these explicitly prodemocracy activities need not require large amounts of money, though certainly more is needed than the $12 million Washington currently spends. In 1992 it allotted $2 million to further civil and political rights and roughly $10 million to back democratic change in African countries. A fund of $25 to $40 million would seem more appropriate given the expanding opportunities in the more than 30 African countries undergoing political liberalization." Carol Lancaster, "Democracy in Africa," *Foreign Policy*, vol. 85 (Winter 1991–92), p. 164.

12. Confidential interview, Washington, January 1992.

simultaneously marginalized from and dependent on the international economy.[13] Private investment has all but vanished from Africa; loans and foreign aid are the sole source of external capital.

Foreign investors have little interest in Africa. The return on investments there "fell from 30.7 percent in the 1960s to just 2.5 percent in the 1980s."[14] Africa's collapse has contributed to the development of what the United Nations calls the "strategic triad" in investment: 80 percent of investment flows remain in the United States, the European Community, and Japan. Although total investment in the developing countries has increased, the *share* of total investment in those countries dropped by 7 percent during the 1980s. Three-fourths of that share went to ten countries: China, Hong Kong, Malaysia, Singapore, Thailand, Argentina, Brazil, Colombia, Mexico, and Egypt. Countries in the world's lowest income categories—many of them in Africa—received 0.7 percent of international investment in the third world.[15]

Africa will not see a new infusion of investment capital any time soon. A 1991 U.N. report states that declining worldwide foreign direct investment in developing countries is probably not going to grow in the near future, "despite efforts by nearly all of those countries to open up their economies to foreign direct investment and to liberalize their policy regimes."[16] Regionally centered trading blocs in North America, Europe, and East Asia, as well as moves to formalize them, raise the possibility of further marginalization of Africa. The U.N. report warns that developing countries face a stark choice if they want to remain in the world economy: join one of the three existing regional blocs or form one of their own.

While Africa was becoming marginalized, it also became more dependent on the IMF and the World Bank. Many African governments

13. Our analysis draws from Thomas M. Callaghy, "Africa and the World Economy: Caught between a Rock and a Hard Place," in John Harbeson and Donald Rothchild, eds., *Africa in World Politics* (Boulder, Colo.: Westview Press, 1991), pp. 39–68.

14. Callaghy, "Africa and the World Economy," p. 40.

15. Centre on Transnational Corporations, *World Investment Report, 1991: The Strategic Triad in Foreign Direct Investment* (New York: United Nations, 1991), p. 13.

16. Centre on Transnational Corporations, *World Investment Report, 1991*, p. 83.

borrowed to keep pace with social demands. Other governments borrowed to enrich the elite. Overwhelmed by debt, African governments had to bargain with the World Bank and the IMF, because these international actors controlled access to loans and influenced the willingness of foreign governments to provide assistance. In the 1980s the World Bank, in congruence with renewed favor in the United States for laissez-faire capitalism, demanded programs of severe economic reforms for the continuation of aid. By the end of the 1980s the major donor nations of the North had added political conditionalities to such aid.

Leaders in Southern Africa now find international capitalism to be the only game in town. The referees are the World Bank and the IMF; the rules are structural adjustment programs and aid conditionalities. The leaders of Southern Africa also know that they face fresh competition from the countries of Eastern Europe and the former Soviet republics. They have discovered that, in the words of Joan Robinson, "the misery of being exploited by capitalists is nothing compared to the misery of not being exploited at all."[17]

CHANGE AND THE ANALYSIS OF CONFLICT IN SOUTHERN AFRICA

In Southern Africa, as elsewhere, change takes place along different dimensions, at different rates, and sometimes in different directions. In any population we can differentiate dimensions of change in institutions (formal rules); informal constraints (norms and conventions); organizations and coalitions (groups of actors pursuing common goals); leverage (resources available to achieve goals); and structures (long-standing macrosocietal patterns of economic, political, and cultural interactions).[18] Change along one dimension need not affect other

17. Joan Robinson, *Economic Philosophy* (Chicago: Aldine Publishing, 1963), p. 45.

18. These dimensions are derived from Douglass North, *Institutions, Institutional Change and Economic Performance* (Cambridge University Press, 1991); Gabriel A. Almond and others, *Crisis, Choice, and Change* (Little, Brown, 1973); and Ernest J. Wilson III, "A Research Agenda for Reforming State and Market in Africa: A Modified Structuralist Paradigm," paper delivered at the Colloquium on the Economics of Political Liberalization in Africa, Center for Interna-

dimensions. Norms and conventions at times seem impervious to change in formal institutions. At other times formal institutions persist in the face of dramatically changed societies. In fact, powerful theories of politics have been built on the alleged implications of nonsynchronic change, as, for example, when formal institutions remain frozen while change occurs in informal conventions,[19] distributions of power,[20] or long-standing economic patterns.[21]

History matters in the study of change. It used to be axiomatic that if a society wanted to get from point x to point z, it was important to spell out the dimensions of obstacle y. Yet studies from economics suggest another consideration: the ability of a society to get from x to z depends also on how it got to x.[22] In other words, paths of change can narrow and eliminate options. Institutional legacies accumulated on the road to x, and the persistence of the mental models associated with those institutions, stand in the way of a simple progression to z.

What this means for the study of change in Southern Africa is that "what's past is prologue," *and*, as William Faulkner put it, "the past is never dead. It's not even past." In Southern Africa change must confront the structural and institutional legacies of apartheid and colonialism as well as the mental models and social repertoires of the past that people carry with them into the future.

The nonsynchronic aspect of change is crucial for understanding present developments in Southern Africa. Two examples stand out. First, since 1990 there has been a basic disjunction between governmental policies of change in South Africa and attitudes and values of some

---

tional Affairs, Harvard University, March 6–7, 1992.

19. Alexis de Tocqueville, *The Old Regime and the French Revolution*, trans. Stuart Gilbert (Doubleday, 1955).

20. George F. Kennan, *Memoirs, 1925–1950* (Little, Brown, 1967), p. 229.

21. Leon Trotsky, *The Russian Revolution: The Overthrow of Tzarism and the Triumph of the Soviets*, ed. F. W. Dupee (Doubleday, 1959). For a stimulating and incisive analysis of South Africa that combines elements from Trotsky and Tocqueville, see Robert M. Price, *The Apartheid State in Crisis: Political Transformation in South Africa, 1975–1990* (Oxford University Press, 1991).

22. This concept, called path dependency, was developed by W. Brian Arthur in "Competing Technologies, Increasing Returns, and Lock-in by Historical Events," *Economic Journal*, vol. 99 (March 1989), pp. 116–31. The concept has become a central part of Douglass North's approach to institutional change. See North, *Institutions, Institutional Change and Economic Performance*.

officials within the government. The South African government pledged itself to the U.N. mandate to neutrally oversee the Namibian elections and transition, embarked on a democratic transition itself, and hailed the dawn of a new era of nonracialism in South Africa. Concurrently, elements within that same government surreptitiously and illegally violated the pledge of neutrality in Namibia; trained former Namibian counterinsurgency fighters for clandestine action against citizens of the new South Africa; and funded, armed, and trained Inkatha Freedom Party forces for action against the African National Congress.[23] More recently, members of the South African Defence Force officially participated, for the first time, in a meeting of military representatives from all the countries of the region in May 1993; two of the South African officers stunned other participants when they asserted that South Africa still might need to fight an anticommunist insurgency in the region.

A second gap exists between policies, institutions, and values, on the one hand, and patterns of economic and social behavior, on the other. Profound change in policies and institutions in South Africa may gain legal equality for the black majority. But change in the structural legacy of white domination will not match the pace of formal political change. Ownership of capital, resources, and land, as well as vast differences in life expectancy, infant mortality, employment, and literacy, will continue to disproportionately benefit white South Africans.

Here the contrast between Southern Africa and Eastern Europe is informative. The revolutions in Eastern Europe discredited an ideology and a way of life. The transition to democracy and capitalism in Eastern Europe takes place amid a radical shift in social and economic patterns of behavior. In South Africa apartheid as an official policy is on its deathbed, but apartheid as a way of life—a way of structuring life chances, economics, and job opportunities—will prove tenacious. So will the racism that apartheid nurtured. Thus in South Africa apartheid as a formal model will end; apartheid as a mental and social model will persist.

23. Eddie Koch and Philippa Garson, "The Third Force: Two Hit-Squad Men Speak," *Weekly Mail*, January 4–24, 1992, p. 1.

THE INTERDEPENDENCE OF SECURITY IN SOUTHERN AFRICA

Until recently the study of international security presumed that security was a problem for integrated nation-states facing threats from other such integrated states. International relations could therefore be considered apart from comparative politics. Security studies could claim to be simply "the study of the threat, use, and control of military force."[24]

The breakup of the former USSR and Yugoslavia, however, illustrates a reality familiar to those who study regional security in the third world: the existence of the state cannot be taken for granted. As Barry Buzan observes,

> The concept of national security requires national objects as its points of reference, and in very weak states such as Lebanon, Mozambique, Chad and Uganda, these hardly exist. To view such a state in the same security terms as one would view Sweden or Japan is misleading. When there is almost no idea of the state, and the governing institutions are themselves the main threat to many individuals, national security almost ceases to have content.[25]

In this book we treat security in Southern Africa as an interdependent relationship that encompasses the individual, national, and regional levels. In much of the region the state itself has been the biggest threat to individual security; in others that threat has been the absence of a functioning state. Where the state cannot or will not protect its people in their daily lives, individuals live out a Hobbesian nightmare. In Southern Africa the most physically insecure people are women and children, who bear the brunt of violence.

24. Stephen M. Walt, "The Renaissance of Security Studies," *International Studies Quarterly*, vol. 35 (June 1991), p. 212. This twenty-eight-page article, which purports to be an assessment of the current state of security as well as a call for future research, does not refer at all to the third world or the South or its periphery, nor does it suggest that civil war and internal disorder might be areas for security studies.

25. Barry Buzan, *People, States and Fear: An Agenda for International Security Studies in the Post–Cold War Era*, 2d ed. (Boulder, Colo.: Lynne Rienner Publishers, 1991), p. 101.

If the very units that constitute a region are themselves in question, then internal disorder becomes regional disorder. Conflicts within countries in Southern Africa frequently visit neighboring territories. Insurgents cross borders with impunity in search of safe-haven; armies cross borders to find and destroy them. Victims of domestic violence flee their countries to escape conflict and thus overtax the carrying capacity of their neighbors.

Even if states are well defined, internal conflicts often become regional ones. For instance, in its attempt to maintain apartheid at home, the South African government set out to punish any country in the region that supported the struggle against apartheid within South Africa. In turn, conflicts between the nations of Southern Africa exacerbate tensions and conflicts within those nations.

Other, less martial changes in one country also ripple throughout the region. The end of one-party rule in Zambia fueled demands for an end to the one-party regime in Tanzania and to the autocracy in Malawi. People in South Africa look to Namibia and Zimbabwe in the hope of seeing racial reconciliation. And, of course, the region is so intertwined economically that the development of individual countries can be impaired or promoted by the economic actions of neighbors.

For analytic purposes we have to treat the national and regional levels as distinct. Nonetheless, we maintain that regional security in Southern Africa depends on security within states as much as on security between states.

CONFLICT RESOLUTION: BUILDING INSTITUTIONS AND ORGANIZATIONS

Conflict in Southern Africa takes many forms. Among other things it can be manifest or latent, and it can arise from differences over values, interests, or resources. We therefore define conflict broadly, as a social situation in which at least two parties try to acquire the same set of scarce material or immaterial resources at the same time.[26]

Conflict resolution is best understood as a *process* that involves one or several of four different strategies:

26. Peter Wallensteen, "Understanding Conflict Resolution: A Framework," in Peter Wallensteen, ed., *Peace Research: Achievements and Challenges* (Boulder, Colo.: Westview Press, 1988), p. 120.

—Moving the system of actors, issues, and actions away from a focus on incompatibility toward a focus on compatibility.

—Reducing the level of destructive action by various means and transferring the conflict from a violent to a nonviolent level, albeit without removing any of the basic incompatibilities.

—Solving the basic incompatibilities as they are perceived by the parties so that the parties voluntarily express satisfaction with the outcome.

—Transforming entire conflict formations and changing the relationship between the parties from one of conflict to one of peace.[27]

Conflict resolution has succeeded ad hoc in Southern Africa only when violence has erupted and continued for years. Violence itself has been a strategy for conflict resolution, a strategy that has exacted an enormous toll. The challenge for the future of Southern Africa will be one of *peacebuilding*. Institutions and organizations must be created at the local, national, and regional levels to bound conflict within and between nations so that conflicts can be resolved without violence.

The creation of new institutions in Southern Africa will depend on the interests and resources of the different actors in the region. The effects of violence have driven those actors to see some mutual interest in resolving future conflict. But any new political or economic institution—whether federalism, consociationalism, or parliamentary democracy at the national level or customs unions, security regimes, or free trade zones at the regional level—will have distributional consequences, and actors will of course try to create arrangements favorable to their own interests. This poses a grave problem for Southern Africa, where power and economic relationships are so asymmetrical. How can those with preponderant economic, political, and military strength be persuaded to take part in arrangements that would lead to an equitable sharing of power and resources? We return to this question throughout the book.

ORGANIZATION OF THE BOOK

The book is divided into three parts. Part 1 focuses on those elements of past conflict and conflict resolution that will play a part in future efforts

27. Wallensteen, "Understanding Conflict Resolution," pp. 123–25.

at building security in Southern Africa. Part 2 turns to the present and examines conflict and conflict resolution at the national level in Southern Africa. Part 3 examines potential interstate conflict issues and the capacity of the region to construct strategies for resolving those issues.

Part 1: Past Conflict

Chapter 2 describes conflict legacies distant in time that continue to affect possibilities for stable peace. It argues that the eventual conjunction of settler colonialism, racism, and the mineral rush of the late 1800s led to an integrated economic region predicated on white domination. Global changes after World War II as well as domestic changes in South Africa prompted sustained resistance to such domination, but in the early 1970s Southern Africa remained the last redoubt for colonialism.

Chapter 3 examines developments in the region after the Portuguese withdrawal from Southern Africa. South Africa's rulers, confronting hostile states outside its borders and greater opposition within, initiated a regional war that would last more than a decade, with devastating consequences. By the end of the 1980s policies of regional destabilization and limited domestic reform had brought the National Party to a dead end from which only negotiation could deliver it.

Chapter 4 compares the successes and failures of conflict resolution efforts from 1974 to 1992 and seeks lessons that might be drawn from those attempts at peacemaking. It also notes that many important conflict issues remain unresolved, and attempts at their resolution will be constrained by compromises reached in the past.

Part 2: National Conflict in Southern Africa

As the overriding conflict in Southern Africa—the attempt by South Africa to maintain white supremacy in the region and at home—draws to a close, new problems and conflict issues will come to the fore. Chapters 5, 6, and 7 map out these likely conflicts and examine the capacity of national institutions to resolve them.

Chapter 5 focuses on South Africa's second interregnum and the attempts by political parties and societal actors to resolve the conflict legacies of apartheid. From 1990 to 1994 conflict resolution in South Africa exhibited two contradictory impulses—one toward problem solving and cooperation and the other toward political predominance.

Although problem solving narrowed differences among elites over issues of political participation, violence and security, and economic strategy, conflict resolution remains incomplete in South Africa. The new government of Nelson Mandela faces major challenges in creating a secure, just nation.

Chapter 6 presents a country-by-country survey to uncover existing and potential intrastate conflict issues in Southern Africa. Chapter 7 explores the capabilities and the institutions that will be needed for the individual countries of the region to provide security for their peoples. Since most of the countries of Southern Africa are simultaneously implementing programs of economic liberalization and democratization, the chapter also examines possible trade-offs among state building, democracy, and economic structural adjustment.

Part 3: The Regional Question

Chapter 8 examines possible interstate conflict issues that Southern Africa will confront in the near future and evaluates the potential for resolving them without violence. In addition to tensions caused by the spillover of domestic conflicts, the region will face crises caused by interdependency, such as shortages of resources, large-scale labor migration, and the need for regional responses to drought, development, and disease. Southern Africa will also face conflict arising from South Africa's dominant economic and military position in the region. The chapter concludes by assessing norms and institutions that could foster cooperation within the region.

Chapter 9 summarizes our findings. Regional security in Southern Africa hinges on national and regional processes. At the national level, the key process is the consolidation of viable states and civil societies; at the regional level, cooperation depends on norms of amity and the creation of institutions and organizations to promote security and equitable development. We conclude by suggesting ways that international action and policy can act as midwife to a new Southern Africa.

PART 1

Past Conflict

Chapter 2

Setting the Stage

A regional security complex is "a set of states whose major security perceptions and concerns are so interlinked that their national security problems cannot reasonably be analyzed apart from one another. . . . Security interdependence is markedly more intense between the states inside such complexes than it is between states inside the complex and those outside it."[1] Southern Africa forms such a complex, ranging from Angola, southern Zaire, and Tanzania in the north to South Africa in the south.

The present-day Southern African regional security complex emerged only recently. Economic and political ramifications of the mineral revolution of 1870–1920 linked the Portuguese presence in Angola and Mozambique to the British and Dutch settlements in South Africa. The sense of regional security interdependency intensified in the 1960s when wars for national liberation began in the Portuguese colonies, independence came to the British colonies, and armed struggle started against the white settler communities in Southern Rhodesia, South Africa, and South-West Africa.

Cumulative legacies of conflicts over race, land, labor, and political rights created the current Southern African security complex, which developed in four stages. The first stage of encounter is marked by two separate historical processes: the Portuguese invasion of what is now Angola and Mozambique, starting in the late 1400s, and the Dutch and British invasion of South Africa, beginning in 1652 and in the early 1800s, respectively. The second stage can be traced to the discovery of gold and diamonds in South Africa near the end of the nineteenth century and the frenzied search for minerals elsewhere in Southern

1. Barry Buzan and others, *The European Security Order Recast: Scenarios for the Post–Cold War Era* (London: Pinter, 1990), pp. 13–14.

Africa. Further evolution to a third stage took place after World War II, when international norms against racism and colonialism led to a great global wave of decolonization. The final stage in the creation of the Southern African security complex began in the mid-1970s with the collapse of the Portuguese empire and the regional destabilization begun by South Africa.

This chapter focuses on the first three stages. The more recent past is covered in chapter 3.

THE FIRST STAGE: ENCOUNTERING THE OTHER

For at least the last 500 years violent conflict has been endemic in Southern Africa. Portugal introduced the slave trade to the coast of what is now Angola in the early 1500s and to Mozambique in the 1600s. Between 1500 and 1800 the Portuguese exported more than three million slaves from Angola alone.[2] The trade in human lives decimated African societies, in some cases prompting violent resistance toward the European intruders but for the most part engendering a permanent state of internal war since many African rulers embraced the slave trade in order to profit from it. The most enduring *political* effect of the slave trade on the peoples of Angola was to splinter the Kongo Kingdom and other nascent states in the region into competing, armed, slave-raiding bands.[3] Similarly, in Mozambique, *prazos*, or plantations based on slave labor, became de facto independent feudal enclaves supplied by marauding warrior groups.

Portugal's presence in Angola and Mozambique was minimal, however, limited to small armed settlements on the coasts of the Atlantic and Indian oceans. By 1850, for example, there were only about 2,000 Portuguese in all of Angola (out of the total African population of

2. Paul E. Lovejoy, *Transformations in Slavery: A History of Slavery in Africa* (Cambridge University Press, 1983), pp. 73–74.

3. Lovejoy (*Transformations in Slavery*, pp. 73–78) refers to the period as one of "warlordism" in Angola. On the general effects of slavery on political and social life in Africa, see Mbaye Gueye, "The Slave Trade within the African Continent," in *The African Slave Trade from the Fifteenth to the Nineteenth Century* (Paris: Unesco, 1979).

5,500,000). In 1860 the Portuguese began a prolonged attempt to create a firmer hold in Angola, which was repelled in 1870 when a series of rebellions forced them to evacuate their garrison in the capital of the remnant Kingdom of the Kongo. In Mozambique Portuguese control was even more tenuous. In 1860 there were only about 100 Portuguese living in Lourenço Marques (now Maputo).[4]

The political disintegration caused by the overseas slave trade had long-lasting effects. Even when the overseas trade was abolished in the 1860s, the warlords of Angola and Mozambique continued to deal in slavery until the 1920s.[5] Corrupt Portuguese authorities in Luanda and Lourenço Marques continued to export slaves to São Tomé and Madagascar.

Portugal gradually turned to the production of rubber and coffee in Angola and cotton in Mozambique, substituting forced labor for slavery. It also used its colonies as dumping grounds for its criminals. The combination of violent coercion and exploitation eventually earned the Portuguese colonial system the epithet of *Raubwirtschaft*, or robbery economy.[6]

To the south of the Portuguese slave ports in what is now the Western Cape of South Africa, a small band of Dutch settlers arrived in 1652 to set up a way station for the Dutch East Indies Company. The settlers traded with the indigenous Khoisans—metal, tobacco, and liquor for Khoisan cattle—to supply East Indies–bound ships with food and provisions. Members of the settlement eventually moved inland, appropriating large tracts of land for grazing, along with any livestock that was on it. The Boers (as they called themselves) clashed with the African

4. Angolan figures are from Gerald J. Bender, *Angola under the Portuguese: The Myth and the Reality* (University of California Press, 1978), p. 20. The number for Lourenço Marques is from Jeanne Penvenne, "We Are All Portuguese! Challenging the Political Economy of Assimilation: Lourenço Marques, 1870–1933," in Leroy Vail, ed., *The Creation of Tribalism in Southern Africa* (University of California Press, 1989), p. 262.

5. Allen Isaacman and Anton Rosenthal, "Slaves, Soldiers, and Police: Power and Dependency among the Chikunda of Mozambique, ca. 1825–1920," and Linda M. Heywood, "Slavery and Forced Labor in the Changing Political Economy of Central Angola, 1850–1949," in Suzanne Miers and Richard Roberts, eds., *The End of Slavery in Africa* (University of Wisconsin Press, 1988).

6. William Minter, *King Solomon's Mines Revisited: Western Interests and the Burdened History of Southern Africa* (Basic Books, 1986), p. 30.

inhabitants over the seizure of land and livestock. From the mid-1700s to the mid-1800s a series of wars were fought along the frontier of white expansion, first to the north and then to the east of the Cape. The intrusion of the settlers and their expropriation of land and cattle disrupted the already fragile carrying capacity of the South African ecology.

Even before the new intruders came, shortages of resources had fueled wars among African communities. Early frontier wars between the Boers and the Xhosas in the late 1700s were fought not only because the Boers were encroaching on Xhosa lands but because intra-Xhosa warfare drove some Xhosas toward the Boer settlements. Recent studies have concluded that the series of deadly wars fought between Africans in Natal in the 1820s, the Mfecane, or "Great Crushing," was caused by a crisis of drought, overgrazing, and expansion to find water and land for survival.[7]

The civil servants of the Dutch East India Company who administered the Cape Colony considered the Boer-African frontier wars a nuisance. As far as they were concerned, Cape Colony was simply a depot for ships serving the Asian trade, and its stability and security were being endangered by the willfulness of the Boer settlers. For example, toward the end of the 1770s the inland Boers found themselves overextended in a guerrilla war with the region's San peoples. Given the Boers' precarious hold in the interior, such a war should have bred caution, which was the course urged by Cape Colony administrators. Instead, the settlers chose to provoke additional African resistance from the Xhosa peoples by continually raiding their cattle. One historian sees in this early episode basic tendencies that would resonate throughout South Africa's history:

> This narrow self-interest and severely limited sense of collective obligation came to the fore in this first, curious "war" as the strangest and most dangerous side of the frontier character. It meant that the frontier Boers seldom appeared to recognize either their own best interests, or the ultimate consequences of their actions. They would, it would often seem, carelessly bring a storm of ruination

---

7. Elizabeth A. Eldredge, "Sources of Conflict in Southern Africa, ca. 1800–30: The 'Mfecane' Reconsidered," *Journal of African History*, vol. 33 (1992), pp. 1–35.

and havoc upon themselves and their neighbors for the sake of apparently negligible gain or stubborn grievance.[8]

Two patterns describe relations between Dutch settlers and Africans in this period. First, the early Cape Dutch East India economy was based on slavery, which bred a patriarchal master-servant relationship between the Cape gentry and their slaves inside the colony.[9] That mode of slavery, although grounded ultimately on force, demanded reciprocity and obligations from the master. Boers who ventured to the frontier hoped to replicate such a relationship as a way to affirm their social status. On the other hand, relations between Boer and African on the frontier frequently were marked by acknowledged interdependence: "Proximity and intimacy achieved familiarity, sensual gratification, shared lifestyle and mutual convenience, but not tolerance or understanding."[10]

When the British seized the colony from the Dutch in 1806, the tension between settlers and colonial authorities intensified. The Cape became part of the British empire during the most dynamic period of Britain's industrial revolution. Although the British seized the Cape to secure the sea route to Asia, on which so much of its trade depended, it quickly sought to establish a prosperous, capitalist colony there.

Violence soon erupted between Boer slaveholding farmers and the British, who implemented legislation conducive to the free labor market requirements of the new era. The British colonial government crushed a series of minor rebellions by Boer farmers in the first three decades of the 1800s and abolished slavery in 1834.

British liberalism in the Cape was "Janus-faced."[11] On the one hand, British liberalism could value free labor and conceive of education, wealth, and religious instruction as steps to equality, although that view was usually laced with skepticism that the African could ever

8. Noel Mostert, *Frontiers: The Epic of South Africa's Creation and the Tragedy of the Xhosa People* (Alfred A. Knopf, 1992), p. 232.

9. Clifton C. Crais, *The Making of the Colonial Order: White Supremacy and Black Resistance in the Eastern Cape, 1770–1865* (Witswatersrand University Press, 1992), pp. 33–35.

10. Mostert, *Frontiers*, p. 241.

11. Martin Legassick, "The State, Racism and the Rise of Capitalism in the Nineteenth-Century Cape Colony," *South African Historical Journal*, vol. 28 (1993), pp. 329–68.

achieve true equality. The "enlightenment" face of British liberalism outlawed slavery, and when it resurrected various prohibitions on free labor, it did so in nonracial terms. When Britain devolved a measure of self-government to the Cape Colony, it insisted on a color-blind franchise with voting restrictions limited to property or legal employment. Yet British liberalism was capable of appalling atrocity. In the Eastern Frontier of the Cape, where interaction between white and black was most acute, the British settlers of Grahamstown in 1820 injected the most virulent racism known in South Africa. That racism arose when the Xhosa peoples refused to give up their traditional agricultural way of life to become laborers for the white economy. The settlers soon characterized the Africans as the antithesis of progress, describing them as "libidinous, uncontrolled, lazy and disrespectful of established authority."[12]

The British colonial army fought a series of wars in the Eastern Cape between 1811 and 1855. During that time the African went, in British eyes, from noble savage awaiting religious and economic conversion to "irreclaimable." Such wars differed dramatically from the frontier wars of the 1700s and the African wars of the same period, when rival groups fought limited conflicts over land, cattle, and resources. The military campaigns against the Xhosa and their allies eventually became total wars, with the Xhosa character at the root of the conflict, according to the British. By the 1850s scorched-earth tactics, indiscriminate slaughter, and induced famines had destroyed the social order of the Xhosa peoples.

By depicting the African as the antithesis of progress, liberalism could justify atrocity. British colonial representatives thought the destruction of Xhosa traditional institutions and way of life was necessary for the group's advancement, which recalls the comment made by an American soldier in Vietnam that "We had to destroy the village to save it." The perception of the African that developed in the early nineteenth century became the chief justification for British colonialism throughout Africa in the late nineteenth century.

British state building in the nineteenth century yielded another far-reaching legacy, that of using the state to enforce racial categorization and discrimination. "Pass laws," which restricted the movement of Africans in white areas, and "native reserves"—isolated, usually barren

12. Crais, *Making of the Colonial Order*, p. 129.

areas where Africans were forced to live—were inventions of the British colonial state. They were inventions that would be used repeatedly throughout the region in the twentieth century.[13]

The British wars on the Eastern Frontier made the Boers who had settled there intensely insecure. Frustrated by British edicts on the "proper" treatment of Africans and endangered by British inability to provide protection against the Africans they had provoked, the Boers set out on "the Great Trek" away from the Cape and the reach of colonial authority. This expansion, once again, led to bloodshed between the white settlers and the African inhabitants of the distant lands, in this case the Zulu empire.

The Boers established a series of short-lived "republics" in Natal and the Transvaal, but both were subsequently annexed by the British. Maintaining authority over the frontier Boers overextended the British, who saw no practical reason to keep the "trekkers" in the British sphere anyway. Britain ceded authority to the Boers to establish the Orange Free State in 1854, thus signaling its desire to limit its commitment in the region.

Despite the mythology that has developed in contemporary South Africa, there was little cohesive ethnic identity among the Boers in the human mid-1800s. As one historian notes, "Instead of the growth of a unifying ethnic consciousness, extreme individualism, self-aggrandizement, and even anarchy prevailed in the early years of the Transvaal and the Free State."[14] Political identity was focused on local and regional ties, not ethnic or protonational ones.

From 1750 until 1870, twenty-nine separate wars or skirmishes—between Boers and Africans, British and Africans, Boers and British, and Africans and Africans—were fought in what is now South Africa. No one victor emerged. By 1870 there was a delicate balance of power in the region. The British colony in the Cape had about 180,000 European settlers; tensions still ran high along the Eastern Frontier. In Natal a small British presence lived uneasily with Zulus to the north. Two Boer republics, the Transvaal and the Orange Free State, with a combined population of about 30,000 Europeans, maintained a fragile hold in the interior of South Africa. Population growth and resource scarcity (espe-

---

13. Crais, *Making of the Colonial Order*, p. 3.
14. Hermann Giliomee, "The Beginnings of Afrikaner Ethnic Consciousness, 1850–1915," in Vail, ed., *Creation of Tribalism*, p. 24.

cially land for cattle grazing) ensured conflict and instability, but the lack of predominant military strength seemed to ordain a grudging coexistence between Africans and settlers.[15]

THE SECOND STAGE: TOWARD AN INTEGRATED POLITICAL ECONOMY

The discovery of diamonds and gold in South Africa and the consequent frenzied search for mineral wealth would eventually link the settler colonies in the south to the Portuguese presence in Angola and Mozambique. (See figure 2-1.) The diamonds found at Kimberly in 1867 and the gold discovered in the Witwatersrand in 1886 offered new prospects for wealth, and colonists quickly set out to create the conditions needed for the cheap extraction and production of minerals. The mineral revolution demanded transportation, capital, labor, exploration, and political control, the development of which led to an interconnected region.

Until 1870 only 62 miles of railroad track had been laid in Southern Africa, but between 1870 and 1915, 10,700 miles of railways were constructed in the region.[16] (See figure 2-2.) Johannesburg became the hub of the rapidly emerging regional economy. The lure of instant wealth brought an explosion of European immigration. In 1865 the European population of South Africa was about 200,000. By 1905 it was more than 1,100,000.[17]

The frenzied exploitation of Southern Africa's mineral wealth was equaled only by the frenzied exploitation of labor. The low quality of the gold in the Witswatersrand meant that the ore could be mined profitably only with cheap labor. To ensure an adequate supply of cheap manual labor, colonial authorities forcibly dispossessed Africans of land and consequently an independent means to earn a living. For decades afterwards hundreds of thousands of Africans drawn from Bechuanaland (Botswana), Basutoland (Lesotho), Northern Rhodesia

15. See A. Atmore and S. Marks, "The Imperial Factor in South Africa in the Nineteenth Century: Towards a Reassessment," *Journal of Imperial and Commonwealth History*, vol. 3 (1972–73), pp. 107–08.

16. A. J. Christopher, *Southern Africa* (Hamden, Conn.: Archon, 1976), p. 175.

17. Christopher, *Southern Africa*, p. 248.

FIGURE 2-1. *Colonial Southern Africa, circa 1870*

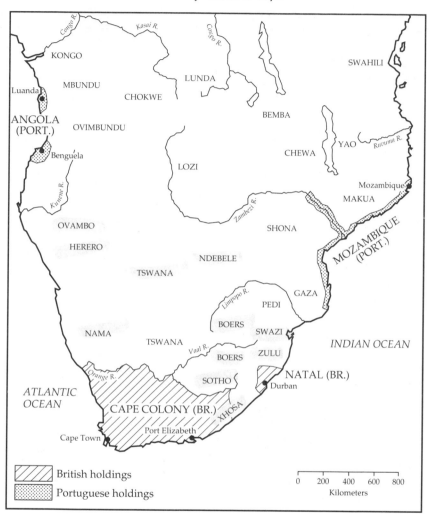

Source: Adapted from William Minter, *King Solomon's Mines Revisited* (Basic Books, 1986), pp. 40–41.

(Zambia), Nyasaland (Malawi), and southern Mozambique entered a regionwide migrant labor pool, working in the mines for cash and then returning to their families, who had been barred from accompanying them. (See figure 2-3.) To prevent unwanted African urbanization, colonial authorities extended the use of pass laws and native reserves.

Legislation to limit African landholding passed in all the territories of South Africa between 1890 and 1913. This last year saw the passage of

FIGURE 2-2. *Development of the Railway Network of Southern Africa, 1860–1910*

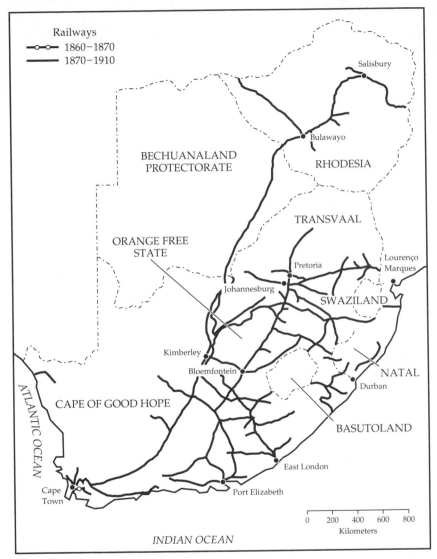

Source: Adapted from A. J. Christopher, *Southern Africa* (Hamdon, Conn.: Archon, 1976), p. 176.

the Natives Land Act, which cemented what would become a crucial distribution conflict for South Africa throughout the twentieth century. Driven by two demands—cheap labor for the mines and protection for white farmers against black competition—the 1913 act set aside 93 percent of South Africa's land for white purchase only. The act crowded

FIGURE 2-3. *Labor Migration Patterns of Southern Africa in 1939 and 1980*

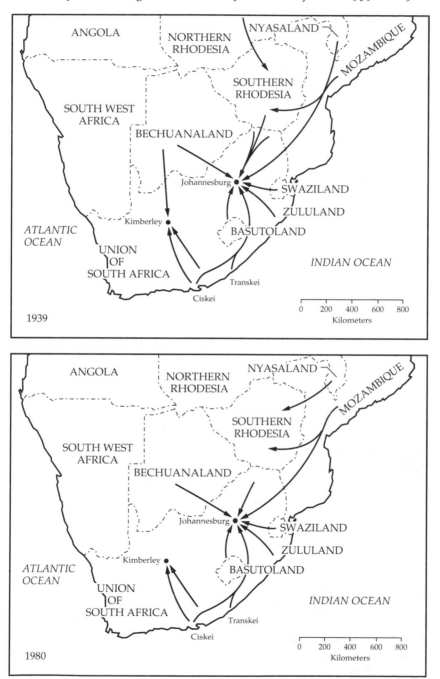

Source: Basil Davidson, *Modern Africa* (London: Longmans, 1983), p. 144.

the African population onto small parcels of land that could not sustain the agricultural needs of so many. (See figure 2-4.) Destitution, disease, and death for those Africans on the reserves were the inevitable result, which forced formerly productive, landowning peasants to labor for white owners of large farms or, alternatively, for the mines.[18] The South African example would be repeated throughout the region.

The appetite for mineral wealth led to widespread exploration into the interior of Southern Africa. Cecil Rhodes's British South Africa Company gathered a force of settlers to invade Mashonaland and Matabeleland (what is now Zimbabwe) in search of gold. They found only small, disappointing gold deposits, but large lodes of chromite and asbestos ensured the newly named Rhodesia its part in the emerging regional extraction network. In Northern Rhodesia lead, zinc, and copper were found; in South-West Africa copper and diamonds were mined. The vast copper holdings of the Belgian Congo served to expand the regional network to the north. Angola joined the regional economy when diamonds were discovered there in the 1920s and the Benguela railroad was completed to provide transit for the Congo's copper riches.

Consolidation of Political Control

The discovery of Southern Africa's vast riches coincided with intense industrial competition among the powers of Europe. The industrialization of Europe demanded more raw materials and new markets. Explorers and missionaries flocked to Southern Africa, and not just for adventurism and Christian love: they came to chart transport routes and find markets, arable land, and minerals.

The Berlin Conference of 1884–85, at which the major European powers divided up Africa, attempted to defuse tensions in Europe by giving the main European actors access to their "fair" share of Africa's riches in "an orderly manner." Of course, each colonial power sought to deny others access to as much of the region as possible without causing war with one another. Nonetheless, the powers saw the advantage of collaboration; they realized that efficient control of a given territory by any colonial power was more to their overall advantage than if none of

18. Colin Bundy, *The Rise and Fall of the South African Peasantry* (University of California Press, 1979).

FIGURE 2-4. *Native Reserves in Southern Africa as of 1913*

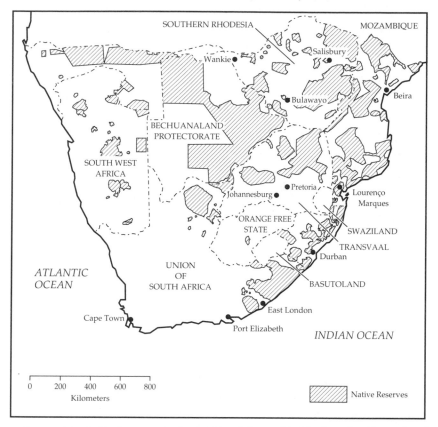

Source: John H. Wellington, *Southern Africa: A Geographical Study*, vol. 2: *Economic and Human Geography* (Cambridge University Press, 1955).

them had control. Boundaries were established based on claims of "effective occupation."

The combination of the need to establish effective occupation, the quest to find mineral riches, and the desire to exploit those riches to the utmost demanded military force on a level unprecedented in Southern Africa. With the exception of the Xhosa frontier wars of the 1850s, wars in Southern Africa until 1870 had been limited in scope and means. But the period between 1870 and 1920 brought wars of domination—and in some cases, extermination—of peoples.

In Angola the Portuguese embarked on a thirty-year campaign of "pacification" to justify their claims to the colony. In Mozambique the

Portuguese defeated the Gaza empire to stake a claim against British encroachment. In German South-West Africa (Namibia), the Germans fought the Herero and Nama peoples in brutal wars we now call ethnic cleansing: 80 percent of the 80,000 Herero people were killed and the rest forced into the surrounding deserts.[19] In German East Africa (Tanzania), German authorities created famine as a weapon to crush the Maji Maji rebellion, killing between 250,000 and 300,000 in the process.[20] In Rhodesia the British South African Company seized cattle and territory and brutally suppressed the Shona and Ndebele people who resisted.

Meanwhile, in South Africa the British imported massive force to stake their claim to the newfound riches. Thousands of troops moved to vanquish the Zulu empire, and nearly a half million troops, as well as Africans from the Cape Colony, set out to suppress Boer independence in the South African war.

The result, British military victory in 1902 and political compromise, led to the establishment of the Union of South Africa in 1910. The various South African colonies were united under a single parliament based in the Cape and an executive civil service in Pretoria. While the Cape retained its property-based, nonracial franchise, the rest of the Union denied Africans the vote. Peace was easy, said Lord Milner,

19. A 1904 proclamation of the German commander in South-West Africa read: "The Herero nation must leave the country. If it will not do so I shall compel it by force. . . . Inside German territory every Herero tribesman, armed or unarmed, with or without cattle, will be shot. No women and children will be allowed in the territory: they will be driven back to their people or fired on. These are the last words to the Herero nation from me, the great General of the mighty German Emperor." Quoted in Helmut Bley, *South-West Africa under German Rule, 1894–1914* (Northwestern University Press, 1971), pp. 163–64.

The commander considered the genocide justified because "a reconstruction of the old tribal organisation would lead to renewed bloodshed sooner or later. He understood the uprising as the first sign of a race war which would confront all European colonial powers in Africa. Therefore, any complacence on the part of the Germans would further the idea . . . that Africa belongs only to the Africans." From the staff records of General von Trotha, quoted in Tilman Dedering, "The German-Herero War of 1904: Revisionism of Genocide or Imaginary Historiography?" *Journal of Southern African Studies*, vol. 19 (March 1993), pp. 83–84.

20. John Illiffe, *A Modern History of Tanganyika* (Cambridge University Press, 1979), p. 200.

British high commissioner to South Africa: "You only have to sacrifice the 'nigger' absolutely."[21] But the peace that concluded the South African War of 1899–1902 would also postpone for nearly ninety years the resolution of the conflict over black political participation.

The dictate of effective occupation set by the Berlin Conference posed significant problems for the Portuguese. Their claims to Angola and Mozambique were based on their holds of Luanda (a port in Angola) and Lourenço Marques (now called Maputo, in Mozambique) and assertions that they had occupied the area for 400 years. The Portuguese presence had always been minimal, however, and it never amounted to effective, sustained administration of either country. Indeed, as late as 1912–13 the Portuguese governor of the Congo district of Angola confessed that "Portugal only ruled a narrow strip of land along the coast and as recently as 1902 Africans who lived less than a kilometer from the coast had imposed taxes and fines on the Portuguese traders."[22]

The Berlin dictate set the Portuguese on a thirty-five-year campaign of repression to establish administrative control of Angola. They tried to do so with military force and vast quantities of alcohol, which was the chief Portuguese export to that colony.[23] The military campaign against Angola met heavy local resistance. Nonetheless, at the end of 1920 Portugal could claim direct administrative presence, however tenuous, in the whole territory. There was roughly one *posto*—the most local office in the administrative hierarchy—for roughly every 14,808 Africans and for every 4,334 square kilometers of territory.[24]

21. Quoted in Mostert, *Frontiers*, p. 1273.

22. Lawrence W. Henderson, *Angola: Five Centuries of Conflict* (Cornell University Press, 1979), p. 106.

23. "The official yearbook for 1898 reveals that 30 percent of all Portuguese engaged in Angolan commerce were exclusively involved in the wholesale or retail sale of alcohol. This figure does not include the even greater percentage of Portuguese traders in the interior who relied on rum and wine as almost their only item of barter with Africans." By 1926 Portuguese traders imported 8,010,000 liters of alcoholic beverages into Angola, which, per capita, amounted to almost twenty-five times more alcohol than was imported into the French and British West African colonies that same year. Bender, *Angola under the Portuguese*, p. 146.

24. Numbers derived from Henderson, *Five Centuries of Conflict*, p. 118; and Bender, *Angola under the Portuguese*, p. 20.

Southern Mozambique, because of its proximity to the Transvaal and its port of Lourenço Marques, was quickly incorporated into the regional economy. Angola, because Portugal lacked the capital to explore adequately and to exploit the mineral wealth of that area, was not. Without railroads, which the Portuguese could not afford to build, Angola could not benefit unilaterally as a shipping depot for the mineral riches of the Congo. Portugal was forced to contract out concessions to finance the Benguela railroad, which was finally completed in 1929. Similarly, Portugal chartered more than half of Mozambique to concessionary companies controlled by British, German, and French capital. Not until 1942 had the Portuguese government bought out the concessions in Mozambique.[25]

The years immediately following World War I finalized the Southern African regional system that would last until the 1960s. (See figure 2-5.) German defeat in the war led to a League of Nations mandate of South-West Africa to South Africa. In 1923 the settlers of Southern Rhodesia opted against union with South Africa and earned the ambiguous status of "self-governing" colony. The High Commission Territories of Bechuanaland, Swaziland, and Basutoland remained protectorates of Britain. These territories, together with Southern Rhodesia and colonies in Nyasaland, Northern Rhodesia, and Tanganyika (Tanzania), gave Britain the strategic balance to thwart any expansionist ambitions of South Africa and to protect the interests of British capital throughout the region.

What united the colonial authorities and settler communities was both the determination to appropriate the riches of Southern Africa and the exploitation of Southern African peoples in that pursuit. But the bond was imperfect. Portugal remained resentful of its dependence on British and South African capital for exploiting Angola and Mozambique, and both the Southern Rhodesians and the Portuguese were wary—with good reason—of the regional aspirations of the South Africans. Some South African leaders after 1910 expressed interest in northern expansion, possibly even into southern Mozambique. Most South African leaders claimed that South Africa's natural sphere of influence ran at least to the Zambezi river, through Zambia to the northern

25. Bertil Egero, *Mozambique: A Dream Undone* (Uppsala, Sweden: Scandinavian Institute of African Studies, 1987), p. 48.

FIGURE 2-5. *Southern Africa in 1945*

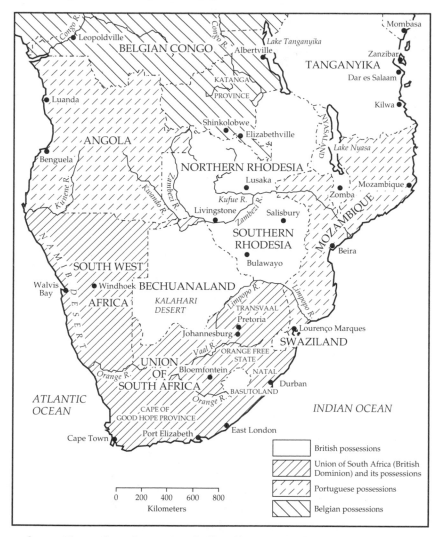

Source: Thomas Borstelmann, *Apartheid's Reluctant Uncle: The United States and Southern Africa in the Early Cold War* (Oxford University Press, 1993).

borders of Botswana and Zimbabwe, down into the Mozambique channel. South African General Jan Smuts had proclaimed that South Africa's perimeter of defense extended all the way to Kenya. As late as 1962 South Africa planned to incorporate the British High Commission Territories into the Union, and similar plans were voiced for Namibia.

Legacies of the Consolidation

During the first stage of regional consolidation in Southern Africa, the colonial powers and settler regimes created states, imposed economic and political patterns of racial marginalization and exploitation, and forced together cultures unused to being governed in one territorial unit. Three legacies from this period are crucial to understanding Southern Africa as it exists today: the totally inadequate basis for viable states in the Portuguese colonies; the economic distortion and disruption of African life; and the emergence of ethnicity as a way to cope with that disruption.

THE PORTUGUESE DENOUEMENT. In the Portuguese colonies, states were established in name only. Farmers and traders, not bureaucrats, constituted the most important Portuguese presence from 1920 to 1960. When the colonial administration in Angola set exorbitant taxes and insisted on enforced labor to meet them, hundreds of thousands of Africans fled across borders, which led to a crisis of depopulation of Angola's interior.[26] Another indicator of the lack of state control and penetration is that by 1953 only fifty-three miles of paved roads existed in Angola, and most other roads were often unfit for travel.[27] Unlike Britain, Portugal devolved little authority on its representatives in its possessions. The metropole monopolized legislation, economic planning, and labor policy affecting the colonies.

By almost any standard, Portuguese colonialism was the harshest, most exploitative variety in a continent of colonial exploitation. Its system of forced labor was particularly brutal, prompting Portugal's own minister of colonies in the mid-1940s to excoriate the "blind selfishness" of the white settler farmers, whose greed was leading to the mass migration of able, healthy Africans. "To cover the deficit [caused by depopulation] the most shameful outrages are committed, including forced labour of independent self-employed workers, of women, of children, of the sick, of decrepit old men, etc. Only the dead are really exempt from forced labour."[28]

The living standards of Africans in Angola fell dramatically in the forty years following Portugal's establishment of an administrative pre-

26. Bender, *Angola under the Portugese*, pp. 108, 142.
27. Bender, *Angola under the Portugese*, p. 102.
28. Quoted in Bender, *Angola under the Portugese*, pp. 108, 143.

sence. Angola's best farming lands were reserved for whites while blacks were often resettled to provide cheap labor for the settlers. Even as late as 1942 the forced labor system paid workers less than $1.50 a month. Little attempt was made to educate Africans; indeed, little attempt was made to educate white settlers: "In 1952 . . . Angola had 14,898 primary school students (more than two-thirds of whom were white) compared with African enrollments the same year of 418,898 in Ghana and 943,494 in Zaire."[29]

Portugal's legacy of exploitation and failed state building is not much different in Mozambique. In the 1960s a Mozambican's life expectancy was between 25 and 33 years, about that of an African male in the Cape Colony at the turn of the century.[30] Eduardo Mondlane, the American-trained sociologist who was the first president of FRELIMO,[31] found that in some rural districts of Mozambique villagers had never seen a Portuguese before the war of independence in the 1960s.[32] Many villagers do not realize even now that they live in a place called Mozambique.[33]

ECONOMIC DISTORTION AND DISRUPTION. Regional economic integration based on mining cemented patterns of domination and subordination in Southern Africa. Investments in railways, roads, energy, and communications complemented investments in mineral production and cash crops. The entire region was drawn into a system that served the interests of mining and plantation capital.

The migrant labor system and native lands policies devastated African populations. Legislation increasingly institutionalized segregation and racism not only in South Africa but also in the British and Portuguese colonies. In economic terms, the colonial division of labor in its

29. Bender, *Angola under the Portugese*, p. 152.

30. Allison Butler Herrick and others, *Area Handbook for Mozambique* (Washington: American University Press, 1969), p. 117; and Norman Bromberger and Kenneth Hughes, "Capitalism and Underdevelopment in South Africa," in Jeffrey Butler, Richard Elphick, and David Welsh, eds., *Democratic Liberalism in South Africa: Its History and Prospect* (Wesleyan University Press, 1987), p. 214.

31. Frente de Libertação de Moçambique, a Mozambican nationalist movement.

32. Eduardo Mondlane, *The Struggle for Mozambique* (Penguin Books, 1969), p. 102.

33. William Finnegan, *A Complicated War: The Harrowing of Mozambique* (University of California Press, 1992), p. 18.

Southern African form crushed traditional socioeconomic systems. Forced labor, land distribution policies, taxes, and deportations to native reserves fragmented local socioeconomic networks while imports hindered local production. Lack of investment in the traditional sector—either for immediately productive purposes or for health care and education—coupled with military oppression underscored the continued subjugation of the colonized. The economic exploitation and disenfranchisement that Southern Africans experienced was so total that even today many people in the region equate capitalism with domination, exploitation, repression, and racism.

THE CRYSTALLIZATION OF ETHNICITY. Until the 1900s the political and social affiliations of Africans were varied and flexible. Primary attachments were to local chieftains, but such attachments were not fixed.[34] Myriad examples of war within African groups, for example, among the Ovimbundu of Angola, the Xhosa and Zulu of South Africa, and the Shona of Zimbabwe, illustrate that Africans' ethnicity did not confer their primary political identity.

The fragmentation of rural societies and communities and a rapidly changing environment created deep identity crises for many Africans, providing fertile ground for the crystallization of ethnicity. This ground was tended by missionaries who, through their studies of tribal languages, introduction of written language, and emphasis on tribalism and tradition, implanted in Africans a new awareness of ethnicity.[35] Ethnic ideologies were shaped and taught at missionary schools.

The missionary emphasis on ethnicity corresponded to the British conception of Africans as "tribal beings." It also reinforced the British system of indirect rule, whereby African leaders served as intermediaries between the colonial administrators and the people. Ethnic identity gave these leaders status and power. As Leroy Vail put it, "Forward-looking members of the [African] petty bourgeoisie and migrant workers alike attempted to shore up their societies and their own positions in them by embracing ethnicity and accepting tribal identities."[36]

34. Leonard Thompson, *A History of South Africa* (Yale University Press, 1990), pp. 113, 123.

35. Leroy Vail, "Introduction: Ethnicity in Southern African History," in Vail, ed., *Creation of Tribalism.*

36. Vail, "Introduction: Ethnicity in Southern African History," p. 14.

Most local African elites oscillated between collaboration and resistance in their dealings with the colonizers, depending on their immediate perceptions and calculations of group interests and power. Only in South Africa and Mozambique was there anything resembling modern nationalism. The African National Congress, formed in 1912, called for national citizenship in South Africa as well as greater unity among all Africans. In Mozambique Africans with some measure of wealth and education tried for a short time in the 1920s to insist that "We are all Portuguese!"[37]

Perhaps the most intense new ethnicity was Afrikanerdom, which developed around the turn of the century. A coherent and compelling mythology and group identity grew out of the war between Britain and the Boers, in which entire Boer families were herded into concentration camps; the Boers' impoverishment and bitter envy of newcomers who enjoyed the riches of the mining revolution; and the establishment of organizations such as the Broederbond.

did this ethnicity coincide w/ Calvinist orientation?

THE THIRD STAGE: GLOBAL DECOLONIZATION AND SOUTH AFRICAN APARTHEID

Two processes set the twists and turns of the Southern African regional security complex after World War II: the development of apartheid in South Africa and global decolonization. The collision of these processes led to a thirty-year regional war that has still not ended.

The international political climate in the aftermath of the Second World War posed major challenges for white domination in Southern Africa. Nazi atrocities and genocide produced worldwide awareness of racism and staunch resolution to protect basic human rights.[38] The United Nations, in response to rising demands for political independence among colonized peoples, lobbied for the end of European colonialism and enshrined political self-determination as a key principle of international order. These developments threatened the settlers and colonists in Southern Africa.

37. Penvenne, "We Are All Portuguese!"
38. Paul Gordon Lauren, *Power and Prejudice: The Politics and Diplomacy of Racial Discrimination* (Boulder, Colo.: Westview Press, 1988), pp. 166–86.

The force of these nascent norms was tempered, however, by the emerging division of the world into a bipolar structure, defined by the United States as a struggle between a "free world" and communism. The face-off between the United States and the Soviet Union solaced Southern African whites, who shrewdly calculated that joining Western allies in the global struggle against communism would help them avert international and domestic appeals for internal political reform.

The emerging international normative order could not by itself end white domination in Southern Africa. Indeed, the postwar history of international involvement there shows public condemnation of apartheid and colonialism standing alongside increased ties between the region and the international economy. International attention focused on the region only when episodic, direct violence brought media scrutiny. International pressure for change followed—not led—domestic pressure in Southern Africa.

The regimes of Southern Africa followed different strategies for meeting the challenges of the new international environment. Although the different strategies sometimes exacerbated conflicts among the white settlers and colonists in the region, the wars of national independence eventually drove the white regimes to cooperate on security matters.

Apartheid and the Triumph of Afrikanerdom

International changes were not the only ones that challenged racism in South Africa. Major domestic changes wrought by World War II also did. Meeting the wartime needs of the Western allies fostered a manufacturing boom in South Africa. South African industry grew tremendously and brought more and more blacks into the industrial workplace and urban communities. Even so, there was a shortage of labor during this growth period. Accordingly, black wages rose sharply, black trade unions made solid gains, and the number of blacks living in urban areas more than doubled.[39]

The increased economic strength of an African urban, organized, industrial work force led to growing political strength for organizations that challenged white political domination in South Africa, notably the African National Congress (ANC) and the South African Communist

39. Robert M. Price, *The Apartheid State in Crisis: Political Transformation in South Africa, 1975–1990* (Oxford University Press, 1991), pp. 15–17.

Party. These two groups worked together to organize nonviolent mass action campaigns to win for blacks basic political, economic, and social rights.

These domestic changes struck at the heart of Afrikanerdom. Afrikaner leaders feared the massing together of blacks in cities and bridled at black demands for political change. Afrikaner farmers wanted stricter controls on labor mobility because the departure of black farm workers for the cities and for higher wages was creating a shortage of cheap labor in the countryside. Afrikaners' self-proclaimed racial superiority over black Africans was melting away as blacks made economic gains despite racist legislation. Moreover, Afrikaners, whose place in the South African hierarchy was inferior to that of the English-speaking population, feared that English-dominated business would accede to African demands for reform. A unified Afrikaner response was needed not only to stand up to internal demands for change, they thought, but to roll back black economic gains and to upgrade the status of Afrikaners.

Apartheid came to South Africa when the National Party (NP), representing Afrikaner extremism, won a plurality of seats in the 1948 elections. The NP put in place a vigorous set of laws and policies that sought to regulate all relations between races in South Africa. What distinguished apartheid from earlier economic, political, and legal domination by whites over blacks was "the completeness with which racial separation was sought, and in the locus within the state of racial control."[40]

In pursuing apartheid the National Party had three aims: "(1) to create a completely segregated society, in keeping with the precepts of Afrikaner politico-religious doctrine, and in so doing to preserve Afrikaner identity; (2) to secure white political supremacy and its resulting economic privileges from potential internal and external threats (the former represented primarily by the black majority and the latter by an international community increasingly inhospitable to notions of racial rule); and (3) to move the Afrikaner community into a position of social and economic parity with the English-speaking community, which had dominated the modern economy and urban sector since the dawn of capitalist economic development in South Africa."[41]

40. Price, *Apartheid State*, p. 19.
41. Price, *Apartheid State*, p. 23.

To accomplish these goals the National Party established a totalitarian police state to control blacks. Laws such as the Population Registration Act, the Prohibition of Mixed Marriages Act, the Immorality Act, the Reservation of Separate Amenities Act, and the Group Areas Act strictly segregated South Africa by race. Forced removal of entire communities led to the violent uprooting of over 3.5 million people.[42] Enforcement of laws restricting black movement in the country (pass laws) led to 5.8 million prosecutions in one decade alone.[43] The success of such draconian coercion depended on restricting violence to the black townships and thereby enabling white South Africans to remain oblivious to the harshness their way of life inflicted on millions. The security of white South Africans came to rest on the insecurity of black South Africans.

Once the National Party had captured the South African state, it molded a bureaucracy, judiciary, police force, and military to serve the interests of the minority. It legislated away voting rights for its "coloured" and Indian populations. Through the force of law and packing the judiciary, the apartheid state effectively gave the government the right to detain and arrest anyone, indefinitely. Rights to free speech and assembly did not exist for the majority.

The National Party transformed the state into an employment agency for poor Afrikaners, which meant that the South African government became a bloated bureaucracy with a vested interest in preventing any reform. By 1970 half of all employed Afrikaners worked in the public and semipublic sectors. Eighty percent of all state jobs were held by Afrikaners.[44] By 1977 Afrikaners held 90 percent of the top executive and managerial state positions.[45]

The National Party also established a welfare economy for Afrikaners and intervened actively to assist Afrikaner business. The state increased by almost 500 percent the amount of capital it placed in Afrikaner-owned banks. It awarded important contracts to Afrikaner business and established state-run industries with Afrikaner directors to compete with English-owned enterprises.[46]

42. Thompson, *History of South Africa*, p. 194.
43. Price, *Apartheid State*, p. 20.
44. Price, *Apartheid State*, p. 25.
45. Thompson, *History of South Africa*, p. 199.
46. Dan O'Meara, *Volkskapitalisme: Class, Capital, and Ideology in the Develop-*

South Africa's apartheid policy received only muted international criticism during the 1950s. While the United Nations drew attention to South Africa's racist policies, the major European powers and the United States remained silent for the most part. The United States had its own problems with segregation at home, and the virulent anti-communism of the McCarthy years made it loath to criticize South Africa, which justified its political repression by claiming it was suppressing communism. Both Britain and the United States supplied South Africa with arms. Furthermore, the United States ensured South African access to international capital through the World Bank and the Export-Import Bank and actively cooperated with South Africa in the processing of uranium for atomic energy.

Because of its economic investment and historical involvement in Southern Africa, Great Britain worried more about a resurgent, active South African role in the region than about apartheid. Immediately after the war Britain had refused requests by the South African government to incorporate the High Commission Territories into the Union of South Africa. Britain also pushed through a plan for federation of Southern Rhodesia, Northern Rhodesia, and Nyasaland to counter the rise of Afrikaner power in South Africa. The federation, established with scant consideration for the opinions of Africans in those territories, gave the Southern Rhodesian settler regime more influence in the affairs of the other colonies and led to industrial polarization, with disproportionate capital investment and federal revenues going to Salisbury.[47]

Southern Rhodesia's whites were strengthened too by a British campaign to increase emigration to the colonies. Many of the whites in Southern Rhodesia in the 1960s were newcomers; 43 percent of eligible voters in 1969 had been born in England or other crown colonies.[48] It

---

ment of Afrikaner Nationalism, *1934–1948* (Cambridge University Press, 1983), p. 250.

47. Philip Paul Jourdan, "Provisional Implications for the SADCC Mining Sector of a Post-Apartheid South Africa," report prepared for the SADCC Mining Sector Coordinating Community Unit, Ministry of Mines, Lusaka, Zambia, March 1992, p. 68.

48. Stephen John Stedman, *Peacemaking in Civil War: International Mediation in Zimbabwe, 1974–1980* (Boulder, Colo.: Lynne Rienner Publishers, 1991), pp. 40–41.

was these recently arrived individuals, for the most part, who made up the most virulently racist part of the Southern Rhodesian settler community. Having rapidly attained upward mobility in life-style and possessions in their new location, they were determined not to relinquish it.

By the late 1950s Britain was firmly caught between two cross-pressures. It wanted to protect its economic interests in Southern Africa, but it had committed itself to global decolonization. As Britain brought many of its former colonies to independence, it sought to retain leadership over them through the Commonwealth. As the Commonwealth grew into a multiracial institution, Britain had to refrain from a full embrace of South Africa. Consequently, even as Britain offered vocal support for peaceful change and majority rule in the region, it increased its lucrative economic dealings with South Africa.

Portugal steadfastly rejected the international norm of decolonization. The African colonies made profits for the metropole and, Portuguese leaders thought, ensured Portugal's status as a European power. Moreover, the Portuguese had developed a mythology about its colonialism. The ideology of "lusotropicalism" held that the Portuguese were uniquely able to understand black peoples; therefore Portuguese colonialism was not racist. Because of the self-proclaimed absence of racism among the Portuguese people and because Portugal's culture induced affinity with all tropical peoples, Portugal's interactions with Africans were supposedly egalitarian and harmonious.[49] But the myth of lusotropicalism did not obscure the reality that Portuguese colonialism was the most exploitative in Africa.

Portugal responded to the new international environment by appealing for new emigrants to its colonies. In Angola the white population grew from 44,083 in 1940 to 172,529 in 1960; in Mozambique it expanded from 27,400 to 97,200 during the same period and doubled—to over 200,000—from 1960 to 1970.[50] In 1951 Portugal declared Angola and Mozambique to be provinces, not colonies. The next year Portugal successfully lobbied the North Atlantic Treaty Organization for a pledge of assistance to Portugal if any of its "overseas territories" was threatened.

Both Britain and Portugal remained concerned about South Africa's regional ambitions. A booming economy led South Africa to believe—

49. Bender, *Angola under the Portuguese*, pp. 3–18.
50. Finnegan, *Complicated War*, p. 29.

rightly—that it was *the* regional giant. Afrikaner politicians spoke of the entire region as South Africa's natural sphere of influence; its natural defense perimeter was said to stop at the Zambezi river. South African leaders even claimed that they could serve as a bridge between Europeans and Africans in the region, since the Afrikaner wars with the British had made them, they maintained, profoundly anticolonialist. (Most African nationalists, however, recognized the paternalism in that claim and rejected it out of hand.)

Global Decolonization Comes to Southern Africa

By the late 1950s and early 1960s the global trend of decolonization had helped foster independence in more than thirty African countries. Some Southern African states, such as Tanzania, Malawi, Zambia, Botswana, Lesotho, and Swaziland, were decolonized peacefully. In others, namely, the Portuguese colonies, Southern Rhodesia, South-West Africa, and South Africa, the liberation process was violent and protracted.

Apartheid stifled a liberal response to the new demands for political independence and economic justice in South Africa, while Portugal's authoritarian government invoked lusotropicalism to nourish the myth that Portugal's presence as a colonizer was a positive force for African development. Also standing in the way of peaceful change was a great wave of new immigrants, who had heeded British and Portuguese summonses to the region.

Insurrection mounted first in Angola. Portuguese settlers responded to a surprise uprising in March 1961 with vigilante violence and indiscriminate slaughter of blacks; the colonial army bombed vast territories with napalm. By the end of the summer more than 50,000 Africans and 2,000 whites had been killed, and nearly a tenth of the African population of Angola had crossed the border into Zaire.[51] As would happen also in Rhodesia and South Africa, the refugees became a willing pool of recruits for the fight against the settler state.

Inside South Africa black opposition to the white regime took the form of "defiance campaigns" against unjust laws in the late 1950s and protests against the pass laws in the early 1960s. The Sharpeville massacre of 1960, at which sixty-seven unarmed, peaceful demonstrators

51. Bender, *Angola under the Portuguese*, p. 158.

were gunned down by the South African Police, marked a turning point for the antiapartheid movement, however.[52] Many Africans no longer believed it was possible to eradicate apartheid by peaceful means alone. In 1961, after long debate, the African National Congress abandoned its almost fifty-year commitment to nonviolent change and launched an armed struggle against the white regime. A rival organization, the Pan Africanist Congress of Azania (PAC), also turned to guerrilla tactics.

The Sharpeville massacre riveted international attention on South Africa. The brutal force used against the demonstrators elicited world-wide condemnation and increased the normative pressure against the white regime. The obvious potential for political instability drove inter-national investors to look elsewhere to place their money.

The South African government responded immediately. It restored investor confidence in the economy by quickly clamping down on the opposition: the government banned the ANC and the PAC within days of the Sharpeville massacre and dramatically increased spending for the military and domestic arms production.[53] It reacted to international condemnation by declaring South Africa a republic and pulling out of the Commonwealth.

The National Party also formulated a longer-term strategy. In an attempt to meet international demands for self-determination but still maintain the racial segregation embraced by most white South Africans, the government established Bantustans, or black homelands. Swaths of barren territory—about 13 percent of South Africa's land—were carved out and millions of blacks forced to move to them. Such "separate development," South African leaders declared, would be akin to formal decolonization. From 1961 to the mid-1970s, when Pretoria formally recognized the Bantustans as "independent sovereign homelands," South Africa quested for international acceptance of the homelands policy as a way out of its race dilemma.

52. Leonard Thompson and Andrew Prior, *South African Politics* (Yale University Press, 1982), p. 15.

53. Between 1959–60 and 1966–67, defense spending rose from 39.2 million rand (7 percent of the total budget) to 213 million rand (17 percent of the budget). In 1960–61 South Africa spent 315,000 rand on arms manufacturing; by 1964–65 it spent 33 million rand. James Barber and John Barratt, *South Africa's Foreign Policy: The Search for Status and Security, 1945–1988* (Cambridge University Press, 1990), pp. 101–03.

A Regional War

Other nationalist movements in Southern Africa also turned to guerrilla warfare during the mid-1960s to earn independence. In 1964 FRELIMO began a protracted war to overthrow the Portuguese in Mozambique; in 1965 the Zimbabwe African People's Union (ZAPU) started a guerrilla war in Rhodesia; in 1966 the South West African People's Organization (SWAPO) initiated a war for Namibian independence.

The almost simultaneous outbreaks of armed opposition in the region brought dramatic responses from the white regimes. By 1965 Portugal had 50,000 troops in Angola and, in conjunction with its increased military effort to stop the new insurrection in Mozambique, was spending almost half of its national budget on defense. In 1965, to preempt British pressures for majority rule in Southern Rhodesia, the white settlers under the leadership of Ian Smith unilaterally declared their independence from Britain. And, as mentioned above, South Africa dramatically increased its military spending and domestic arms production.

The concurrent threats to the white regimes brought them into active cooperation to maintain racial domination in Southern Africa. South Africa, Portugal, and Rhodesia shared military intelligence. South Africa provided military assistance to both regimes. South Africa and Mozambique became Rhodesia's economic lifelines when the United Nations in 1966 voted to impose sanctions on the renegade colony.

Such cooperation, however, was counterbalanced by purely nationally based interests. Even at the height of military and political cooperation among the regimes, the Portuguese colonies and Rhodesia refused to accept a free-trade zone with South Africa for fear that it would harm their burgeoning industry.[54] Rhodesia's dependence on South Africa and Mozambique to break sanctions often led to bitterness over the added costs that middlemen placed on key goods. South Africa and Rhodesia occasionally clashed over Rhodesia's unwillingness to negotiate a settlement to its crises with Britain and its majority.[55]

54. Kenneth W. Grundy, *Confrontation and Accommodation in Southern Africa: The Limits of Independence* (University of California Press, 1973), p. 253.
55. The South African attitude toward Rhodesia was shaped by the historical differences between the two countries. National Party leaders argued that

South Africa's regional strategy in the 1960s sought to prop up the colonial regimes in Angola, Mozambique, and Rhodesia. Pretoria also tried to use its economic power to co-opt the newly independent countries of the region into accepting South Africa's legitimacy. South Africa's long-held goal of incorporating the High Commission Territories was stymied when Britain formally granted independence to Botswana, Lesotho, and Swaziland.[56] Nevertheless, these countries' economic ties to South Africa and their landlocked status made them extremely vulnerable to South African actions. South Africa also had extensive economic ties to Zambia and Malawi. In the end, though, South Africa was unable to translate its overwhelming economic power into political acceptance of its regional agenda. Only Malawi established full diplomatic relations with Pretoria, and no regime signed a nonaggression pact that Pretoria had sought in the 1960s.

South Africa's objectives on the regional level—political, economic, and military hegemony and regional acceptance of apartheid at home—were never accepted by the majority of the other states in the region. The common antipathy against white minority rule provided a basis for unity among the new countries of Botswana, Zambia, and Tanzania.

Tanzania and Zambia were crucial in the formation of regional cooperation for liberation. Both countries provided supply and training bases for the liberation movements in Angola and Mozambique. Zambia, at enormous cost and despite U.N. dispensation, upheld the U.N. economic boycott of Rhodesia. Later in the 1960s it provided assistance to guerrillas fighting the Smith regime in Rhodesia. In 1969 another step was taken toward regional cooperation when the Conference of Heads

---

Southern Rhodesia's fate was separate from that of South Africa because the colony decided in 1923 not to join South Africa and because its constitution was not specifically based on race. (Southern Rhodesia used a property-based franchise, which at least theoretically was color-blind.) South Africa felt that the declaration of independence in 1965 destabilized the region and imperiled South Africa's ability to maintain its policies of apartheid at home and in South-West Africa.

56. As late as 1963 South Africa put forward a proposal to incorporate the High Commission Territories into South Africa. See Ronald Hyam, *The Failure of South African Expansion, 1908–1948* (New York: Africana Publishing, 1972), pp. 184–98; and James Barber, *South Africa's Foreign Policy, 1945–1970* (Oxford University Press, 1973), pp. 168–70.

of State and Governments of East and Central Africa adopted the "Manifesto on Southern Africa" (better known as the Lusaka Manifesto), which pledged the region to work for nonracialism throughout Southern Africa.

Disagreements over which of the competing liberation parties to support sometimes marred regional unity against colonialism and apartheid. Except for SWAPO in Namibia, the insurrectionists had been divided from the start. By 1966 there were three armed liberation movements in Angola—FNLA, MPLA, and UNITA.[57] In Zimbabwe two different movements competed for the mantle of black representation—ZAPU and ZANU (Zimbawe African National Union). In Mozambique two movements, FRELIMO and COREMO,[58] fought the Portuguese until COREMO dissolved; FRELIMO itself suffered from internal divisions. And in South Africa, the ANC and PAC held forth different visions of a postapartheid South Africa.

Movements were split by ethnic and regional affiliations, personality clashes among leaders, competing ideologies, and external patrons. The divisions only grew worse over time, as the colonial and settler states seized upon the differences within and among the nationalist parties in order to sow disunity and weaken the struggle for independence. Prospective patrons were forced to choose among different claimants to legitimacy and effectiveness.

International support for the decolonization movements came from the United Nations, which claimed more and more newly independent states as members, and the newly formed Organization for African Unity. The former voted for a voluntary arms embargo against South Africa in 1962; the latter organization established the struggle against apartheid and colonialism as a priority for continental action and pledged military training and equipment to freedom fighters in Southern Africa. Financial support for the nationalist movements came from the Scandinavian countries as well as from Eastern-bloc countries, which also provided military assistance and training.

The major Western powers found themselves caught in contradictions. Britain, France, Germany, and the United States had economic

57. FNLA, MPLA, and UNITA are acronyms for Frente Nacional de Libertação de Angola, Movimento Popular de Libertação de Angola, and União Nacional para a Independência Total de Angola.
58. COREMO stands for Comitê Revolucionário de Moçambique.

and strategic interests in Southern Africa, interests that they believed were more threatened by Africans coming to power than by settler regimes maintaining white domination.[59] Moreover, very strong lobbies within those powers accepted the claims of South Africa and Portugal that the colonial and settler presence in Southern Africa provided a bulwark against communism and that the "free world" needed the strategic assistance of Portugal and South Africa.

All of these Western powers, however, were publicly opposed to colonialism and racism. In the United States the public commitment against racism and colonialism and the governmental fear of revolution and majority rule led to a "speak loudly . . . but carry a small stick" policy.[60] In fact, the United States actively assisted the South Africans and Portuguese in their attempts to maintain domination. The American policy paper NSSM-39, issued in 1969, argued that the white regimes of Southern Africa were there to stay and that economic and political ties could be used to moderate the consequences of racial rule.[61]

NSSM-39 signaled that the major Western power still viewed South Africa as an ally in good standing. This evaluation, combined with South Africa's ability to contain armed resistance and two decades of stunning economic growth, created an optimistic white political elite. As the 1960s came to an end Pretoria could claim a special role for South Africa in the continent's affairs. In accordance with its "special role," it began to formulate a policy that would use South Africa's enormous economic power to force regional acceptance of its dominant position. South Africa also more frequently cast the conflict throughout the re-

59. For example, British investment between 1964 and 1966 was more profitable in South Africa than anywhere else in the world; and the *Wall Street Journal* in 1970 reported that investments in South Africa were the most profitable international investment of 260 American companies. See Barber and Barratt, *South Africa's Foreign Policy*, p. 99. British capital investment in South Africa increased from 290 million British pounds in 1962 to 641 million pounds in 1969. See Minter, *King Solomon's Mines Revisited*, p. 178.

60. Herman Cohen, former U.S. assistant secretary of state for African affairs, "A View from Inside," in Harvey Glickman, ed., *Toward Peace and Security in Southern Africa* (New York: Gordon and Breach, 1990), p. 216.

61. Mohamed A. El-Khawas, ed., *National Security Study Memorandum 39: The Kissinger Study of Southern Africa* (Westport, Conn.: Lawrence Hill, 1976), pp. 76–182.

gion as one of South African virtue versus communist-inspired aggression, a portrayal that led in the 1970s to "the institutionalization of forms of self-deception and delusion."[62]

Similar optimism prevailed in Rhodesia. Rhodesian counterinsurgency forces had been extremely successful at finding and killing guerrilla fighters who entered the country. The lack of protest—a result of state coercion—was misinterpreted by the Smith regime as African satisfaction with their third-class lot. As late as 1972, when a new Zimbabwean guerrilla infiltration of Rhodesia was set to begin, Smith had proclaimed that his country had "the happiest Africans in the world."[63] The cumulative weight of international sanctions had yet to be felt, and therefore Rhodesians believed that they would never pinch tightly. And tensions between Rhodesia and South Africa were at their nadir: South African soldiers and police helped patrol within Rhodesia, and South African reconnaissance equipment, especially helicopters, assisted Rhodesia's counterinsurgency battalions.

Even Rhodesia's status with its former ruler seemed on the brink of resolution. After two unsuccessful negotiations to end Rhodesia's rebel status, the two countries in 1971 reached an agreement that put the prospects of majority rule sometime in the mid-twenty-first century. Before the agreement was finalized, however, Britain insisted that Rhodesia's blacks, who made up 95 percent of the population, be canvassed about their support for the proposition. For the first time in Rhodesia's colonial history, the majority were asked their opinion on the political makeup of their country. Not surprisingly, they overwhelmingly rejected the Smith-Home agreement and left Britain saddled with its "Rhodesia problem."

The event that most shook white optimism in Southern Africa occurred in 1974 when a group of disgruntled army officers in Portugal, tired of fighting unwinnable colonial wars in Africa—wars that had taken the lives of more than 13,000 soldiers—overthrew the dictatorship of Marcello Caetano. Portugal's new leaders rapidly began to decolonize Angola and Mozambique, more concerned with hastening their withdrawal than with creating stable transitions to independence. In less than a year and a half, Portugal had withdrawn from Africa,

---

62. Grundy, *Confrontation and Accommodation*, p. 244.
63. David Martin and Phyllis Johnson, *The Struggle for Zimbabwe: The Chimurenga War* (London: Faber and Faber, 1981), p. 1.

leaving an immature revolutionary movement, FRELIMO, in power in Mozambique and an internationalized civil war in Angola, where South African and Cuban troops would confront each other.

The rapid collapse of the Portuguese colonial empire deprived South Africa of two vital buffer states and gave a moral and material boost to liberation movements in Zimbabwe, Namibia, and South Africa itself. For Zimbabwe, Mozambique now afforded a 600-kilometer border that rebels could cross for sanctuary and equipment and return to fight the white regime stronger than before. The regional balance of forces altered almost overnight.

Chapter 3

A Ride on the Whirlwind, 1975–90

In the three decades following World War II, the Portuguese, Dutch, and British presences merged in the full-blown regional war that pitted newly independent African states and national liberation movements against the colonial and settler regimes. The collapse of Portuguese colonialism transformed the regional war, hastening Zimbabwean independence, emboldening resistance to apartheid in South Africa, and prompting large-scale South African destabilization of its neighbors. Between 1975 and February 1990 (when the South African government released Nelson Mandela from prison, thus ushering in the promise of a new era in Southern Africa), the amount of death and destruction in Southern Africa surpassed that of the period of colonial consolidation.

SOUTHERN AFRICA IN THE 1970S: THE WEIGHT OF THE PAST

When Angola and Mozambique came to independence in 1975, Southern Africa began to suffer fully the consequences of cumulative long-term economic, political, and social legacies from its deep past. For the former British colonies of Tanzania and Zambia, the mid-1970s meant coming to terms with their economic and political inheritances. Because independence was based on arbitrarily drawn colonial borders, the new nations of Tanzania and Zambia were amalgams of different populations and groups, who had been taught by British missionaries to think of themselves as having separate identities. Zambia holds 72 ethnolinguistic groups; Tanzania has 120.[1]

1. Ieuan LL. Griffiths, *An Atlas of African Affairs* (London: Methuen, 1984), p. 130; and Rodger Yeager, *Tanzania: An African Experiment* (Boulder, Colo.: Westview Press, 1982), p. 35.

All of the countries of the region lacked human capital at independence. In Tanzania, "there were only twelve African civil engineers, eight African telecommunication engineers, nine African veterinarians, and five African chemists. No Africans had been trained as geologists or mechanical or electrical engineers."[2] In Zambia 108 Africans had received university education.[3]

The newly independent countries were also constrained by the legacy of the mineral revolution—they were vulnerable economically to the apartheid regime in South Africa. Botswana, Lesotho, and Swaziland came to independence enmeshed in a formal trade relationship with South Africa, the South African Customs Union. Botswana and Lesotho sent more than 50 percent of their exports to South Africa; those two countries and Swaziland got more than 65 percent of their imports from South Africa. While Zambian exports to South Africa made up 2–8 percent of its total trade in 1964–68, Zambia imported about 23 percent of its goods from South Africa.[4] Of the six countries that came to independence in Southern Africa in the 1960s—Botswana, Lesotho, Malawi, Swaziland, Tanzania, and Zambia—only one, Tanzania, was not landlocked and dependent on transport routes through the Portuguese colonies or South Africa. Migrant labor into the South African mines remained an important source of capital for Mozambique, Botswana, and Lesotho.

Like the other newly independent countries of the region, the Portuguese colonies that gained independence lacked national coherence. Angola comprises eight ethnolinguistic groups; Mozambique has nine.[5] But the tasks of nation building and development were compounded in the Portuguese colonies by a dearth of human capital even greater than that suffered by the British colonies. Two examples suffice: In 1975 when Portugal exited from Mozambique, there were three black doc-

2. Robert Mortimer and others, *Politics and Society in Contemporary Africa* (Boulder, Colo.: Lynne Rienner Publishers, 1988), p. 228.

3. Mortimer and others, *Politics and Society*, p. 228.

4. Numbers are from Kenneth W. Grundy, *Confrontation and Accommodation in Southern Africa: The Limits of Independence* (University of California Press, 1973), p. 35.

5. Lawrence W. Henderson, *Angola: Five Centuries of Conflict* (Cornell University Press, 1979), p. 40; and William Finnegan, *A Complicated War: The Harrowing of Mozambique* (University of California Press, 1992), p. 27.

tors and one black lawyer; 90 percent of the population was illiterate.[6] In Angola at independence, there was not a single African businessman or bureaucrat.[7]

In Angola, Mozambique, Tanzania, and, to a lesser extent, Zambia, the ruling elites borrowed ideas of nation building and policies of socialist development from Western experience, but those ideas conflicted with traditional society and customs. Pursuing a policy style that Goran Hyden characterizes as "We must run, while others walk,"[8] the ruling parties believed that modernization could be imposed from above. They treated traditional social relationships as barriers to development. While the attempt to modernize from above resulted in gains in literacy, health care, and education, the militaristic treatment of citizens produced alienation and disengagement. For the Portuguese ex-colonies, that alienation was aggravated by attacks from internal parties supported by the Rhodesians and South Africans and by the economic strains of the regional war.

In Angola the MPLA, with Cuban and Soviet assistance, had thoroughly routed its domestic opponents in 1976. South Africa, however, continued to supply UNITA with arms and equipment to keep it alive as a threat to the regime. Moreover, South Africa often invaded southern Angola to attack SWAPO guerrillas who had taken refuge there.

In Mozambique, FRELIMO's support for Zimbabwean independence incurred high costs for the new country. Physical hardship was felt through a series of Rhodesian air and land attacks. Economic hardship came in March 1976 when Rhodesia closed its border to economic trade with Mozambique. The Mozambicans retaliated by refusing to renew economic relations with Rhodesia, a decision that resulted in the loss of approximately $556 million, more than two years' worth of all exports from Mozambique.[9] To counter Mozambican support for the Zimbabwean guerrillas, the Rhodesian Central Intelligence Organiza-

6. Per Wastberg, *Assignments in Africa: Reflections, Descriptions, Guesses*, trans. Joan Tate (Farrar, Straus, and Giroux, 1986), p. 115.

7. Gerald J. Bender, *Angola under the Portuguese: The Myth and the Reality* (University of California Press, 1978), p. 201.

8. Goran Hyden, "Administration and Public Policy," in Joel D. Barkan, ed., *Politics and Public Policy in Kenya and Tanzania*, rev. ed. (Praeger, 1984), p. 107.

9. Carol B. Thompson, *Challenge to Imperialism: The Frontline States in the Liberation of Zimbabwe* (Harare: Zimbabwe Publishing House, 1985), p. 79.

tion (CIO) equipped and trained a group of former Portuguese settlers to destabilize Mozambique. In 1980, at Zimbabwean independence, the CIO turned over command of MNR (or RENAMO, Resistência Nacional Moçambicana, as it was known later) to the South African military, who turned it into a devastatingly effective killing machine.[10]

Zambia, which provided support and bases for ZIPRA (Zimbabwean People's Revolutionary Army), also bore Rhodesian air and ground attacks. Moreover, Kenneth Kaunda's principled stand to abide by U.N.-imposed sanctions against Rhodesia cost Zambia's economy $744 million between 1969 and 1977.[11]

The costs of regional cooperation to end white rule constantly tested the alliance of Front Line States. By 1978, Zambian citizens often expressed bitterness over Kaunda's support for other people's freedom at their expense.[12] Such bitterness led Kaunda, without consultation with his Front Line allies, to reopen trade relations with Rhodesia, which prompted much criticism from Tanzanian president Julius Nyerere and Mozambican president Samora Machel.

South Africa's Disarray

Portugal's withdrawal from Southern Africa posed several choices for South Africa. In Mozambique, Portugal had handed over power to Mozambique's only liberation movement, FRELIMO; South Africa had to decide whether it should live with or actively undermine the new regime, whose rhetoric was decidedly revolutionary. In Angola, where three armed movements vied for power, the situation was more fluid. Should South Africa intervene to prevent the most radical of the parties,

10. For an account of the Rhodesian role in founding MNR and transferring it to South Africa, see Ken Flower, *Serving Secretly: An Intelligence Chief on Record Rhodesia into Zimbabwe, 1964–1981* (London: John Murray, 1987), pp. 140–41, 262, 273. Flower was head of the Rhodesian Central Intelligence Organization.

11. Estimate of Sir Robert Jackson, ex-coordinator of U.N. assistance to Zambia, in Ronald T. Libby, *The Politics of Economic Power in Southern Africa* (Princeton University Press, 1987), p. 243. Libby points out (p. 244) that the figure almost certainly "deflates the real cost to Zambia. It does not include the extra recurrent and capital costs arising from rerouting Zambia's external trade, the congestion surcharges at Indian and Atlantic ocean ports, increased storage charges, nor state subsidies paid to transport agencies such as Zambia Railways."

12. Libby, *Politics of Economic Power*, pp. 242–45.

the MPLA, from coming to power? Should it stay on the sidelines and try to engage whichever party came to power?

Victories by ideologically hostile regimes in the former Portuguese colonies also raised questions about South-West Africa and Rhodesia: Could these white states survive? Would it be possible to establish friendly black regimes in those countries that would enjoy international legitimacy?

The South African state was divided from the start on these questions. One policy line, associated with then–Prime Minister John Vorster, suggested reaching some kind of *modus vivendi* in the region. Through a combination of economic incentives and veiled threats, a policy of détente hoped to produce regional acceptance of apartheid. An opposing line, associated with the ministry of defense and its chief at the time, P. W. Botha, held that South Africa could not countenance independent regimes that might support the overthrow of South African apartheid. The struggle between these two foreign policy courses led to contradictory South African actions throughout most of the 1970s.

Initially, under Vorster, South Africa tried to pursue regional détente in order to co-opt the liberation movements. Part of the strategy involved quiet diplomacy with Kenneth Kaunda of Zambia to find ways to negotiate a solution to the war in Rhodesia. Vorster had decided that the white position was untenable in that country. The best that could be hoped for, he thought, was a political settlement that would protect white property and bring to power a black regime friendly to South Africa. In coordination with Kaunda, Vorster agreed to pressure Ian Smith to release imprisoned nationalist leaders and to negotiate with them over majority rule. Kaunda, joined by Julius Nyerere, would pressure the various competing liberation groups to unify. The exercise led to talks between Smith and some of the nationalist leaders in August 1975 at Victoria Falls but failed to produce a settlement.[13]

Vorster also hoped that an end to settler rule in Rhodesia would alleviate international pressure on South Africa to withdraw from Namibia. The South African leader seemed to think that decolonization could be partial in the region. If Pretoria aided the quest for peace in Rhodesia, then the international community might abide South African racial domination in Namibia and at home.

13. Stephen John Stedman, *Peacemaking in Civil War: International Mediation in Zimbabwe, 1974–1980* (Boulder, Colo.: Lynne Rienner Publishers, 1991), pp. 67–68.

To the new FRELIMO regime in Mozambique, Vorster offered recognition and a policy of noninterference, accompanied by an implicit threat against Mozambican support for South African resistance fighters. Vorster's policy immediately came under attack within his government. The ministry of defense, plotting without Vorster's approval, loaded planes and helicopters to attack the government in Mozambique. The renegade plot was thwarted at the last moment by the South African Bureau of State Security.[14]

All of the latent tensions within the South African government came to a head over Angola. The South African foreign ministry preferred to recognize whatever government came to power, even the Marxist MPLA party, while the military insisted that South Africa intervene to ensure that a friendly regime took office. The military's approach, and the policy line of P. W. Botha, won out.

The full story of the South African invasion of Angola has yet to emerge. Some argue that the initial military operation to keep the MPLA from power was ordered by Botha without Vorster's approval, a scenario that one analyst rightly calls improbable.[15] More likely is that Vorster was persuaded to go along with the military because he thought he would get U.S. support for the invasion and because Kenneth Kaunda had clearly indicated that Zambia did not want the MPLA in power. Furthermore, the situation on the ground would have allowed Vorster to reconcile divergent policies toward Mozambique and Angola: FRELIMO was the sole independence movement in Mozambique when the Portuguese overthrew their own government in Lisbon. In Angola three different parties—the MPLA, FNLA, and UNITA— competed for power in 1975, and the South Africans and Americans felt that the MPLA was militarily vulnerable.

The South African invasion in 1975 led to a major escalation of the Angolan civil war. Once the South African military, together with Zairian forces, invaded Angola to assist FNLA and UNITA—both of which received American support—Cuban troops and Soviet military aid sprang to the defense of the MPLA. But South Africa did not get the allegedly promised U.S. support for the invasion, and most of Africa

14. Kenneth W. Grundy, *The Militarization of South African Politics* (Indiana University Press, 1986), p. 91.

15. Deon Geldenhuys, *The Diplomacy of Isolation: South African Foreign Policy Making* (Johannesburg: MacMillan South Africa, 1984), p. 82.

recognized the MPLA as the government of Angola. The South African military had to retreat.

The rapid internationalization of the Angolan conflict had important repercussions. It prompted a reevaluation of American foreign policy, which led the United States for the first time to take an active role in working for political settlements in the region. The presence of Cuban troops and Soviet advisers in the region—and the precedent of their intervention—lent urgency to the efforts of the Western powers and African leaders to end the conflicts in Rhodesia and Namibia. For the African heads of state the war underscored the need for unity so that the region would not become more of a superpower battleground.

Détente was temporarily saved by Henry Kissinger, who flew to Lusaka in April 1976 and signaled American willingness to help the regional parties work toward a political settlement on Rhodesia and Namibia. Kissinger acknowledged that the presidents of the newly named Front Line States—Kenneth Kaunda of Zambia, Seretse Khama of Botswana, Julius Nyerere of Tanzania, and Samora Machel of Mozambique—must play a role in bringing peace to the region; he promised to work through them. Kissinger also met with Vorster, providing him with international legitimacy in the hope that he would continue to push the Smith regime to settle. Although the Kissinger intervention led to a meeting of all parties in Geneva in October 1976, it failed to bring a political settlement to Rhodesia, for reasons we discuss in the next chapter. The failure of the Geneva talks, in conjunction with processes and events in South Africa, ended the Vorster approach to change in the region.

South Africa's Domestic Crisis

Divisions within South Africa over domestic issues soon mirrored the governmental split over regional policy. In particular, the precepts of apartheid itself came into question. Apartheid had been designed to promote Afrikanerdom, and it had done so successfully. In 1948 when the National Party had taken power, Afrikaners were mostly indigent farmers and blue-collar workers. By 1970 more than half of all Afrikaners were state employees; less than 10 percent were occupied in agriculture.[16]

16. Robert M. Price, *The Apartheid State in Crisis: Political Transformation in South Africa, 1975–1990* (Oxford University Press, 1991), p. 25; and Heribert

Between 1948 and 1970 South Africa possessed the second-fastest growing economy in the world.[17] During that time the base of South Africa's economy moved from agriculture and mining to manufacturing. Apartheid had well served the interests of mining and agriculture by providing cheap labor, but the expansion of manufacturing demanded a more skilled black work force. Important business interests, as well as some bureaucrats, argued that apartheid's restrictions on labor mobility and failure to provide education for black labor would undermine continued growth of the South African economy. The success of apartheid had begun to contribute to its undoing.

Because apartheid was a shackle on future manufacturing growth, a small constituency for political reform developed. Even the South African military, fearful that a stagnant economy could not support the increased arms spending that a regional war would necessitate, became a voice for political reform. And because apartheid had moved so many Afrikaners out of the agricultural sector, which had supplied a key constituency for apartheid at its inception, the National Party sensed that it had a limited opening to promote change. Some within the South African government began to voice the previously unspeakable: South Africa's survival depended on political reform.

Economic stagnation in the 1970s also helped create the conditions for black rebellion against apartheid. Mobilized by Stephen Biko and other adherents of the black consciousness movement and emboldened by the defeat of colonialism in Angola and Mozambique, students in Soweto went on strike on June 16, 1976, to protest the teaching of Afrikaans in their schools.[18] As it had in Sharpeville sixteen years earlier, the South African regime answered the peaceful demands of Soweto students with lethal force. This time, however, the protests spread across South Africa. Hundreds of blacks were killed over the course of the student uprising, and thousands crossed the border into Mozam-

---

Adam and Hermann Giliomee, *Ethnic Power Mobilized: Can South Africa Change?* (Yale University Press, 1979), p. 169.

17. Dan O'Meara, *Volkskapitalisme: Class, Capital and Ideology in the Development of Afrikaner Nationalism, 1934–1948* (Cambridge University Press, 1983), p. 247.

18. For two attempts to weigh various explanations of the Soweto uprising, see Anthony W. Marx, *Lessons of Struggle: South African Internal Opposition, 1960–1990* (Oxford University Press, 1992), pp. 51–72; and Price, *Apartheid State in Crisis*, pp. 46–58.

bique to train for the overthrow of the white regime. The international community responded with a U.N. arms embargo on Pretoria and a worldwide movement to convince multinational corporations to divest from South Africa.

The Outcome: South Africa's "Total Strategy"

Domestic upheaval coupled with regional threat led to the triumph of the Botha faction. Financial and military circles berated the Vorster government for its inability to handle the new dimensions of South Africa's problems. Business criticized Vorster for his unwillingness to reform apartheid to allow for greater labor mobility, the training of black skilled labor, and recognition of organized black labor. Generals and other senior military strategists leveled attacks on regional security policy, claiming that the invasion of Angola had been bungled and that Vorster's attempt at détente was failed in conception as well as execution.[19]

In 1978 P. W. Botha became prime minister and put in place what Robert Price calls South Africa's "security driven agenda."[20] Apartheid was to be abandoned, reluctantly, to ensure continued white political and economic domination; in its place would be a program of social, economic, and political reforms aimed at drawing what state strategists dubbed "useful blacks" into a new supportive alliance. Purposeful repression would be used to lower black expectations about the extent of change and to alleviate white worries that reform would result in the majority coming to power. Although Botha's program made some concessions to the demands and grievances of selected parts of the disenfranchised majority—for example, black trade unions were legalized and local communities were given state permission to end petty discrimination if they so desired—it resolutely maintained direct white minority control of the political system.

As for regional strategy, top military planners formulated a comprehensive alternative to détente. The new "total strategy," laid out in a 1977 Defence White Paper, argued for the fundamental reorganiza-

19. Robert Davies, Dan O'Meara, and Sipho Dlamini, *The Struggle for South Africa: A Reference Guide to Movements, Organizations and Institutions*, 2d ed. (London: Zed Books, 1988), p. 44.
20. Price, *Apartheid State in Crisis*, p. 45.

tion and buildup of the white state's capacity to intervene militarily in the region. It also held that the mobilization of all available resources—economic, political, social, psychological, and military—was essential to defend South Africa at home and in the region. The South African state, the paper contended, was threatened by a total communist onslaught—a Soviet-orchestrated strategy to take over the whole region—with South Africa the coveted prize.

P. W. Botha adopted the "total strategy" when he assumed the prime minister's office in 1978. Regional policymaking thus changed in at least three significant ways, which had enormous implications for all of Southern Africa.[21]

The decisionmaking process was restructured. Bureaucratic infighting among various ministries, state bureaucracies, and parts of the military and security apparatus was rife in the last years of the Vorster government. The Botha government decided to end the infighting by restructuring the political decisionmaking process. The most notable features of this reorganization were, first, a decisive centralization of power in the hands of the prime minister and (after 1984) the executive state president, with a corresponding diminution of the role of the cabinet and the parliament. Second, a military-dominated extraparliamentary government structure, the National Security Management System, was established alongside—but superior to—the formal government structure at all levels. At the top of this parallel structure was the State Security Council, the main decisionmaking body in South Africa until late 1989.

This administrative change meant that no important decision could be taken in South Africa without the consent of the military. Similarly, the military could reach decisions and implement them (with the concurrence of the state president) without seeking cabinet consent. In sum, "total strategy" emanated from the military, fostered the military's ascendancy to power, and created an independent, unaccountable military organization.

Regional objectives were clarified. Botha fleshed out a concept first suggested by Vorster: a regional economic and security alliance, with South

---

21. This way of analyzing the restructuring of regional policy is from Robert Davies and Dan O'Meara, "Total Strategy in Southern Africa: An Analysis of South African Regional Policy since 1978," *Journal of Southern African Studies*, vol. 11 (April 1985).

Africa as the dominant regional power, should be formed to counteract the influence of "Marxism" in the region. The concept called for regional economic projects and nonaggression pacts that would demonstrate the superiority of capitalism over socialism and Marxism. In return for its support of the Constellation of Southern African States (CONSAS), Pretoria sought regional recognition of the homelands and continued white political domination in South Africa. Strategists hoped that if the region could be lured into acknowledging the legitimacy of South Africa, then international legitimacy would follow.

South Africa formulated other regional objectives. Pretoria wanted regional states to prohibit Namibian and South African liberation movements from operating either openly or clandestinely in their territories; it also wanted regional states to moderate their own antiapartheid stance. Pretoria did *not* want regional states to develop means to defend themselves militarily or to cultivate strong ties—especially military ones—to socialist countries. And Pretoria intended that regional states should maintain and deepen their economic links to, and dependence on, South Africa.

New instruments were created to achieve the objectives. To accomplish its regional goals, the government beefed up SADF (South African Defence Force) capabilities for fighting interstate wars; increased domestic arms production; intensified its nuclear arms development; and reinforced the police and the military to improve their ability to fight a counterinsurgency war.[22]

Pretoria took other, more particular steps to persuade regional states to meet South Africa's newly clarified goals. These included setting up reconnaissance commandos and other special forces for hit-and-run operations; stationing ethnic battalions near the borders for raids into neighboring territories; and establishing surrogate forces, whose recruits came from the country concerned but were supplied, trained, and

22. In F. W. de Klerk's speech of March 24, 1993 that revealed South Africa's nuclear capability, he states that the regional war of the mid-1970s was a decisive influence on South Africa's determination to develop the bomb. According to de Klerk, "The bomb strategy was that, if the situation in Southern Africa was to deteriorate seriously, a confidential indication of the deterrent capability would be given to one or more of the major powers, for example the United States, in an attempt to persuade them to intervene." The text of the speech is in *Argus*, March 25, 1993.

led by the SADF, in particular by the directorate of special tasks within the SADF's Department of Military Intelligence (DMI).

Surrogate forces were considered the most important of the new military instruments created within the framework of "total strategy." South African strategists valued them especially for two reasons. First, the cost of training, equipping, and commanding the surrogate forces was small compared with the damage they could inflict on the target state. Second, they constituted a low-risk option in terms of overt exposure of their South African patronage. Although the surrogate forces were externally generated and controlled, they had the potential to build a domestic constituency and base of support that could render future assistance moot.

South Africa also formulated specific new policies to further regional dependence on its economy. Attacks on transportation lines that bypassed South Africa would force countries to rely solely on South African ports, and closing down a country's exports and imports could force concessions. Barring migrant labor from South Africa could financially devastate recalcitrant neighbors. The precise mix of economic carrots and sticks Pretoria wielded would be determined by a country's willingness to advance South Africa's objectives.[23]

THE 1980S: REGIONAL DESTABILIZATION AND DOMESTIC EMERGENCY

Regional and international developments lent impetus to South Africa's pursuit of a "total strategy." A political settlement to the Rhodesian war in 1980 had led to the election of Robert Mugabe in Zimbabwe. Mugabe and his party, the Zimbabwe African National Union, were publicly committed to socialism and deeply antagonistic to South Africa.

Zimbabwean independence encouraged other African states in the region to band together to reduce their economic vulnerability to South Africa. In 1980 representatives of the Front Line States (at the time, Angola, Botswana, Mozambique, Namibia, Tanzania, Zambia, and

---

23. See Deon Geldenhuys, "Some Strategic Implications of Regional Economic Relationships for the Republic of South Africa," *ISSUP Strategic Review* (University of Pretoria), January 1981. Perhaps inadvertently, this article presented the apartheid regime with a comprehensive list of economic warfare tools to be used against neighboring countries.

Zimbabwe) and Lesotho, Malawi, and Swaziland met in Lusaka, Zambia, to form the Southern African Development Coordination Conference (SADCC, but known now as the Southern African Development Community). Among the group's major goals were the "forging of links to create a genuine and equitable regional integration" and "the reduction of dependence, particularly, but not only, on the Republic of South Africa."[24] SADCC's immediate priority was to establish alternative transportation routes to minimize reliance on South African ports.

South African strategists believed that Mugabe's election and the formation of SADCC meant that regional co-optation had to be replaced by coercion and destabilization. Moreover, Pretoria was heartened by Ronald Reagan's election in the United States. South Africa welcomed Reagan's hard-line anticommunist stance, thinking that the new administration's policy toward the region—"constructive engagement"—would provide carte blanche for South Africa to attack neighboring states.

Pretoria actively pursued regional destabilization from the second half of 1980 to the end of 1983. SADF raids, sabotage, kidnappings, bombings, and assassinations struck throughout the region. South Africa also introduced or stepped up the activity of surrogate forces in Lesotho, Mozambique, Zambia, and Zimbabwe. Frequent troop incursions and, twice, large-scale invasions took place in southern Angola. In response to some criticism from business interests inside South Africa and from several Western governments about the widespread, indiscriminate destabilization, targets began to be chosen more selectively, but destabilization nevertheless continued and intensified.

South African state unity about regional goals, tactics, and strategy reached its pinnacle early in the 1980s. Both critics and admirers of the South African regime have posited that South African political elites were unified throughout the 1980s and followed a coherent strategy in dealing with their simultaneous crises.[25] In retrospect, however, it

24. SADCC, *Southern Africa toward Economic Liberation: A Declaration by the Governments of Independent States of Southern Africa*, statement presented at Lusaka, Zambia, April 1, 1980 (London, 1980).

25. For the critical side, see Price, *Apartheid State in Crisis*, pp. 99–101. Price admits, however, that on regional matters important divisions existed among policymakers; see p. 95. For a fawning treatment of the South African state and its reform attempts, see James M. Roherty, *State Security in South Africa: Civil*

seems likely that the coherence of the South African state splintered after 1982. Instead of sustaining its unity, the state dissolved into acrimonious debates about what could be accomplished in the region, what the goal of total strategy should be, and the extent of domestic concessions necessary to maintain white domination at home.

As differences grew among military strategists about the goals of regional destabilization, an important factional dispute broke out about the purpose of the proxy forces. One side, associated with the Department of Military Intelligence and Special Forces, supported the overthrow of the MPLA in Angola and FRELIMO in Mozambique and their replacement with governments subservient to Pretoria's demands. The other side, led by the foreign ministry, saw the surrogate forces creating crises of ungovernability that would compel the current governments to accede to South Africa's wishes.[26]

The latent splits among factions did not surface until increasing international criticism, especially from the United States, forced South Africa to make choices over the purpose of regional destabilization. In particular, the United States argued that if South Africa's goal was to create a secure region, then it needed to marry its military attacks to viable political goals. Unbridled destruction of the region, U.S. policymakers insisted, would only exacerbate South Africa's insecurity.

Chester Crocker, the American assistant secretary of state for African affairs, believed that creating a region amenable to South African security would comfort the National Party enough that it could proceed with domestic reforms. Crocker put forward a peace plan for Angola and Namibia that demanded Cuban withdrawal from the region as a price for Namibian independence. Crocker also coaxed Samora Machel into seeking common ground with Pretoria and encouraged Mozambique to pursue economic and political relations with the West.

Crocker's memoirs provide a glimpse into the deep divisions about regional policy that existed in the South African security establishment. He describes a U.S.–South African meeting in Cape Verde in 1983 as "somewhere between Club Med and an adult-style *Lord of the Flies*":

> Like paint remover, the non-stop alcohol intake stripped away any veneer of Afrikaner solidarity. They disagreed about everything:

Military Relations under P. W. Botha (Armonk, N.Y.: M. E. Sharpe, 1992).

26. Price, *Apartheid State in Crisis*, p. 95.

Savimbi's prospects in Angola, the relative importance of the Angolan war for South Africa, the role being played by the United States, the hopes for Namibia's internal parties, how to handle growing black unrest at home, and the right course in Mozambique. So deeply did they disagree about Mozambique that Botha excluded Van der Westhuizen from our restricted discussion of that topic. Later, when Cabelly [special assistant to Crocker] approached the fuming "Wessy" to compare notes, he growled: "You're wasting your time talking to them [Botha, Malan, Fourie, Barnard, Geldenhuys]—*I run Mozambique.*"[27]

In early 1984, anxious to break out of its international isolation and gain political recognition as a peaceful, responsible regional power, Pretoria negotiated with Angola and Mozambique. The nonaggression pact between South Africa and Mozambique—the Nkomati Accord, named for the river that separates the two countries—marked the peak of this phase, which also included a South African agreement to withdraw troops from Angola.[28] P. W. Botha was richly rewarded by the Western powers for his newfound posture as regional peacemaker: that summer he was invited to make state visits to West Germany and Great Britain.

South Africa's regional peace offensive formed part of a dual strategy for addressing what by 1984 had become an increasingly sickly economy. Between 1980 and 1985 the South African gross domestic product had increased by only 4 percent; the population had grown by 12 percent. South Africa needed international legitimacy to bolster investor confidence and foreign capital investment, and Pretoria hoped that Botha's program of domestic reform and the new regional policy would provide it.

As South Africa turned to negotiation in the region, the National Party set in place what was to be a key building block in its attempt to

27. Chester Crocker, *High Noon in Southern Africa: Peacemaking in a Rough Neighborhood* (W. W. Norton, 1992), p. 216. The Botha that Crocker refers to is Pik Botha, then minister of foreign affairs. The other personalities are Magnus Malan, minister of defense; Brand Fourie, deputy minister of foreign affairs; Neil Barnard, head of the national intelligence service; Janie Geldenhuys, chief of the SADF; and Pieter van der Westhuizen, chief of staff for intelligence for the SADF.

28. The Nkomati Accord is described in detail in chapter 4.

reform apartheid. A new tricameral constitution, approved in a whites-only referendum in November 1983, came into effect in 1984. South Africans classified by apartheid as "Coloureds" and "Asians" were to be represented in parliament, although in separate, racially exclusive chambers. A ratio of four votes for the white chamber to every two for the Coloured and one for the Asian ensured a white majority of votes on "general affairs." South Africans classified as Blacks continued to be excluded in the parliament.

The tricameral scheme proved to be an important spur to mass protest campaigns. The majority of Coloureds and Asians boycotted elections for the new parliament. The United Democratic Front (UDF)—a confederation of previously disparate antiapartheid organizations, local community associations in the black townships, militant student groups, and organized labor—was launched to campaign against the tricameral system. In September 1984 an uprising in the Vaal triangle area triggered a wave of escalating strikes, protests, and riots that continued until June 1986.[29]

These developments led to further international isolation, notwithstanding continuing attempts by the Botha government to capitalize on its regional accords. By mid-1985 the situation had deteriorated so much that even state strategists implicitly conceded that the "total strategy" was failing. For the first time since Sharpeville, the South African government declared states of emergency in parts of the country, and the SADF was sent into the townships to restore order.

The South African government in 1984 began clandestine operations to assassinate UDF organizers, establish black vigilante groups to foment violence in the townships, and train homeland forces to be used against UDF and ANC supporters. One plan, Operation Katz, called for the secret formation of a Xhosa Resistance Movement, which would be a counterrevolutionary ally against the UDF in the Eastern Cape and "would not be traced back to the RSA [Republic of South Africa]."[30] In 1985 a special hit squad was established with orders to "permanently

29. The best account of the insurrection is found in Steven Mufson, *Fighting Years: Black Resistance and the Struggle for a New South Africa* (Beacon Press, 1990).

30. The quotation is from the text of the document; see "Operation Katz," *New Nation*, March 12–18, 1993, p. 12. See also Rich Mkhondo, *Reporting South Africa* (Portsmouth, N.H.: Heinemann, 1993), pp. 75–76; and "The 'Dirty Tricks' Trail Leads to the Top," *Weekly Mail*, March 12–18, 1993.

remove from society" Matthew Goniwe, a high school teacher and UDF activist in the Port Craddock region of the Eastern Cape.[31] A year later the SADF provided special military training in Namibia to police forces affiliated with the Inkatha movement of Mangosuthu Buthelezi.[32]

Western media coverage of South African police and military repression in the black townships increased public demand in Europe and the United States for the imposition of tough economic sanctions. A speech by P. W. Botha to a federal congress of the National Party in August 1985 marked an important turning point in international efforts to isolate South Africa. Heralded in advance as a statement that would map out a new direction, Botha's "Rubicon speech" instead demonstrated to a large international audience that the regime had no credible answers to the deepening crisis. Indeed the xenophobic, threatening tone of the speech goaded foreign bankers into refusing to roll over South African short-term loans, which created what became known as the "debt standstill crisis."

The increasing international isolation, especially the partial sanctions introduced by many countries in 1985–86, exacerbated South Africa's long-standing, precarious economic situation. Transnational companies and international banks lost their confidence in South Africa. The result was a significant net capital outflow between 1985 and 1988, estimated at 25.2 billion rand.[33]

By 1985 Western commercial bankers too had grave doubts about the South African economy. A freeze on new lending was accompanied by reluctance to renew credits. The effects snowballed. With prospects of profits dramatically diminished, private investors were disinclined to enter the South African market. Many foreign investors began to disinvest. Public creditors followed suit and refused new loans and debt renegotiations. More and more countries introduced trade sanctions.

31. Goniwe and three colleagues were murdered on June 27, 1985. An official inquest took place in 1993. South Africans witnessed the unprecedented event of the defense counsel for the SADF accusing the South African police of the killings, as well as the murders of three policemen who supposedly knew of the killings. See "Police Killed Colleagues, Inquest Told," *Weekly Mail and Guardian*, August 13–19, 1993.

32. "New Evidence on Caprivi Hit-Squads," *Weekly Mail and Guardian*, August 6–12, 1993.

33. Price, *Apartheid State in Crisis*, p. 228.

As Alan Hirsch aptly put it, "The ability of the West to take a moral stand in the 1980s was assisted by the illness of the golden goose."[34]

Botha's Rubicon speech also fueled what had become all-out insurrection in the townships. Responding to a call by the ANC to render the townships ungovernable, youths enforced school and consumer boycotts and labor stay-aways, attacked blacks thought to be collaborators, and used hit-and-run tactics to attack police and defense forces in the townships. Attacks by ANC cadres against targets affiliated with the South African state tripled between 1981–83 and 1984–86. "Between August 1984 and the end of 1986, four times more political work stoppages or 'stayaways' were staged than in the entire preceding three-and-one-half decades. . . . The workdays lost to strikes over 'economic' issues jumped over 200 percent between 1983 and 1984, then increased by 80 percent in 1985 and 93 percent in 1986. . . . Concurrently, the number of students boycotting school increased from approximately 10,000 in 1983 to almost 700,000 in 1985, swelling the ranks of militant youth available to 'man the barricades.' "[35]

The regime responded to the deepening crisis by intensifying repression and imposing a nationwide state of emergency in June 1986. Over the next six months the government detained without charge over 29,000 people.[36]

South Africa coupled repression at home with more violence in the region. Any hopes that South Africa was sincere in its "peace offensive" of 1984 were short-lived. American attempts to press further negotiations on Angola foundered in May 1985 when the SADF tried, unsuccessfully, to sabotage oilfields in Cabinda, Angola. In Mozambique, South Africa failed to abide by the Nkomati Accord and continued to supply MNR with personnel and provisions.

In 1986 the SADF carried out raids in Mozambique, Botswana, and Zimbabwe. Worst hit was undoubtedly Mozambique, which first suffered a massive 1986 MNR invasion from Malawi into northern Mozambique, aimed at dividing the country; that attack was followed by

34. Alan Hirsch, "The Paperback which Reveals a More Likely Commonwealth Line," *Weekly Mail*, August 18–24, p. 14.

35. Price, *Apartheid State in Crisis*, p. 193.

36. Leonard Thompson, *A History of South Africa* (Yale University Press, 1990), p. 236.

major infiltrations of men and equipment from South Africa, which led to, among other things, several large-scale massacres.

Zimbabwe and Tanzania rallied to assist FRELIMO. Both countries sent approximately 10,000 troops into Mozambique. Both countries chided Malawi for its support of MNR and threatened military action should Malawi dictator Hastings Banda refuse to take steps to shut down MNR operations.

1986–89: DOMESTIC AND REGIONAL DEAD ENDS

In 1986 South Africa's domestic crisis prompted a review of state strategy, which took place within the military-dominated institutions of the National Security Management System. "Total strategy" fell out of favor. The top military and government officials responsible for state strategy (securocrats, as they were called in South Africa) turned instead to "winning hearts and minds" (WHAM). The securocrats believed that black mass protests stemmed from bread-and-butter issues rather than political ones and that blacks could be bought off or neutralized by material concessions. Hoping to seize the initiative and forestall "a revolutionary onslaught," South Africa embarked on upgrading economic and social facilities in selected townships.

Pretoria hoped that WHAM would depoliticize black communities. Circumstances had forced the Botha regime to "accommodate" Africans within the political system, but domestic and international pressures to negotiate obliged Pretoria to acknowledge that it could no longer unilaterally implement political reforms. Any new dispensation would have to be the product of negotiation if South Africa were to succeed in gaining legitimacy. By early 1986 government leaders had edged toward accepting the necessity for negotiation, yet their vision of any new dispensation and of the negotiating process itself remained narrow.

The narrowness of vision became clear in May 1986 when the Commonwealth Eminent Persons' Group (EPG), which was composed of former heads of state, visited South Africa. The purpose of the EPG was to canvass black and white opinion in South Africa and to promote a "possible negotiating concept."[37] During the group's visit, the SADF

37. *Mission to South Africa: The Commonwealth Report, The Findings of the Commonwealth Eminent Persons Group on Southern Africa*, foreword by Shridath

made devastating raids on the capitals of Botswana, Zimbabwe, and Mozambique, thereby scuttling the group's efforts.

Stiffer sanctions from the United States and the European Community followed the failure of the Eminent Persons' Group, which drove further wedges between big business and the South African state. Some corporations in South Africa began to meet unilaterally with the African National Congress in Lusaka and elsewhere. The message from private citizens and business seemed to be that if the National Party was unwilling to make peace, they would have to do it themselves.

The National Party, however, believed that it could dictate the pace and outcome of change. It still insisted that any new constitution must continue to provide for racially differentiated political representation. Separate, racially exclusive political structures were to deal with "own affairs," while a complex array of joint bodies operating at local, regional, and national levels would introduce a modicum of power sharing for "general affairs." The negotiating forum (which Botha called "the Great Indaba") was to be a purely advisory body. The minority government and its allies and confidants were to have at least parity with other participants in the negotiations, and the regime would retain the power to decide whether to accept the forum's recommendations.

Achieving these goals was seen to depend on cultivating a "moderate" black leadership as a credible alternative to the existing national liberation and mass democratic movements. The "moderates" were to become the main negotiating partners in the Great Indaba, and "revolutionaries" were to be excluded unless they first capitulated. The 30:20:50 formula in vogue among state strategists captured the essence of the approach. According to the formula, 30 percent of blacks were moderates, 20 percent supported revolutionary organizations, and 50 percent were undecided. The task of WHAM was therefore to neutralize the "revolutionaries" through repression, enhance and consolidate an alternative "moderate" leadership through concessions, and through both processes win over the undecided majority.

The capstone of WHAM was to be a series of elections in October 1988 for black local authorities. When these failed to attract credible candidates or sufficient voters, it was clear that WHAM had failed.

Ramphal (Harmondsworth, U.K.: Penguin Books, 1986). The group reported that the South African government remained hostile to the fundamental right of one-person, one-vote.

Those blacks who cooperated with WHAM at the local level suffered community ostracism and often became targets of violence. Instead of black township administration tied to the state, the people relied on civic associations that could combine the provision of local services with active opposition to apartheid. Dual power—official government structures versus autonomous community-based organizations—came to be the norm at the local level.[38]

By 1989 the South African government's war against its own people had not solved the crisis of ungovernability. Indeed, government repression further isolated South Africa internationally and contributed to the downward economic spiral. The economic decline fed domestic unrest, which in turn fostered more repression. A new leader, F. W. de Klerk, recognized South Africa's security contradiction.[39] On September 20, 1989, he told South Africans, "We must accept the risk that goes with new initiatives. The risk of staying in a dead end street is far higher. Everything we do, we do it to avoid revolution."[40]

Nor had South Africa's war against its neighbors solved its security problems. At the end of 1987 South Africa fought its largest pitched battle in Angola against FAPLA (the Angolan army) and Cuban troops. After sending in more than 6,000 troops and saving its Angolan ally UNITA from an MPLA offensive, South Africa found itself unable to finish off the attacking force. A military stalemate developed around the Angolan town of Cuito Cuanavale. The introduction of new weapons by the Cubans and Angolans ended South African air superiority and made the costs of any South African attack prohibitive. Then in a militarily audacious move, Cuba moved 15,000 of its troops close to the Namibian border. The resulting strategic dilemma led directly to South African participation in talks with the United States, Angola, and Cuba. Those talks led to the Tripartite Agreement of December 1988, which paved the way for Namibian independence.

38. Mufson, *Fighting Years*, pp. 104–33; and Price, *Apartheid State in Crisis*, pp. 202–17.

39. The notion of security contradiction comes from Price, *Apartheid State in Crisis*, pp. 297–98.

40. Mkhondo, *Reporting South Africa*, p. 17. De Klerk was to repeat the metaphor two years later when asked why he embarked on negotiations: "If we continued as we were, we were in a cul-de-sac." *Reporting South Africa*, p. 19.

After Cuito Cuanavale, Pretoria began to see negotiations in a different light, as a way to seek political solutions to both internal and regional security problems. Several developments explain South Africa's changing perceptions.

—The military stalemate at Cuito Cuanavale had highlighted the limitations of militaristic aggression as a means of guaranteeing long-term security for apartheid.

—"Total strategy" and its "WHAM" successor had failed to create a supportive alliance capable of resolving the domestic crisis of apartheid; moreover, white political cohesion on the future path of South Africa had gradually dissolved.

—The pressures of international isolation, particularly exclusion from the "normal facilities" of international financial markets, had profoundly harmed South Africa's faltering economy.

—The changing international environment, particularly the adoption of glasnost, perestroika, and "new thinking" in the Soviet Union, had led to growing cooperation between the Soviet Union and the West in seeking political solutions to regional conflicts and lessened the perceived threat of international communism.

Each of these developments was important, but it was their joint impact that was decisive. The events at Cuito Cuanavale merit special comment, however. The confrontation at Cuito Cuanavale, though not a military defeat for SADF, proved to be a political setback with wide-ranging ramifications. It revealed the dangers inherent in trying to achieve political goals with outmoded military means, and it also reduced the standing of the military within the apartheid state in general. The internal balance of forces within the ruling white minority shifted.

The business community, both English and Afrikaner, tended to favor a negotiated solution to the Angolan and Namibian wars. A negotiated solution, they thought, would further peace and stabilize the regional security situation, and thus enhance the hopes for a political settlement within South Africa. Foreign affairs officials and many senior military officers, who grasped the international political implications arising from continued militarism, also probably favored a negotiated settlement, but they were wary of compromising South Africa's national security. At least parts of the military and security apparatus saw Namibian independence as a "sellout" that marked a decided deterioration in South Africa's security.

Two policy options emerged for short- to medium-term South African regional policy. The first one, based on détente and a reorientation of regional strategy, emphasized the importance of regional economic cooperation and peaceful relations among the countries of Southern Africa. This option held that destabilization had served its purpose and that the time was ripe to reintroduce the total strategy as it was originally conceived, together with a brushed-up version of CONSAS. Internal negotiations would be undertaken so the international community would be placated enough to remove sanctions.

The second option rested on a mixture of continued confrontational military behavior and Afrikaner nationalist fundamentalism. Its advocates stressed the rule of force and emphasized the traditional Afrikaner precepts of white supremacy. They eschewed internal negotiation and threatened to undermine peacemaking in the region and in South Africa.

South African regional policy began to show gross contradictions. In Mozambique, South Africa invested in the Maputo harbor and agro-industries and offered to assist FRELIMO in other areas, including gas exploration and tourism. Pretoria furnished nonlethal military aid to the Mozambican armed forces for the defense of Cabora Bassa power lines. At the same time, however, elements of the SADF continued to help the MNR.

Having unleashed a total war, the South African state found that it was not easy to jettison the personnel and organizations that waged the war. Having established proxies to do their bidding, South African leaders found that those proxies had agendas of their own. Having organized networks of sadistic killers, the South African government discovered that those assassins did not desist when some within the state wanted them to stop.

CONCLUSION

The South African state under P. W. Botha created a constituency for regional and domestic destabilization, even when such destabilization could undermine official policy. And the new leadership that chose the path of negotiation feared that the warlords would turn their wrath on those who challenged them. Advocates of negotiation also feared that their own early complicity in the dirty wars would become known.

Finally, one cannot discount that the new leadership believed it could harness the warlords to weaken the ANC as a bargaining partner.

The authorities in Pretoria could not ignore the new circumstances that prevailed after Cuito Cuanavale. The military option in Angola had become extremely costly in military, political, and economic terms. Pretoria's known involvement in destabilization elsewhere in the region, most notably in Mozambique, had become costly diplomatically and ideologically and had increased South Africa's international isolation precisely when economic pressures dictated a major effort to reduce isolation. At the same time, the government needed space, time, and a degree of legitimacy to tackle the question of how to proceed with domestic restructuring, including negotiating with the ANC.

The withdrawal of South Africa from Angola, the formal independence of Namibia, and the freeing of Nelson Mandela in February 1990 raised hopes that the thirty-year war against white domination in Southern Africa was coming to a close. By concentrating solely on conflict in Southern Africa, we have tried to show what conflict resolution has been up against in the region. We have therefore not focused until now on the many attempts to resolve the myriad conflicts of the region. To complete the picture of past legacies, we turn in the next chapter to a comparison of different attempts by various parties in the region—often with involvement from international third parties—to resolve their conflicts.

Chapter 4

Conflict Resolution: Experiences, Lessons, and Legacies

Conflict in Southern Africa has been widespread, intense, and protracted. Yet between 1975 and 1993 negotiation, mediation, and problem solving went hand in hand with the region's wars, leading sometimes to successful peacemaking. British mediation at Lancaster House in 1979 ended Zimbabwe's thirteen-year civil war. American mediation brought an end to the interstate war between South Africa and Angola in 1988 and paved the way for Namibian independence and the end of civil war there in 1989. In May 1991 participants in the Angolan civil war, with help from American, Russian, and Portuguese mediators, agreed to end their conflict. (One of the parties to the agreement, UNITA, rejected the settlement a year later, however, plunging that country back into civil war.) In October 1992, as the Angolan agreement unraveled, the main antagonists in the Mozambican civil war accepted a far-reaching peace agreement.

Conflict and conflict resolution in Southern Africa provide a bountiful harvest, perhaps the best in the world, for the current study of peacemaking. Negotiated settlements of civil war are rare, yet Southern Africa has seen three in thirteen years.[1] The ending of civil war in Namibia and U.N.-sponsored elections there in 1989 established that the United Nations could play a role in resolving civil wars. And the breakdown of the U.N.-monitored cease-fire and elections in Angola in October 1992—at a time when the international community demanded

---

1. In the twentieth century only about 15 percent of civil wars have ended through negotiation; most end through elimination or unconditional surrender of one of the antagonists. See Stephen John Stedman, *Peacemaking in Civil War: International Mediation in Zimbabwe, 1974–1980* (Boulder, Colo.: Lynne Rienner Publishers, 1991), pp. 4–8.

U.N. intervention in scores of civil wars—demonstrated the dangers and limits of peacemaking in civil war.

In this chapter we examine the successes and failures of conflict resolution in Southern Africa. By comparing successful and failed cases of negotiation we can derive lessons for the larger study of conflict resolution. We also seek to determine whether settlements and compromises aimed at ending hostilities have in fact redressed the fundamental conflicts that led to war. Such knowledge enables informed speculation about the likelihood of renewed violent conflict in the future. The terms of settlement also establish the constraints under which future conflict resolution must take place.

We begin by discussing the Alvor agreement of 1975, which failed to create a peaceful transition to independence in Angola. Then we look at the various attempts in the 1970s to resolve the Zimbabwean civil war, which culminated in the political settlement at Lancaster House, and we evaluate the effectiveness of the Lancaster agreement in bringing peace to Zimbabwe. Next we analyze the mediation of the Namibian conflict and explain its intertwining with attempts to end the interstate war in Angola. We examine the attempt by Mozambique and South Africa to reach a bilateral security agreement at Nkomati in 1984, and we also describe the attempts to end the domestic components of the Angolan and Mozambican wars. The chapter concludes by comparing all these cases.

ANGOLA: THE ALVOR AGREEMENT

The April 1974 coup in Lisbon put in power a military government with divided thoughts about its colonies in Africa. Some officers urged a transfer of power to African nationalist groups; other Portuguese authorities still insisted that the African colonies were vital parts of the empire. Those who argued for Portuguese withdrawal—the officers who had executed the Lisbon coup—prevailed. But unlike other colonial powers in Africa, Portugal had no experience with decolonization and therefore no real sense of how to bring its colonies to independence peacefully. Nor was a peaceful transfer of power Portugal's immediate priority—the new military government wanted to cut its losses as quickly as possible.

Three liberation movements competed for power when the Portuguese empire collapsed: the Movimento Popular de Libertação de Angola (MPLA), the União Nacional para a Independência Total de Angola (UNITA), and the Frente Nacional de Libertação de Angola (FNLA). Each had received international assistance in the preceding twelve years: the MPLA from the Soviet Union, Cuba, and Congo; the FNLA from the United States and Zaire; and UNITA from Zambia and, ironically enough, Portugal itself.[2] China at different times gave aid to all three movements.

The aims and makeup of the three liberation movements differed dramatically. UNITA and the FNLA were very much the creation of individuals—Jonas Savimbi and Holden Roberto, respectively—and their programs reflected this fact. Roberto's ideology was a mishmash of beliefs unified by enthusiasm for capitalism and suspicion of *mestiços*.[3] At its inception as the União das Populaçoes de Angola (UPA), the FNLA was deeply rooted in the traditions of Bakongo society. In fact, Roberto's earliest goal had been to restore the old Kongo kingdom in northern Angola and southern Zaire, until the United States stressed that such separatism would not win U.S. support. The UPA then changed its name and began to project a more national-oriented, Angolan image. UNITA's ideology, originally one of self-reliance, Maoism, and African socialism, has changed over the years in direct relation to Savimbi's opportunism.[4] The MPLA, on the other hand, was Marxist and nonracial. More than the other two movements, the MPLA consistently advanced a national project for liberation.

Each of the movements had particular ethnic constituencies and strengths. The MPLA drew its greatest support from the poor neighbor-

2. For example, in 1969 Savimbi established a working relationship with the Portuguese secret police, and in 1971 UNITA and the Portuguese military agreed that UNITA forces would have control over the Luena area in the central highlands in exchange for stopping MPLA's westward movement. Instances of other such collaborative agreements between UNITA and the Portuguese military are many. See William Minter, ed., *Operation Timber: Pages from the Savimbi Dossier* (Trenton, N.J.: Africa World Press, 1988); and Joseph Hanlon, *Beggar Your Neighbours* (London: CIIR and James Currey, 1986), pp. 155–56.

3. People of mixed African and white descent.

4. As Larry Napper points out, UNITA in 1974 had "few established programmatic positions." Larry C. Napper, "The African Terrain and U.S.-Soviet Conflict in Angola and Rhodesia: Some Implications for Crisis Prevention," in Alexander George, ed., *Managing U.S.-Soviet Rivalry: Problems of Crisis Prevention* (Boulder, Colo.: Westview Press, 1983), p. 156.

hoods of Luanda and the surrounding region. The FNLA was based in the Bakongo peoples in northern Angola, UNITA in the Ovimbundu of the central highlands. But "it would be an oversimplification and a distortion to describe the conflict between these movements as ethnic (or tribal) in its essence. All tried to gain support among a wide range of groups in Angola. All had some success."[5]

A halfhearted attempt by the Portuguese to broker a settlement among the warring parties resulted in the Alvor agreement, signed in January 1975. The liberation parties agreed to elections, power sharing, and integration of their armies in anticipation of the Portuguese departure in November 1975. The agreement fell far short of its goal.

Within months the MPLA, FNLA, and UNITA had resumed fighting, this time at more intense levels with arms and advisers from external sponsors.[6] Instead of establishing an orderly, peaceful transition to independence in Angola, the Portuguese had created a situation ripe for international intervention.

Because the three liberation movements in Angola had different strengths, constituencies, and interests, they placed unequal stress on the several aims of the agreement. The FNLA military forces, although insignificant in the early 1970s, had been reconstructed in Zaire with U.S. assistance after the Lisbon coup. Its army was therefore strong, and the FNLA believed that it could gain power unilaterally. Of the three signatories to the Alvor agreement, it was the least committed to power sharing. The MPLA, which advocated a socialist transformation, found its support limited mostly to Luanda, the Angolan capital. While it agreed on the principle of power sharing, the MPLA was not committed to holding elections. UNITA, the weakest party militarily, felt that it had strong political support. It therefore had the most stake in the

---

5. James Voorhees, "Soviet Policy toward the Conflict between South Africa and Angola in the 1980s," Ph.D. dissertation, Johns Hopkins University, 1992, p. 63.

6. This account of the Alvor agreement is based on F. W. Heimer, *The Decolonization Conflict in Angola, 1974–1976: An Essay in Political Sociology* (Geneva: Institut Universitaire de Hautes Etudes Internationales, 1979); Napper, "African Terrain," pp. 155–86; Alexander George, "Missed Opportunities for Crisis Prevention: The War of Attrition and Angola," in George, ed., *Managing U.S.-Soviet Rivalry*, pp. 187–224; and John A. Marcum, *The Angolan Revolution*, vol. 2: *Exile Politics and Guerrilla Warfare (1962–1976)* (MIT Press, 1978).

successful implementation of the agreement, since it believed it would win an election.

Angola quickly became part of the global competition between the United States and the Soviet Union. Within two weeks of the signing of the Alvor agreement, the U.S. government voted to send approximately $300,000 to the FNLA. That aid bolstered the FNLA's already dominant military and sundered its frayed commitment to the negotiated transition. It also signaled that the United States was not committed to the Alvor compromise, a message noted by the Soviet Union. The MPLA soon found itself under siege from the FNLA army, which was supported by Zairian forces. Cuban advisers and Soviet equipment arrived in May and June 1975 to help the MPLA hold Luanda. In July the MPLA mounted a successful counterattack and was poised for overall victory by the end of the summer.

South Africa and the United States could not countenance an MPLA victory.[7] In August South Africa sent troops more than 100 miles into Angola and offered assistance to UNITA, which Savimbi accepted. The United States embarked on a $32 million covert aid program to stop the MPLA. South Africa, believing it would have U.S. support, invaded Angola in October to eliminate the MPLA. The MPLA, in response, called for Soviet matériel and intervention from Cuban troops to repel the South African challenge.

The United States and South Africa hoped that the FNLA and Zairian forces would take Luanda and proclaim independence by November 11, the day scheduled for the Portuguese departure. South African forces, aided by UNITA, would assist by conquering as much of the country as possible up to Luanda. Zairian president Mobutu Sese Seko committed two elite battalions from his country to help the FNLA, while South Africa sent two airplanes—far ahead of its advancing columns—loaded with artillery and gunners to shell Luanda from the south. However, Cuban forces and Soviet equipment had just arrived. FNLA and Zairian forces fled and South African defense minister P. W. Botha ordered a frigate up the coast to evacuate the artillery and gun-

---

7. John Stockwell relates that the U.S. government in July 1975 decided to give massive support to the FNLA and UNITA and to encourage South Africa to side with UNITA. This eventually led to coordination between the CIA and South Africa on escalated action against the MPLA. See Stockwell, *In Search of Enemies: A CIA Story* (W. W. Norton, 1978).

ners. When November 11 arrived, it was the MPLA that declared independence for Angola. The Portuguese left, without any commitment to the agreement they had helped mediate.[8]

What went wrong? Why did the Alvor agreement prove so ineffective at binding the Angolans to a peaceful settlement of their competition? First, the agreement was not based on a full, honest commitment to a peaceful transition and power sharing. The signatories and their external backers had different visions of post-colonial Angola. The liberation parties shared a desire to oust Portugal, but the MPLA desired a socialist transformation and Roberto and Savimbi put forth various scenarios based on capitalism, traditionalism, and African nationalism. Moreover, at least one party—the FNLA—believed that it could prevail unilaterally through war. U.S. assistance promoted that belief.

Portuguese ineptitude also marred the Alvor agreement. The agreement did not establish security arrangements that might have minimized violence among the parties. The Portuguese were unwilling to actively monitor the cease-fire and transition, and they did not call upon any international organization to help enforce a cease-fire. Indeed, it seemed as if the designers of the agreement believed that the transition was to take place in a regional and international vacuum. They did little to anticipate the external involvement that came to pass, and therefore did not try to bring on board the actors who subsequently contributed to the escalation of the conflict. In other words, they made no attempt to create an environment that might have given the settlement a chance.

MEDIATION IN ZIMBABWE: FROM FAILURE TO SUCCESS

The chaotic decolonization of Angola brought a new, acute awareness of the potential for escalation and superpower confrontation throughout Southern Africa. That awareness produced different reactions from different players. It compelled Southern African heads of state to make

8. The South African presence became untenable once the U.S. Congress adopted the Clark amendment in December 1975 prohibiting U.S. covert aid to Angola. South African forces were withdrawn by March 1976, and more than three years would pass before they attempted another large-scale invasion.

a unified effort to resolve the Zimbabwean civil war. It also drove South African prime minister John Vorster to seek the installment of a friendly black regime in Rhodesia, one that would both reject social transformation and allow white domination to continue in a different guise. Further intransigence from Rhodesian prime minister Ian Smith, Vorster believed, would lead to increased violence and victory for revolutionaries who could endanger South African security. The precedent of Cuban intervention in Angola raised the possibility of like intervention in Rhodesia.

In the mid-1960s two liberation parties—the Zimbabwe African Nationalist Union (ZANU) and the Zimbabwe African People's Union (ZAPU)—organized armies to overthrow the white settler regime of Ian Smith and the Rhodesian Front. The ensuing civil war claimed between 20,000 and 30,000 lives, mostly civilians, from 1966 through 1980. The issues at stake included the political demand for "one person, one vote," an end to institutionalized racism, and the economic redistribution of wealth and land.[9] And again, as in the Angolan war against Portugal, the black struggle against the white government was compromised by "struggles within the struggle"—personal, ethnic, and ideological divisions.[10]

ZANU and its military arm ZANLA (Zimbabwe African National Liberation Army), which bore the brunt of the fighting for liberation, had support from the majority Shona-speaking population of Zimbabwe. The main regional sponsor was FRELIMO; after Mozambique gained independence from Portugal, the FRELIMO government gave ZANU arms and sanctuary. International support for ZANU, the more radical of the liberation movements, came mostly from China. Robert Mugabe eventually led ZANU, but he did not consolidate his position until 1978, after a series of bitter, violent interparty battles.

ZAPU, led by Joshua Nkomo, and its army ZIPRA (Zimbabwe People's Revolutionary Army) received sponsorship from Zambia and the Soviet Union. Its main source of strength within Zimbabwe stemmed from the Ndebele of Matabeleland, who make up 15 percent of Zimbabwe's population. In addition to the two armed liberation

9. This discussion of Zimbabwe is based on Stedman, *Peacemaking in Civil War*.

10. Masipula Sithole, *Zimbabwe: Struggles within the Struggle* (Harare: Rujeko, 1977).

parties, two prominent politicians—Bishop Abel Muzorewa and Reverend Ndabaningi Sithole—led political parties without armies inside Zimbabwe.

Four times during the 1970s would-be mediators attempted to resolve the conflict. In 1974 Kenneth Kaunda of Zambia and John Vorster of South Africa pressured the parties to attend a peace conference, which eventually convened at Victoria Falls in August 1975. The mediation strategy called for Kaunda and Julius Nyerere of Tanzania to impose unity on the nationalist parties while South Africa pushed Smith and the Rhodesian Front to settle. The mediators' goal was to gain commitment to a gradual, five-year transition to majority rule. Little preparation was made for the meeting, and in the end the conference furthered the distance between the competing liberation movements as well as between blacks and whites in Zimbabwe.

The U.S. government actively joined the search for a mediated peace in Zimbabwe, prompted by the collapse of the Portuguese in Angola and the failure of the United States and South Africa to prevent the MPLA from gaining power. In April 1976 in Lusaka, U.S. secretary of state Henry Kissinger publicly committed the United States to ending white rule in Rhodesia and Namibia. He assured Kenneth Kaunda that he would work with the presidents of the Front Line States to bring peace to the region. Kissinger also sought cooperation from South Africa to bring majority rule to Rhodesia in exchange for support for Vorster at home.

In short, Kissinger revived the Kaunda-Vorster strategy. South Africa, by threatening to abandon its ally in Rhodesia, would gain Ian Smith's public commitment to majority rule. The Front Line States would work to promote unity among the nationalists. Kissinger promised to develop specific proposals for a transition, with help from the Front Line presidents. In private, however, Kissinger added a different twist: his goal was to devise a solution that would isolate ZANU and its Mozambican ally FRELIMO.[11]

In September 1976 Kissinger met Ian Smith in Pretoria. The South African threats had produced their intended effect: Smith agreed to majority rule. Smith, who thought that Kissinger was bargaining on behalf of the liberation movements and their sponsors, requested that his government control police and security during the transition.

11. Stedman, *Peacemaking in Civil War*, pp. 89, 99–103.

Kissinger acceded, but he cautioned that the Front Line presidents would have to concur.

Kaunda expressed serious reservations about Smith's stipulation. Kissinger then traveled to Dar es Salaam, where he did not convey Smith's request at all; he simply informed Nyerere that Smith had agreed to majority rule. Then, in an ambiguously worded telegram, Kissinger signaled to Smith that the Front Line leaders had agreed to government control over police and security during the transition. To move the peace process forward, Kissinger had resorted to "lying to both sides."[12]

Kissinger's "lies" kept the mediation effort afloat and led to a peace conference in Geneva in October 1976, chaired by Ivor Richard of Great Britain. Since there was no prior agreement about possible solutions to the war, the conference dissolved into fractious disputes over every detail. On the Rhodesian side, Smith claimed that he had clinched a deal with Kissinger—his purpose in Geneva was simply to sign it. The nationalists rejected that position out of hand because the British and Kissinger had told them that everything was up for negotiation. The conference ended in December 1976 without firm agreement on any details of a transition to majority rule. All of the contending parties— the two armed nationalist movements now forged into an alliance called the Patriotic Front (PF), the two parties without armies, and the Rhodesian Front—postured, blustered, and insulted one another, but they did not engage in serious negotiations.

In 1977 David Owen of Great Britain and Cyrus Vance of the United States initiated a series of informal consultations known as the Anglo-American process. These talks led to a set of detailed proposals for a constitution, transition, and cease-fire, which Rhodesian whites rejected. They chose instead to ally themselves with the two African nationalists without armies, Sithole and Muzorewa.

The new alliance between Muzorewa, Sithole, and Smith, known as the internal settlement, established a transitional government of national unity that the whites hoped would gain international legitimacy and end support for the guerrillas. The enterprise was undermined

12. This was the judgment of an aide to British prime minister James Callaghan, as quoted in David Martin and Phyllis Johnson, *The Struggle for Zimbabwe: The Chimurenga War* (London: Faber and Faber, 1981), p. 253. See also Stedman, *Peacemaking in Civil War*, pp. 85–125.

from the start. The white government watered down and vetoed proposed reforms that might have gained majority support. The black nationalists, knowing that the transitional government would eventually hold an election for a new prime minister, subverted each other in the hope of gaining future advantage.

Parliamentary elections were held in April 1979 in the bastard state of "Zimbabwe-Rhodesia." Abel Muzorewa's party, the United African National Council, won 68 percent of the vote, and Muzorewa became prime minister. His victory set the stage for one final round of negotiations.

Pressure mounted in the United States and Britain for recognition of the Muzorewa government. The common assumption was that Britain's newly elected prime minister, Margaret Thatcher, would recognize Muzorewa, but she did not. Following advice from the British foreign secretary, Peter Carrington, and from the Carter administration in Washington, Thatcher withheld recognition in the hope that one final mediation effort would end the war. In September 1979, under Carrington's leadership and with legitimacy conferred by a Commonwealth Heads of State conference held a month earlier, the British brought all of the parties together at Lancaster House. The conferees reached a negotiated settlement of the war in December.

The grueling four-month conference proceeded in stages as the participants collided over a new constitution, the arrangements of a transitional government, and the details of a cease-fire. The new constitution guaranteed white overrepresentation in the legislature for seven years, protected the pensions of white civil servants, and, most important, prevented any new government from redistributing land unless done by a "willing seller" to a "willing buyer," with the government compensating the owner at market prices. The "willing seller, willing buyer" rule would stay in place for ten years, at which time it could be overturned by a two-thirds vote in parliament. The transition called for the white police and army to maintain security, but under the command of a British governor; Patriotic Front troops were accorded legitimacy by also being placed under the command of the governor. Since a British governor would take control of the government, Muzorewa had to step down as prime minister during the short four-month election campaign. As for the cease-fire, PF troops were to be massed at sixteen holding camps and were to retain their arms. Rhodesian troops were to remain confined to their bases, and a small international Commonwealth force was to monitor the cease-fire.

Between the signing of the Lancaster House agreement and the attainment of independence, Zimbabwe was "a tinderbox."[13] Josiah Tongogara, ZANLA's military commander and a voice for compromise at Lancaster House, died in a car accident in Mozambique in December. ZANU-PF (ZANU's new name) jettisoned its partner in the Patriotic Front, ZAPU, in order to compete in the elections separately, thus fanning rumors that Muzorewa and Nkomo would unite to oppose Mugabe. Twenty-two thousand guerrillas marched into assembly camps in the first two weeks of the cease-fire, but many of the best fighters were kept out of the camps as a fail-safe measure. Rhodesian troops, who were supposed to be kept at their bases, violated the terms of the cease-fire with impunity. South Africa moved three army divisions to the Zimbabwean border. Twice Mugabe narrowly escaped assassination attempts. One aide to the British governor described the transition as "a gigantic game of bluff, keeping just enough Rhodesians obeying the Governor long enough to pull it off."[14] When the people of Zimbabwe finally voted February 27–29, 1980, Mugabe and ZANU-PF won an overwhelming majority. Mugabe used his election-night address to declare a policy of racial reconciliation.

What accounts for the successful termination at Lancaster House? How did negotiations there differ from previous attempts at settlement? Changed circumstances in four areas proved crucial for the resolution of the Zimbabwean civil war. These were changes in the military balance, in the political parties, in learning by the mediator, and in the leverage wielded by the mediator.

First, the Rhodesian military and Central Intelligence Organization felt they were losing the war and needed a settlement. However, only half the Patriotic Front—ZAPU—believed that a negotiated settlement was preferable to continuing the war. The other half, ZANU, thought it could win an outright victory, but only with continued support from Mozambique, ZANU's principal regional sponsor. Mozambique, for its part, had been ravaged by the war and wanted a speedy conclusion of it. Since Mozambican leaders believed ZANU would win any election held in Zimbabwe, they pressed for settlement. Pressure from Mozam-

13. The situation was described thus by Lord Soames, who was the newly arrived British governor of Rhodesia. Stedman, *Peacemaking in Civil War*, p. 201.
14. Stedman, *Peacemaking in Civil War*, p. 202.

bique particularly impressed the general in charge of ZANU troops, Josiah Tongogara, who became a fervent supporter of a settlement.

Second, the makeup of the warring parties differed at Lancaster House. On the PF side, ZANU was more unified than it ever had been in its struggle against the Rhodesian Front. Robert Mugabe had consolidated his position to become the unchallenged leader of the party. On the Rhodesian side, Ian Smith no longer negotiated for the whites. The election of Abel Muzorewa put a more conciliatory, less ideological, and less skillful negotiator in charge of the Rhodesian delegation. Moreover, Muzorewa had the support of the top white military and intelligence leaders, who believed he offered the best hope for a favorable settlement.

Third, the settlement terms met the minimal needs of the participants. That they did so was the result of another factor contributing to success: the British had studied the previous settlement efforts and had learned what each side would accept and what they would reject.

Fourth, Britain as mediator had the leverage to dictate the settlement to the participants—simply knowing what terms were acceptable would not have sufficed. The British had decided that the parties, left to their own devices, would never settle. Therefore the British felt that they had to become arbitrators and dictate terms to the combatants. To do so they used the regional sponsors of the Patriotic Front, Zambia and Mozambique, to pressure the Front. In order to command Rhodesian acceptance, the British held out the tacit promise of recognition of the Muzorewa government if the talks failed. Also, with Muzorewa in power Great Britain had direct influence with the Rhodesian government and no longer needed South Africa to apply pressure. This proved significant because South Africa would have participated actively in the mediation process only if it could have secured a pledge to prevent Mugabe's victory. But the British government could live with Mugabe coming to power, although it did not prefer that outcome.

The Aftermath of Lancaster House

Examining what happened after the Lancaster House agreement was signed is as instructive as examining how the agreement was reached. The Zimbabwean experience shows that problems encountered in the aftermath of settlement can grow out of the process by which war was ended.

The terms of the Lancaster House agreement dealt with only one aspect of the conflict in Zimbabwe: the political domination of whites over blacks. The Lancaster House settlement clearly changed that. The last thirteen years have not led to racial harmony in Zimbabwe, but at least there is racial coexistence, thanks to the settlement and President Robert Mugabe's policy of racial reconciliation.

Racial reconciliation, however, was bought at high cost. The Lancaster House agreement increased black political participation only in exchange for constraint of economic demands for redistribution. It is a cliché that for a negotiated settlement to emerge, all of the parties must gain. In Zimbabwe two important constituencies lost: land-poor Africans and the guerrillas who fought the war.

Although manifest conflict between whites and blacks has dissipated, conflicts among blacks have become more prominent. Mugabe's decision to jettison Nkomo and ZAPU for the post–Lancaster House elections set the stage for a bloody struggle between the two parties. ZAPU cached arms and ammunition, in violation of the settlement. Mugabe refrained from acting at first, then authorized an all-Shona brigade to engage in a scorched-earth campaign in Matabeleland against ZAPU dissidents. ZANU-PF harassed ZAPU members of parliament and jailed prominent leaders of the party.

ZAPU rebels, often called "super-ZAPU," rebelled against Mugabe's government because they felt Nkomo and ZAPU had not received appropriate recognition for their part in the fight for independence. Evidence linked the rebels to South Africa, which raised fears that Zimbabwe would suffer massive South African destabilization, as Mozambique had. Internally, the rebels took advantage of discontent among the landless in Matabeleland and of fear among the Ndebele. Not until 1987 did ZAPU and ZANU sign a unity agreement that incorporated ZAPU into ZANU-PF.

Three points are important. First, since the constitution was dictated by the British, the parties never became normatively committed to it. This was particularly so for ZANU. Although Robert Mugabe came to power through the Lancaster House agreement, the process had humiliated him. One British diplomat at the talks commented afterward, "Mugabe was screwed at Lancaster House."[15] In the years following the conference Mugabe scrupulously honored the terms of Lancaster

15. Interview with a member of Lord Carrington's staff, May 1987, London.

House, but he made it clear that those terms constituted odious interference and worked to repeal them as soon as the agreement allowed. Second, although the agreement addressed the participation conflict between whites and blacks, it did not anticipate the black-versus-black confrontation and conflict in post-independence Zimbabwe. Third, by buying white support with promises not to redistribute land and wealth, the agreement did nothing to alleviate the unequal allocation of resources which had always been part of the conflict. In essence, then, the Lancaster House settlement was an agreement to delay the resolution of important parts of the conflict.[16]

ZANU-ZAPU Reconciliation and the Matabeleland Conflict

The post-independence violence in Matabeleland provides an important case for the discussion of conflict resolution in the region. By the mid-1980s the alarming number of guerrilla attacks on white farms in Matabeleland, multiplying stories about ex-ZIPRA soldiers turning to "banditry," and evidence of South African support for dissident Zimbabweans prompted a massive coercive response from the Zimbabwean state in Matabeleland. An international human rights group estimates that 1,500 Ndebele civilians were killed in 1983 when members of a North Korea–trained Shona battalion conducted a search-and-destroy mission around Bulawayo, the capital of Matabeleland.[17]

The unrest in the region, combined with the state's use of force to quell the rebellion, threatened to set off a large-scale ethnic war in Zimbabwe, a war that would have been devastating for the new country. Yet by 1987 ZAPU and its former ally ZANU had reached a political agreement that ended the violence in Matabeleland and set on course the slow process of regional reconciliation.

The conflict in Matabeleland stemmed from claims by former ZAPU members that they had been reduced to political impotence. Poor, rural

16. The best concise analysis of the aftermath of the Lancaster House agreement is in Jeffrey Herbst, "Racial Reconciliation in Southern Africa," *International Affairs*, vol. 65 (Winter 1988–89). See also Stephen John Stedman, "The End of the Zimbabwean Civil War," in Roy Licklider, ed., *Stopping the Killing: How Civil Wars End* (New York University Press, 1993), pp. 125–63.

17. Lawyers Committee for Human Rights, *Zimbabwe: Wages of War* (New York, 1986).

blacks, angry because their land poverty had not been redressed, swelled the discontent. Adding to these material grievances, leaders on both sides gave vent to inflammatory rhetoric and tactless policies that conferred an ethnic undertone to the conflict.

Tensions subsided in December 1987 when ZANU-PF and ZAPU reached a unity agreement that merged the two parties and gave ZAPU representation in the cabinet. The agreement ended the political conflict between the two parties and relieved regional strains, but it also established a de facto one-party state and therefore contained the seeds of new conflict. While many hailed the agreement as an example of pragmatism winning out over parochial interests, critics charged that the agreement to end the political and regional conflict had been bought at the cost of democracy.

The terms of the peace agreement between ZANU-PF and ZAPU were for the most part dictated by ZANU. Since his assumption of power in 1980, Robert Mugabe had advocated a one-party state as the appropriate regime for bringing stability and development to Zimbabwe. ZANU-PF insisted that ZAPU would have to meet ZANU's terms in any unity agreement, and not the other way around.

The unity agreement resulted from pragmatism on the part of leaders of ZAPU and ZANU-PF. At the end of 1987, Joshua Nkomo had tired of his exile from formal political power. ZAPU had little to show for its opposition to ZANU-PF; its regional base of support still existed, but it had suffered from its exclusion from power. Continued intransigence could mean losing control of disaffected party members. On ZANU's part, there was a sobering awareness that continued violence could provide greater opportunities for South African destabilization. ZANU was concerned also about the reactions of productive white farmers, many of whom threatened to emigrate. What difference did a black government make, some white farmers asked pointedly, if arms had to be taken up again to protect property?

NAMIBIA AND THE ''CONTACT GROUP''

Had it been left to the international community, Namibia's fate would have been determined in 1971, when the world court declared South Africa's continued colonization of South-West Africa to be illegal. South Africa, however, refused to budge. With the fall of Portuguese colonialism in the north, Namibia was all the more strategically important to South Africa. It served as a buffer zone between South Africa and Angola and as a staging area for incursions into Angola. South Africa tried to legitimate its hold in Namibia by setting up an internal settlement similar to the one attempted in Zimbabwe-Rhodesia. But in one important respect the proposed Namibian internal settlement was very different from the Rhodesian one: the regime that Pretoria would bestow upon Namibia would keep apartheid structures in place with no pretense to nominal black control. The South African settlement, known as the Turnhalle Project, would freeze SWAPO—the sole liberation movement in Namibia—out of the new government.[18]

U.N. Security Council Resolution 385, passed in 1976, "called for free elections under U.N. supervision and control for the whole of Namibia as one political entity, adequate time to establish the supervising machinery, withdrawal of the South African administration and South African military forces, release of political prisoners and return of exiles, and end of racial discrimination—without spelling out further details."[19] The prospect of an independent but apartheid Namibia threatened to preempt the U.N. resolution and consolidated international reaction against South Africa. The United Nations brandished the stick of sanctions against South Africa. That threat in turn alarmed the United States and Great Britain, which feared sanctions would jeopardize their extensive economic interests in the region.

Representatives of the United States, Britain, Canada, West Germany, and France began an intensive search for a negotiated peace in Namibia. The mediation effort became known as the Contact Group.[20] Unfortunately, the Contact Group suffered from a major constraint, namely, its *raison d'être*. Since the Contact Group undertook the mediation effort to preclude imposition of U.N. sanctions against South Africa, it lacked from the beginning potential sticks for gaining South African compliance.[21] And South African compliance was essential, because South

18. SWAPO is the acronym for South West Africa People's Organization.

19. I. William Zartman, *Ripe for Resolution*, 2d ed. (Oxford University Press, 1989), p. 192.

20. The most comprehensive study of the diplomacy of the Contact Group is in Vivienne Jabri, *Mediating Conflict: Decision-making and Western Intervention in Namibia* (England: Manchester University Press, 1990).

21. On the purpose of the Contact Group, see Jabri, *Mediating Conflict*, p. 97.

Africa had the upper hand militarily in the territory and could not be defeated by SWAPO. Since SWAPO could come to power only through an internationally brokered settlement and elections, it was a more pliable participant in the negotiation effort.

South Africa faced a dilemma. An internal settlement would install a regime amenable to Pretoria, but it would not be a legitimate regime.[22] South Africa wanted to fulfill both conditions because it wanted good relations with the Contact Group nations. But since the solution that would provide a legitimate regime would put SWAPO in power, a legitimate solution would not yield a friendly solution. South Africa therefore continued to pursue its unilateral alternative while paying lip service to the Contact Group in the hope of gaining terms that would prevent SWAPO from coming to power.

From April 1977 to September 1978, the Contact Group in consultation with the Front Line States extracted concessions from SWAPO to pacify South African concerns. SWAPO agreed that the South African Defence Force could keep a minimal presence inside Namibia during a political transition and that the transition and election would be jointly supervised by a U.N. representative and the South African administrator general. SWAPO also accepted that the small enclave of Walvis Bay on the Namibian coast would remain under South African jurisdiction for the time being; its status would be resolved by negotiations after Namibian independence.

The Group also worked on South Africa. The effort seemed to achieve "astonishing results. . . . [The Western powers] persuaded [Vorster] to nullify his constitutional initiative, to agree to end apartheid in Namibia, and to hold free elections in which SWAPO could participate."[23] U.N. Security Council Resolution 435, adopted in September 1978, set out a general framework for the transition to independence. But every time South Africa seemed close to agreeing to the resolution, it backed away and "raise[d] new issues (such as that of UN impartiality) or exaggerate[d] existing ones just as others had been resolved."[24]

22. Zartman, *Ripe for Resolution*, p. 189.

23. Robert S. Jaster, *The 1988 Peace Accords and the Future of South-Western Africa*, Adelphi Papers 253 (London: Brassey's for the International Institute for Strategic Studies, 1990), p. 11.

24. Jabri, *Mediating Conflict*, p. 127.

Faced with South African intransigence, the Contact Group finally considered sanctions to force Pretoria to settle. South Africa avoided that penalty by agreeing to keep talking, an offer the Contact Group accepted. From then until the election of a new American president, the mediation exercise became one of "talking without negotiating."[25] South Africa began to build an internal settlement that would provide a black alternative to SWAPO.

The Contact Group failed to resolve the Namibian conflict for two reasons. First, the Group lacked the resolve to give teeth to their efforts by imposing deadlines and making alternatives painful to South Africa. I. William Zartman eloquently describes the situation thus: "When sanctions of any kind are feared more by those who would apply them than by the target, it is clear that deadlines are in the hands of the latter, and the mediator has neither leverage nor determination."[26] The goal of the Contact Group—to avoid sanctions—foreclosed the means to resolve the conflict. Second, important changes were taking place within South Africa to negate any move toward negotiated settlement. In particular, P. W. Botha replaced John Vorster in 1978, intent on implementing South Africa's "total strategy" to domestic and regional security problems.

ANGOLA, CUBA, AND SOUTH AFRICA: LINKAGE, PART ONE

Nineteen-hundred eighty proved to be a mixed year for South Africa. On the one hand, Pretoria's hopes for a Muzorewa-led Zimbabwe friendly to South African interests were deflated when Robert Mugabe won election. On the other hand, Ronald Reagan's election to the White House in the United States gave South Africa time "to build up a credible non-SWAPO opposition in Namibia."[27] His election and promise to roll back communism encouraged South Africa's use of force in

25. The phrase "talking without negotiating" comes from Robert O. Matthews, "Talking without Negotiating: The Case of Rhodesia," *International Journal*, vol. 35 (Winter 1979–80), pp. 91–117.

26. Zartman, *Ripe for Resolution*, p. 200.

27. Gerald J. Bender, "Peacemaking in Southern Africa: The Luanda-Pretoria Tug-of-War," *Third World Quarterly*, vol. 11 (April 1989), p. 16.

the region. Pretoria took over the reins of the MNR (Mozambique National Resistance),[28] supported UNITA in Angola, and carried out increasingly larger invasions of Angola.

Unlike the Carter administration, the Reagan regime believed that the conflicts in Angola and Namibia could be linked so as to promote peace. In particular, the United States would push for Namibian independence from South Africa, along with South African withdrawal from Angola, in exchange for Cuban withdrawal from Angola. The architect of Reagan's Africa policy, Assistant Secretary of State for African Affairs Chester Crocker, also initiated "constructive engagement," which sought to prod change in the region with incentives to and dialogue with South Africa.[29] From 1981 to 1988 Crocker insisted on two tenets: one, the United States should talk with all of the parties to the conflict; two, linkage was the only framework that would bring peace to the region. The upshot of that period was bolder, bloodier military moves by South Africa and Angola and, when those failed, a prolonged dialogue about the linkage alternative put forth by Crocker.

U.S. mediation did not start auspiciously. Crocker's linkage proposal met opposition from the Contact Group, which "viewed it as an extraneous issue that would hamper the search for a Namibian settlement."[30] The United States and the Contact Group came to an implicit compromise, however: the United States would continue to insist privately on linkage, but the issue would be hedged in public to avoid scuttling cooperation among the allies.[31] Also agreed to was a de facto division of

28. MNR was later renamed RENAMO, or Resistência Nacional Moçambicana, in rejection of the anglophone term.

29. This discussion of Angola and Namibia draws from Donald Rothchild and Caroline Hartzell, "Great- and Medium-Power Mediations: Angola," in I. William Zartman, ed., *The Annals of the American Academy of Political and Social Science*, vol. 518 (November 1991), pp. 39–57; Michael McFaul, "Rethinking the 'Reagan Doctrine' in Angola," *International Security*, vol. 14 (Winter 1989–90), pp. 99–135; Jaster, *1988 Peace Accords*; Chas W. Freeman, Jr., "The Angola/Namibia Accords," *Foreign Affairs*, vol. 68 (Summer 1989); Gillian Gunn, "A Guide to the Intricacies of the Angola-Namibia Negotiations," *CSIS Africa Notes*, no. 90 (September 1988); and Zartman, *Ripe for Resolution*.

30. Jaster, *1988 Peace Accords*, p. 13.

31. Chester A. Crocker describes U.S.–Contact Group tension and strategy in Crocker, *High Noon in Southern Africa: Making Peace in a Rough Neighborhood* (W. W. Norton, 1992), pp. 120–31.

labor. The Contact Group, in conjunction with the Front Line States, would work on problem solving concerning general constitutional principles for Namibia (phase 1) and transitional arrangements involving a cease-fire, election, and interim administration (phase 2). The United States, under Crocker's lead, would work to win MPLA and South African approval of linkage and a specific timetable for Cuban withdrawal from Angola (phase 3).

According to one analyst, Angola welcomed American mediation because its leaders "recognized that the United States was the only country positioned to negotiate a peace settlement between Angola and South Africa."[32] A more precise formulation would be that some MPLA leaders welcomed U.S. mediation but on the whole the MPLA was badly divided on the question of American involvement. Hence in February 1982 the MPLA and Cuba issued a vague statement that if South Africa implemented resolution 435, then "serious consideration" would be given to Cuban withdrawal from Angola.[33] South Africa accepted the principle of linkage but demanded that Cuban troops leave before the implementation of resolution 435.

The negotiating process crawled during 1982 as the Contact Group and the Front Line States hammered out possible solutions regarding constitutional principles and the transition. The mediators gained limited acceptance on these issues, and by September 1982 they believed that phases one and two were over. SWAPO and the South Africans still differed on some minor details, but no party felt that the distance between them was enough to prevent ultimate agreement. Indeed, the intensive problem solving that the Contact Group engaged in with SWAPO, the Front Line States, and the United Nations provided a quick formula for agreement when South Africa was forced to bargain in good faith years later. By January 1983 the Contact Group had disbanded, after announcing that it had accomplished all that it could.

The successful conclusion of this phase of the negotiations brought into the open the private disagreement between the Contact Group and the United States, however. Linkage was now the only stumbling block to peace. The MPLA was internally divided over the linkage issue, and South African leaders felt no need to make concessions since the status

32. McFaul, "Rethinking the Reagan Doctrine," p. 114.
33. McFaul, "Rethinking the Reagan Doctrine," p. 114; and Bender, "Peacemaking in Southern Africa," p. 19.

quo was comfortable and they knew that the Reagan administration disdained sanctions and would not pressure them.

During this period South Africa intensified its regional destabilization campaign. Part of the U.S. mediation effort was to convince the South Africans that their "total strategy" was not cost effective, and that "far preferable would be a complementary strategy that would engage neighboring states to do their own policing of the nationalist movements to which they gave sanctuary by bargaining the removal of South African destabilization operations against the imposition of neighboring states' control."[34]

From 1981 to late 1983, South Africa invaded Angola at least three times and established bases there with over a thousand troops. The net effect of South Africa's presence was to bolster UNITA, which made major military gains against the MPLA in 1983. The combined UNITA–South African war against Angola was costing the MPLA $2 billion annually in military costs, in addition to $10 billion in damages. But as the war against Angola escalated, so did Cuban and Soviet support for the MPLA.

On December 5, 1983, the United States warned South Africa that its regional destabilization was leading to unacceptable escalation and was too costly a method of maintaining its security. The American warning came the day before the South Africans were to invade Angola in "Operation Askari." Nonetheless, on December 16 South Africa signaled its willingness to withdraw its troops unilaterally from Angola, beginning at the end of January, if the MPLA would show restraint and reciprocity by prohibiting SWAPO from attacking Namibia from Angola. The MPLA dismissed that offer at the beginning of January but only days later sent an urgent message to the United States that it would consider the proposal, provided South Africa would take part in talks to address a litany of Angolan security concerns.[35]

The South African negotiating gambit apparently came from two bureaucratic interests in the government. Pik Botha, representing the foreign affairs establishment, took seriously American calls for a negotiated regional settlement and wanted to convince P. W. Botha that purposeless destabilization was counterproductive. In this instance, Pik

34. Zartman, *Ripe for Resolution*, p. 217.
35. On the events of December 1983 and January 1984 that led to the Lusaka agreement, see Crocker, *High Noon*, pp. 189–98.

Botha received support from Minister of Defence Magnus Malan, who was disquieted by new, sophisticated Soviet and Cuban air defense systems in southern Angola; nor did Malan see any practical reason for keeping 4,000 troops stationed in Angola.

After the MPLA first dismissed Pretoria's offer in early January, the United Nations quickly, overwhelmingly—and without a veto from Western friends—condemned South African regional behavior. P. W. Botha countered by threatening that South Africa would bring Namibia to independence on South Africa's terms, which meant an internal settlement designed to freeze out SWAPO. The United States persuaded the MPLA to focus on South African withdrawal so that negotiations would not become mired in myriad other issues. On the basis of MPLA acceptance, South Africa agreed to negotiate a cease-fire, withdrawal, and monitoring arrangements in southern Angola.

In February 1984 Angola and South Africa signed the Lusaka Accords, which established a cease-fire between the two sides, an agreement on South African departure from Angola, and a joint monitoring commission to police the cease-fire. The cease-fire held between Angola and the South African Defence Force (SADF), but South African withdrawal was delayed because SWAPO, a nonsignatory, kept fighting. South African troops finally left Angola after thirteen months.

In October 1984 Angola put forward a three-year, phased timetable for the departure of some Cuban troops; in exchange South Africa was to implement U.N. Security Council Resolution 435 and stop supporting UNITA. Although Pretoria rejected the timetable, the United States had begun to engage the South Africans in bargaining over specific details of the linkage formula. Internally, however, South Africa was racked by dissension about the goals of its regional strategy and what it hoped to accomplish in Angola.

In March 1985 Crocker presented both sides with new proposals that he believed would bring the parties closer together. But any possibility that the Lusaka Accords would translate into something more was dashed in mid-May when a South African commando, Captain Wynand du Toit, was captured while attempting to sabotage Angolan oil fields in Cabinda, north of Luanda. Angola formally broke off talks with Crocker in July, after the U.S. Congress voted to resume aid to UNITA.

The risks of settlement and internal disunity within the MPLA and the South African government evoked intransigence from Pretoria, which in turn prevented the termination of the war. One analyst argues that if the United States had been willing to use sanctions against South Africa, a settlement could have been made at this juncture.[36] Crocker, for his part, never accepted sanctions as a tool against South Africa, but he did seem willing to explore American recognition of the Angolan regime as a way to put heat on South Africa.[37] This never came to pass, however, because American policy toward Angola became hostage to extreme right-wing groups in the United States, who often worked in conjunction with the South African military and UNITA lobbyists.

The Lusaka agreement yielded ambivalent results for conflict resolution in the region. Crocker contends that the agreement supported those within the MPLA who wanted a regional peace settlement and provided the environment for them to make their timetable offer in October. But Crocker also recognizes a key perverse element of the Lusaka agreement. The cease-fire and other arrangements between the MPLA and South Africa set up a comfortable status quo. The edge to their hostilities was smoothed—there was no longer a pressing need to push negotiations further. A settlement to the conflict would not be reached until the economic and military costs of the conflict became unacceptable and the parties faced a major escalation of the war.[38]

BILATERAL CONFLICT RESOLUTION: THE NKOMATI ACCORD

As mentioned earlier, the United States had urged South Africa to forsake destabilization in favor of bilateral security agreements with the other states of Southern Africa. With American support, Mozambique and South Africa reached an agreement that pledged each side to non-aggression. Signed in March 1984, the Nkomati Accord bound the signatories from interference in the internal affairs of the other. The agreement called for Mozambique to end its assistance to the African National Congress (ANC), in exchange for which South Africa promised to end its support of the MNR. The accord also detailed a major expansion of the economic ties between the two countries. Although

36. Zartman, *Ripe for Resolution*, p. 240.
37. Crocker, *High Noon*, p. 170.
38. For Crocker's analysis of Lusaka, see *High Noon*, p. 198.

Mozambique kept its side of the bargain, South Africa did not. Powerful factions in the South African government had no intention of complying with the provisions of the Nkomati Accord.

Mozambique faced a crisis in 1982 that imperiled the nation's very existence. Although the main explanation for the Mozambican predicament was the South African–sponsored war of destabilization, other problems abounded. Among them were the breakdown of the colonial economy that Mozambique had inherited, the exodus of skilled Portuguese and other settlers, deficient policies adopted by FRELIMO, the crippling cost of implementing international sanctions against Rhodesia during 1976–79, and recurring drought which devastated the rural economy.

The Nkomati Accord was part of Mozambique's response to the crisis. On the global level, FRELIMO pursued maximum political, diplomatic, and economic support from the international community. Regionally, FRELIMO adopted two strategies. First, Mozambique would collaborate with the Front Line States on political and security matters and with members of the Southern African Development Coordination Conference on economic matters. Second, FRELIMO aimed for peaceful coexistence with South Africa.

By late 1983 the war of destabilization, combined with droughts and floods, threatened to destroy the Mozambican economy. At the beginning of 1984 Mozambique canceled its debt repayments and applied for rescheduling with Western creditors. President Samora Machel and the Mozambican government realized that the mounting crisis could be met only by ending the war and reaching an agreement with the International Monetary Fund, which also was the key to accessing the World Bank and a range of public and commercial credit institutions.

Against this general background, FRELIMO had four goals for a *modus vivendi* with South Africa: to avoid a large-scale military confrontation; to end the MNR terror; to achieve a modest measure of economic recovery; and to widen the split between South Africans who saw the advantages of cooperating economically with Mozambique and those who wanted to continue the hard military line.

South Africa saw several reasons to pursue a peace agreement with Mozambique. First, by mid-1983 some strategists in Pretoria were concerned because South Africa had eschewed positive regional action. Destabilization had effectively "softened up" some neighbors, but the region would never accept South African hegemony unless positive economic links were established. Merely throwing one's military might around in the region was not sufficient to win regional cooperation. Moreover, the political costs of destabilization were rising, and the South African economy was suffering its worst recession since the 1930s. South Africa needed to project itself internationally as a constructive force for development to guarantee international capital for investments at home and in the region. Also, the United States and other Western powers began to query South Africa's refusal to reach accommodation with its neighbors. Against this background, some South African policy makers saw the Nkomati Accord as a vehicle to oust the ANC from Mozambique, prevent a buildup of Soviet military equipment and foreign military personnel in Mozambique, and gain international approval as a responsible power committed to regional security and development.

But members of South Africa's military and security branches, and perhaps even P. W. Botha himself, did not accept the arguments for accommodation with Mozambique. The signing of the accord thus proved a disappointing experience for Mozambique. South African military and economic destabilization continued, while economic cooperation with South Africa increased only marginally. Yet Mozambique's crisis situation demanded some kind of agreement. Lacking adequate military muscle, Mozambique's only choice was to try to win a "battle of the minds." Mozambique could only hope that Pretoria's nonimplementation and violation of the Nkomati Accord would expose South Africa to the world as an aggressor. This, as it turned out, was the positive result of the Nkomati Accord for Mozambique. It was clearly a second-best outcome, but it was important for soliciting political support and economic aid from the international community. Of course, much of that aid would have been unnecessary had South Africa complied with the accord.

ANGOLA, SOUTH AFRICA, AND NAMIBIA: LINKAGE, PART TWO

From 1985 to 1987 the MPLA embarked on two major offensives to eliminate UNITA. Both times South African intervention saved its ally. The events surrounding the second offensive in 1987, however, marked a qualitative shift in the military balance of power in the region. The largest SADF involvement ever in Angola began in August–September 1987 when some 6,000 South African troops responded to a concerted effort by Angolan forces to take the town of Mavinga in Angola's Cuando Cubango province. Mavinga, everyone agreed, was strategically important. By taking it, MPLA forces would have a rear base to attack the UNITA headquarters in Jamba farther to the southeast.

South African units, consisting of soldiers from the ethnically composed 32d and 101st battalions as well as white troops from the Permanent Force and units from the South West African Territorial Forces (SWATF), halted the Angolan advance and launched a massive counterattack that forced Angolan troops to withdraw. At Cuito Cuanavale, to the northwest of Mavinga, the Forças Armadas Populares de Libertação de Angola (FAPLA) repelled the SADF-UNITA counterattack; military deadlock ensued. Angolan troops dug themselves in, established firm defense lines, and got more help from the Cubans, including air support. By January 1988 South Africa began to lose air superiority to the advanced antiaircraft missiles, radar, and MiG-23/Su-22 fighters introduced for the defense of the town. SADF strategists argued that the massive land assault required to take Cuito Cuanavale would entail the loss of up to 300 white troops, along with 2,000 SWATF members and an unspecified but large number of UNITA troops.[39] Such substantial losses would be unavoidable since the assault would not receive much air cover from the South African air force.

With these projections in hand, the SADF shelved the plan for an infantry assault and opted instead for a massive artillery barrage. But the defenses held at Cuito Cuanavale, and the military deadlock around the town turned into a strategic disadvantage for Pretoria.

Angola and Cuba combined their military assets with a bargaining strategy. In January a huge influx of Cuban troops was deployed at Cuito Cuanavale, while Angolan and Cuban representatives met with Crocker and evinced flexibility toward previous proposals put forward by the United States. The Angolan meeting with Crocker was followed by American attempts to gain South African commitment to new negotiations. For several months, from January to May, South Africa showed little interest in participating in new talks.[40] But as the stalemate contin-

---

39. *SouthScan*, vol. 2 (May 4, 1988); and *Work in Progress*, no. 54 (1988), p. 7.
40. Jaster, *1988 Peace Accords*, p. 20.

ued and pressure at home intensified, South Africa finally, reluctantly, agreed to meet with the United States, Cuba, and Angola in early May.

In March 1988 more than 15,000 Cuban forces fanned out toward the border with Namibia from the defensive line they had occupied for years along the sixteenth parallel. The move was supported by reinforcements from the sea (at Namibe) and by troops from the Benguela defensive line farther north.

The rapid changes in the deployment of Cuban troops and equipment in the south came as a surprise to the SADF. But, as Robert Jaster remarks, "It is clear that Castro orchestrated the scale and timing of deployment towards the Namibian border so as to put pressure on South Africa at the quadripartite peace talks starting in London on May 3."[41] South Africa asked for assurances at the London meeting that the Cuban troops would not invade Namibia, but none were forthcoming.

May and June were spent in a game of brinkmanship between Cuba and South Africa. Cuba continued to bring more troops into Angola, prompting warnings from the SADF. Two sets of talks at Brazzaville and Cairo did not lead to any South African concessions. Finally, in late June SADF forces attacked Cuban soldiers twenty miles north of the Calueque dam. In retaliation Cuba launched an air attack on SADF positions near the Calueque dam inside Angola, close to the Namibian border. SADF could not repel the attack, in which twelve white South African soldiers were killed.

A diplomatic breakthrough occurred two weeks after the Calueque incident when representatives of the warring parties met in New York: they developed a set of principles to guide the settlement. From July until December representatives met repeatedly to work out the details of a timetable for the withdrawal of Cuban troops from Angola. On December 22, 1988, Cuba, Angola, and South Africa signed a tripartite agreement that ended the war between South Africa and Angola and paved the way for Namibian independence.

Analysts tend to split into two camps to explain what led to settlement. Some emphasize what every side won from the negotiations; others look at what every side stood to lose from continued conflict. Both sides make important points.

What stood to be lost is apparent. Angola's economy was in ruins and approaches to the West for aid and assistance to resurrect it hinged on a

41. Jaster, *1988 Peace Accords*, p. 21.

settlement that would hasten the departure of Cuba and South Africa from the country. Cuba had tired of its lengthy involvement in Angola. South Africa found that its cost of involvement—economic and political—had reached untenable levels. Moreover, the introduction of new weapons systems in southern Angola had annulled South African military superiority in that theater. The Soviet Union, in desperate economic straits at home, could no longer afford Angola's drain on its resources.

Those in the "Who wins?" camp stress that, with this settlement, each side could claim some measure of victory. Angola gained the ouster of South Africa and could take partial credit for Namibian independence. Cuba could boast of its heroic role in preserving Angola and staring down South Africa, and South Africa could claim the triumph of removing the Cubans from the region. The Soviet Union could show the United States its potential for partnership in resolving regional conflicts.

Comparing circumstances in 1988 to those at other times in the conflict helps weigh both sets of contentions. First, every side could claim a victory from the settlement, but so could they have during the previous seven years, when linkage had been on the table. Indeed, the victories earned by participants in 1988 were the victories that Crocker's formula promised from the beginning. While such a "win-win" outcome was a prerequisite for a settlement, it was by no means sufficient to command one. Second, it is also true that in 1988, unlike in other years, the status quo—military deadlock—was taking an enormous toll. Yet the assertion that the situation was a hurting stalemate has to be qualified. The MPLA had decided that UNITA was unbeatable so long as South Africa assisted it. For the MPLA, the settlement was a way to remove what it believed was the chief obstacle to defeating UNITA, not an admission that an outright MPLA victory was unattainable. Third, the suggestion that the new Soviet foreign policy was necessary for settlement ignores the fact that Angola and Cuba had strong incentives to settle regardless of what the Soviet Union wanted. The Angolans' desire for an agreement was evident even in 1984 when the MPLA signed the Lusaka Accords, *against* the advice of the Soviets. In 1988 Soviet advice coincided with the MPLA course, but it is unlikely that Soviet influence determined that course. Where the new Soviet interest in peace in Southern Africa did make a difference, however, was in the internal negotiations between MPLA and UNITA that followed the agreement.

The crucial determinant for the tripartite agreement in 1988 was the military factor. In July 1988 South Africa's overall strategic position was markedly worse than it had been before large-scale fighting began in the late summer of 1987. Most important, South Africa had lost its previously unchallenged air superiority in the region, which obviously had major implications for the situation on the ground. Earlier, South Africa and UNITA had controlled southern Angola for the most part, and they moved with near impunity over most of the area. Control was vital because the area functioned as a buffer zone, separating the SWAPO camps and bases farther to the north from the Namibian border. It also served as the main staging area for UNITA's destabilization war against the MPLA government.

The combined, interlinked effects of the enhanced war-fighting capabilities of FAPLA, MPLA's acquisition of modern war-waging equipment and South Africa's consequent loss of air superiority, as well as distinctly more offensive behavior by the Cuban forces, shrank the South African control zone considerably. In the end, however, it was the escalation of the conflict by the Cubans and the movement of 15,000 troops to the Namibian border that turned the tide toward settlement. The Cuban maneuver provided South Africa with an urgency to settle that had been lacking in previous negotiations.[42] And it was not simply the fact that the South Africans could not dislodge the Cubans that led to the need for settlement; rather, it was the direct threat that the Cubans posed to South African interests in Namibia. As one SADF officer commented, "This was more than we could handle. Had the Cubans attacked they would have over-run the place. We could not have stopped them."[43]

42. Zartman calls the Cuban troop deployment an example of an "escalation to call," where one actor intensifies a conflict but makes it clear that a negotiated settlement is possible and that the escalation is intended to prompt agreement. See Zartman, *Ripe for Resolution*, p. 235. Zartman, Jaster, and Walter Barrows all stress Cuban escalation as the key to the settlement process. See Jaster, *1988 Peace Accords*, pp. 20–23; and Walter Barrows, "Carrots as Well as Sticks in Demilitarizing Southern Africa," in Harvey Glickman, ed., *Toward Peace and Security in Southern Africa* (New York: Gordon and Breach, 1990), pp. 73–74.

43. Jaster, *1988 Peace Accords*, p. 23.

THE NAMIBIAN TRANSITION

It would be an overstatement to say that Namibian independence was an afterthought to the Crocker mediation. Nonetheless, crucial aspects of the election, cease-fire, and constitution for Namibia were up in the air in December 1988. Chester Crocker produced a ready formula for Namibian independence at the tripartite negotiations: U.N. Security Council Resolution 435, refined over the years with the participation of the Front Line States and SWAPO. Yet resolution 435 was at best sketchy on many details of the transition, and SWAPO, a major party in the Namibian conflict, was not a party at all to the tripartite agreement.

Thus significant ambiguities concerning Namibia remained unresolved in the spring of 1989. What would the precise terms of the cease-fire be? How would elections be carried out? How would a constitution be fashioned? These ambiguities were exacerbated by confusion over the basic lines of authority in the territory during the transition. The head of the U.N. Transition Assistance Group (UNTAG) was neither the de facto nor the de jure top official in Namibia during the transition. That position was held by the South African–appointed governor. Moreover, UNTAG's participation in the process was scaled down before the cease-fire even started because of funding cutbacks. The U.N. team was unprepared and severely understaffed on the day that the cease-fire began. SWAPO, out of either ignorance or hope for some kind of tactical advantage, violated the terms of the cease-fire by sending guerrillas into Namibia from Angola. This prompted the SADF to leave their bases to hunt and destroy SWAPO soldiers, a move that was sanctioned by the United Nations. A meeting of the signatories of the tripartite agreement confirmed the need for South Africa to stay committed to the peace process, while the Front Line States pressured SWAPO to desist from actions that might upset the transition.

The most important difference in arrangements between the Namibian and Zimbabwean processes concerned the relationship between elections and constitution making. At Lancaster House, the British insisted that the Zimbabweans agree on a constitution before holding elections. The hope was that the issues that had generated the conflict in the first place would be resolved in the constitution-making phase and that winners in elections would be bound to rules governing political competition and the spoils of victory. In Namibia, elections were to be held first; those who were elected would design a constitution. The resulting document would need approval of two-thirds of the elected parliament to be instituted. When SWAPO failed to gain a two-thirds majority in the first election, it had to engage in hard bargaining with the other parties in Namibia to craft a constitution. Those negotiations went far more smoothly than anyone could have predicted, and in six weeks the document was drafted and approved.

The result of the Namibian process—SWAPO winning a majority of votes but not enough to dictate terms in constitutional negotiations—combined with the active policy of reconciliation pursued by Namibia's first president, Sam Nujoma, produced a compromise similar to Zimbabwe's. The ruling party, by emphasizing reconciliation in the hope of gaining stability and attracting foreign capital and assistance to boost reconstruction, shelved earlier demands for redistribution of wealth, especially land. SWAPO thus gambled that the overall benefits of stability and capitalism would in the long stretch outrun pressures from the dispossessed and party radicals for jobs, land, and income.

ANGOLA: THE INTERNAL SETTLEMENT

After the three-party agreement ending the interstate war in Angola was reached, several African countries tried to step into the breach to mediate a peace between the MPLA and UNITA. The Crocker peace plan had ended the interstate war but introduced fluidity and uncertainty into the civil war. Did the departure of South African troops leave UNITA vulnerable to MPLA attack? Was it possible, or even desirable, for the MPLA to deal UNITA the deathblow that had hitherto been averted? Did the Cuban withdrawal provide an opportunity for UNITA to win outright?

The immediate effect of the resolution of the international component of the war was a renewed attempt by the MPLA to eliminate UNITA. In September 1988 FAPLA initiated another offensive against UNITA, which met with only limited success. The Soviet Union counseled reconciliation between the two parties, a call that was joined by a number of African states.

In early 1989 Angolan president Eduardo dos Santos expressed an interest in seeking an end to the civil war (in response, some analysts believe, to the U.S. linkage of normalization of relations to resolution of the conflict).[44] Savimbi also claimed a willingness to engage in talks. The possibility of bringing the parties together prompted the Front Line presidents, especially Kenneth Kaunda, to start a mediation effort which would be centered in Gbadolite, Zaire. The choice of Zaire—and President Mobutu—was a shrewd one on the part of the Front Line States. Since Mobutu's support was critical to UNITA's ability to keep fighting the war, the FLS sought to commit him to peaceful resolution of the conflict. They believed that by dressing him in the role of peacemaker, he would have an interest in achieving peace. By making one of UNITA's major suppliers a partner in peace, symmetry would be achieved, for the Soviet Union was willing to pressure the MPLA to settle.[45]

The meeting at Gbadolite turned farcical. Mobutu, like Henry Kissinger in Zimbabwe thirteen years earlier, relied on lying to both Savimbi and dos Santos to create the appearance of an agreement, which he then proclaimed to the African heads of state at the meeting. Within a day, the "agreement" unraveled, with Savimbi angrily denying key parts of Mobutu's claims.[46]

Don Rothchild and Caroline Hartzell, who compared the Gbadolite and Crocker mediations, argue that Mobutu failed because he lacked the leverage that the United States had.[47] From what we now know of the meeting, it is clear that Mobutu also lacked a sense of a workable solution that would fulfill the needs of both sides.

In the fall of 1989 the MPLA attempted once again, but failed, to seriously weaken UNITA. Soviet assistance was finally declining; Angola's economy continued its precipitous decline with no relief in sight. As the Soviet Union pursued domestic political change, it urged the MPLA to accept multipartyism and negotiation with UNITA. UNITA's incentives for negotiation came from its belief that it could win an election, as well as from signs that the U.S. Congress would tie aid to progress at the bargaining table. The MPLA and UNITA accepted an offer to mediate from the Portuguese govern-

44. Jaster, *1988 Peace Accords*, p. 48.

45. This interpretation is based on the observations of a member of the Tanzanian foreign ministry who was present at Gbadolite. Confidential interview, May 1991, Washington, D.C.

46. Shawn McCormick, "Angola: The Road to Peace," *CSIS Africa Notes*, no. 125 (June 6, 1991), pp. 3–4.

47. Rothchild and Hartzell, "Great- and Medium-Power Mediations."

ment. The talks yielded little progress until the United States and the Soviet Union joined as active participants.

The length of the transition was a sticking point. The MPLA demanded a three-year interim between settlement and elections, arguing that Angola's frayed infrastructure would require at least that much time to be rebuilt enough to support elections. But the MPLA had a hidden agenda in seeking a drawn-out transition. It believed that a quick election would put it at a disadvantage because the MPLA would be held accountable for the country's devastated economy. UNITA, sensing the MPLA's weakness on this score, wanted elections within a year. Eventually the parties compromised; elections were to be held in fifteen to eighteen months. The MPLA and UNITA signed an agreement in Bicesse, Portugal, on May 31, 1991, to end the Angolan civil war.

One important aspect of the negotiations turned on the parties' choices for interim and long-term institutions. U.S. mediators tried to point out to both the MPLA and UNITA the utility of a constitution that provided a key role for any party that lost an election, to ensure that some amount of power was shared between the antagonists. Both parties, however, insisted on a winner-take-all presidential system. The legislature would be based on proportional representation, but the essential duties and rights of the legislature were never fully spelled out. Apparently each party believed that it could triumph in an election and therefore insisted on institutions that would grant the lion's share of power to the winner.

A final bargain of convenience concerned the interim government. In the Zimbabwean and Namibian examples, the question of who would run the country in the time between agreement and election was a sticking point. In Angola, the MPLA insisted on running the transition, with the United Nations held to a supporting role monitoring electoral registration and voting, the disarmament of troops, and demobilization of soldiers. In theory running the transition could have been an advantage in an election campaign. UNITA, however, eschewed joint administration of the country in the belief that it could garner more popular support by staying outside the government, removed from the taint of inept government policies. The United Nations, for its part, agreed to the arrangements because it wanted to minimize its financial and personnel commitment to Angola during the sixteen-month transition. The United Nations hailed the Bicesse agreement as a bold experiment for future U.N. involvement in peace building because the Angolan parties had agreed to police themselves during the interim.

No event lent urgency to the negotiations, as the Cuban escalation had in the tripartite negotiations of 1988; deadlines and pressure came simply from Soviet and American participation. But two sets of incentives were at work to bring about settlement. First, UNITA attacks in the fall of 1991 and the spring of 1992 had driven home to the MPLA that it could not win a unilateral victory. Indeed, UNITA seemed to be growing more powerful. The Soviet Union, then Russia, pushed for settlement, including cutting off aid and assistance to the MPLA. Second, the United States had also made clear to Savimbi that his support was coming to a close. UNITA desired a settlement also because it was convinced that it would win a free and fair election.

The parties eventually set Angola's first elections for September 1992. The two contending armies were to be disbanded three months before elections, with 120,000 soldiers demobilized and the remaining 40,000 forged into a new Angolan force under the joint command of generals from the two former armies. In contrast to U.N. operations elsewhere, the international community tried to buy peace on the cheap in Angola. The United Nations devoted only $70 million and 800 people to Angola for helping the demobilization, supervising the cease-fire, and assisting in voter registration and the election. In addition, the United States provided $59 million; the European Community pledged $156 million, half of which would be available before elections. Funds committed before the election thus totaled $207 million. In comparison, the successful ending of the war in Namibia, a country with much better infrastructure than Angola's and about a tenth of its population, cost about $430 million and involved nearly 8,500 U.N. personnel. The U.N. peace effort in Western Sahara (population 610,000, not quite 6 percent of Angola's population) was allocated $200 million and 3,700 personnel. In Cambodia, which is less populous than Angola, the U.N. peace-building operation cost $2 billion and involved 20,000 personnel.

The dearth of resources committed to Angola had consequences. The parties themselves were left to carry out the demobilization, and they failed. Margaret Anstee, U.N. special representative of the secretary general, stated that by May 1992 about 70 percent of the estimated 160,000 soldiers had been processed at the assembly points, but only 6,000 had been demobilized.[48] Many soldiers simply left their cantonments with their weapons and turned to banditry. On election day there

48. *SouthScan*, vol. 7 (May 1, 1992), p. 127.

were still two intact armies, one of which—Forças Armadas de Libertação de Angola, UNITA's military arm—emerged better disciplined and provisioned than the other thanks to American "humanitarian" aid to ensure that UNITA's army would be fed, clothed, and paid during its so-called transition to civilian life.[49] The joint leadership of the new Angolan army took charge the day before the election, but there were few integrated units to command.

Both sides delayed demobilizing regular troops, caching large contingents of men and arms in order to be prepared to resume fighting should the peace process derail. UNITA reportedly kept a 10,000–20,000-strong army close to the Namibian border and at other locations and 3,000–5,000 elite troops in Zaire.[50] Beyond the troops withheld from demobilization, each side under the peace accords was granted "personal security" forces, which in fact were each party's most elite soldiers, organized and fully equipped for war.

In general, the ability to implement the Bicesse agreement was hindered by the massive destruction of the countryside and lack of infrastructure and communication in the country. U.N. secretary general Boutros-Ghali stated in June 1992 that the overall situation in Angola was not amenable to the reconciliation process. "The political and security atmosphere throughout Angola remains tense and could yet derail the process if not contained," he said.[51] Neither side trusted the other, and the international commitment to the peace process was insufficient to compensate for that lack of trust.

That the cease-fire held in Angola before the election is something of a miracle. U.N. monitors counted no less than sixteen incidents between January and September 1992 that could have flared into major combat between the two armies. That they did not was attributed to the parties' will to see the process through to elections and their command and control over their armed forces. As official demobilization faltered, however, and soldiers demobilized themselves, U.N. monitors began to

49. Such aid would not have been destabilizing if demobilization had occurred and if the MPLA had adequately fed and paid its own troops.

50. Victoria Brittain, "Angola: The Final Act?" *Southern Africa Report*, vol. 7 (May 1992), p. 20; David Ottaway, "Problem Mounts in Angola as Election Nears," *Washington Post*, April 11, 1992, p. A14; and *Facts and Reports*, vol. 22 (April 17, 1992), pp. 12–13, and vol. 22 (May 1, 1992), pp. 18–19.

51. Quoted in *SouthScan*, vol. 7 (July 3, 1992), p. 198.

fear that the MPLA army no longer had the discipline to obey commands. On the other hand, UNITA's army maintained its discipline, but, neither demobilized nor integrated into a new army, it stood as a potent threat if Jonas Savimbi decided to return to war.

The failure to demilitarize Angola would not necessarily, by itself, have been a problem, except that Savimbi spurned the results of the September elections and plunged the country back into civil war. The terms of the political settlement mandated that the September elections determine the composition of the national legislature and the presidency of the country. A run-off election would be held thirty days after the first results were posted if none of the presidential candidates received a majority. In the legislative elections, the ruling MPLA party outpolled UNITA by a five-to-three margin. MPLA's dos Santos received about 49.5 percent to Savimbi's 40 percent for the presidency.

The election itself ran smoothly and peacefully. One U.N. military commander remarked, without exaggeration, that the polling period was probably the most peaceful two days in the last thirty years in Angola. Multiple, intricate precautions were taken to prevent fraud: representatives of the competing parties were present at the 5,800 polling stations and at every municipal, provincial, and national electoral center. Result sheets were signed off by party representatives at each level, a process that added days to the vote counting. There were numerous logistical foul-ups, but international observers agreed that the elections were free of intimidation and fraud.

Problems emerged as soon as preliminary results were reported, however. The first results came from Luanda, an MPLA stronghold; not surprisingly, they showed the MPLA and dos Santos with a large majority. Savimbi and UNITA immediately cried foul and issued a bombastic five-page memo declaring that the MPLA was engaged in massive fraud and that UNITA would go back to war if it lost the election. When it became clear that returns from the central provinces (UNITA's stronghold) would not offset MPLA's early lead, UNITA withdrew its generals from the joint command of the new Angolan army. Savimbi refused to meet any foreign officials, denounced the United Nations, repeatedly ignored international calls for reasonableness, and demanded a power-sharing agreement in lieu of the elections, a demand clumsily supported by South Africa.[52] His army then launched attacks

52. During the period immediately after the election, as the United Nations

throughout the Angolan countryside, prompting the MPLA to embark on a seek-and-destroy mission in Luanda that left over 1,000 UNITA supporters dead.

Despite international calls for a cease-fire, UNITA continued to shun negotiations and seize territory. The MPLA finally undertook a major offensive in January 1993, hoping to destroy UNITA's center of power in Huambo. Initial MPLA attacks reduced the city to rubble, but UNITA counterattacks repelled the offensive. UNITA managed impressive military gains, and by December 1993 controlled 80 percent of Angolan territory. The resumed civil war is claiming 1,000 lives daily and putting millions of others at risk of starvation, according to U.N. estimates.[53]

MOZAMBIQUE: THE ROME AGREEMENT

While Angola's fragile peace was unraveling, representatives of FRELIMO and RENAMO were putting the finishing touches on a comprehensive peace agreement in Rome. The agreement signed on October 4, 1992, culminated two years of intensive mediation that involved an array of participants, from religious orders in Italy to Portuguese, British, American, and German diplomats, and from the presidents of Kenya and Zimbabwe to a multinational business tycoon.

Preliminary mediation efforts were made by the Mozambican Catholic church in August 1988 with tacit support from the government. Before direct negotiations could proceed, however, RENAMO had to transform itself into a political organization with negotiable aims. In order to do so RENAMO held its first congress in June 1989, roughly thirteen years after the organization was set up by the Rhodesian Central Intelligence Organization. Initially the warring parties agreed on indirect mediation by Robert Mugabe of Zimbabwe and Daniel arap Moi of Kenya. When their efforts stalled, the parties agreed to direct talks in Rome in July 1990, and presidents Moi and Mugabe were

attempted to press Savimbi to honor the election results and participate in a presidential run-off election, South African foreign minister Pik Botha visited Savimbi and unilaterally put forward a plan to shelve new elections and to provide for a government of national unity.

53. *Washington Post*, October 13, 1993, p. A21.

replaced as mediators by three Italian government and church representatives and the archbishop of Beira, Jaime Gonçalves.

The July talks were the beginning of a series of meetings at which the parties tried to find common ground. At the third round of talks in Rome in late 1990, RENAMO and FRELIMO agreed to a partial cease-fire in the Beira and Limpopo transport corridors. The agreement also stipulated a reduction of Zimbabwean troops by about half, from 12,000, and confined them to the corridors. A fourth round of talks in December 1990 established a forty-six-member Joint Verification Committee (JVC) to monitor the cease-fire.[54]

Zimbabwe completed its troop withdrawal by late December, but by early 1991 about thirty violations of the cease-fire had been reported, the vast majority ascribed to RENAMO by the JVC. RENAMO broke off a fifth round of talks in late January, accusing the government of stationing Zimbabwean troops outside the transport corridors. The JVC found no corroborating evidence, but RENAMO resumed attacks in the two corridors nonetheless.

A sixth round of talks was postponed four times while RENAMO repeatedly blocked the peace process. Finally, in May 1991 the parties agreed to an agenda for continuing negotiations. The talks were again interrupted by RENAMO. The seventh round of talks started and broke down in early August, in part because RENAMO introduced a new demand, the suspension of seventeen articles in the new constitution just enacted by FRELIMO.

Negotiations made no progress until October 1991, when a "Protocol on Fundamental Principles" was signed. RENAMO recognized the legitimacy of the government during the transition between a formal cease-fire and elections, thus dropping an earlier demand that the United Nations take over five key ministries during this period. But RENAMO continued its schizophrenic bargaining behavior and on November 9, 1991, presented a document denying the legitimacy of the government and suspending talks indefinitely. During a November visit to Portugal, RENAMO leader Afonso Dhlakama urged greater Portuguese involvement in the peace process, which led later in No-

54. Apart from government and RENAMO representatives, the JVC consisted of members from ten countries jointly selected by the two principal parties: Italy (chair), Congo, France, Kenya, Portugal, Union of Soviet Socialist Republics, United Kingdom, United States, Zambia, and Zimbabwe.

vember to the signing of a second protocol, this one dealing with criteria for and registration of political parties. Early in 1992 FRELIMO and RENAMO signed a third protocol laying out the election process and the contents of an electoral law.[55]

Up to that point in the negotiations, observers believed that RENAMO preferred a power-sharing agreement with FRELIMO over the Western liberal democratic ideas enshrined by FRELIMO in a new Mozambican constitution. RENAMO's erratic negotiating behavior led Mozambican and Western diplomatic observers to query RENAMO's political coherence. Could its leaders deliver on any agreement? Were RENAMO's stated intentions to be taken seriously? As one Western diplomat put it, "The problem is that Renamo don't know what they want anymore. What they claim they want, they already have."[56]

Evidence of dissension within the RENAMO negotiating team in Rome began to emerge in May 1992. Some within RENAMO complained that the organization was not ready for electoral politics because it had not turned itself into a political party. Others, it appeared, never pursued a political role for RENAMO or believed in the possibility of winning an election. For them, the Rome process was a chance to seek a buyout—a guarantee of financial survival for RENAMO leaders and generals in postelection Mozambique—in exchange for ending the war.[57] RENAMO's lack of unified goals obstructed the Rome talks even as the negotiations resolved such issues as the terms for a cease-fire, merging the armies of the two sides, what to do with the soldiers who would be demobilized, electoral law, voter registration, elections, and monitoring.

By mid-1992 three factors conspired to move the peace process forward: strong pressure from external observers to the talks, most notably the United States and Portugal; the gradual abatement of South African

---

55. The account of the negotiating process is derived from official statements of the mediators and involved parties and from various newspaper reports.

56. Economist Intelligence Unit, *EIU Country Report no. 4: Mozambique* (London, 1990), p. 8.

57. See *Facts and Reports*, vol. 22 (June 12, 1992), pp. 14–15. The descriptions of RENAMO's internal problems, its behavior in the negotiations, and the different views its members held on RENAMO's political future are derived mainly from personal communications with individuals close to the negotiating process in Rome.

support to RENAMO and the ensuing breakdown of RENAMO command structures; and the drought that was then being seriously felt throughout Mozambique. According to some observers the drought was especially consequential because RENAMO troops began to leave RENAMO-held areas in search of food.

Following a high-level meeting in Gaborone that included the presidents of Botswana and Zimbabwe, the U.S. ambassador to Mozambique, and the chairman of the Zimbabwe-based Lonrho Corporation, President Chissano of Mozambique announced that he would talk to RENAMO leader Dhlakama to arrive at a cease-fire agreement. This accommodation was a major breakthrough. It symbolized that the extremely prestige-conscious Dhlakama would be treated as an equal by President Chissano.[58]

The October 1992 accord consists of a general peace agreement and seven separate protocols covering different issues linked to war termination, future elections, and international supervision. Specifically, armed forces were to report to forty-nine assembly points, where they would be demobilized under U.N. supervision and assisted in reintegration into their home areas; a new 30,000-member military force made up of soldiers from both sides would be set up. All weapons would be "disposed of" and prisoners of war would be released. Freedom of movement throughout the country was guaranteed. Parliamentary and presidential elections were to be held before October 4, 1993. The United Nations was charged with forming and leading a commission to control and supervise the implementation of the accord.

Sobered by its experience in Angola, the United Nations agreed to assist in peace building in Mozambique. The U.N. Security Council pledged nearly $500 million and 8,000 troops and personnel to create an environment favorable to Mozambican peace. A newly appointed director for the Mozambican mission promised that the Angolan experience would not be repeated—unless the parties carried out their commitments to demobilization, there would be no elections. U.N. rhetoric certainly suggested that the Angolan debacle had been instructive, but the rhetoric was not matched by prompt action. The U.N. plan of assistance was not formulated until December 1992. At the end of 1993 the full contingent of peacekeeping troops was not in place. Soldiers were not demobilized and elections were postponed until October 1994.

58. Confidential communication from a participant in the process.

THE CASES COMPARED

Table 4-1 summarizes conflict resolution efforts in Southern Africa, by country; table 4-2 breaks down the results of those efforts by success or failure at reaching a settlement. Table 4-2 also shows which of the negotiated settlements were successfully implemented and, in the cases of failed conflict resolution, it indicates whether the efforts contributed to future resolution of the conflict.

Among all the negotiations that have taken place, only three—the Lancaster House, tripartite, and Zimbabwean unity agreements—have led to termination of conflict. It is too early to tell whether the Rome accords will be carried out. Among the negotiations that did not terminate the conflict, some did at least contribute to later conflict resolution; others did little to further future mediation efforts or even exacerbated the antagonism among the concerned parties. For instance, the Anglo-American efforts in 1977–78 supplied knowledge and information for the successful Lancaster House agreement in 1979. On the other hand, at Gbadolite and Victoria Falls, no progress was made toward resolving conflict and the warring parties emerged more hostile to one another. A subset of these cases includes agreements that were reached but not implemented, such as Nkomati and Bicesse. In both cases one of the parties to the agreement reneged on its commitments, thereby confirming suspicions about its hostile intentions and deepening mistrust. Mixed cases include the Kissinger-Geneva mediation, which began the intensive problem solving needed for resolving Zimbabwe's war but temporarily drove the parties further apart.

Lessons from Conflict Resolution in Southern Africa

Comparison of the negotiating efforts suggests several important lessons for conflict resolution in Southern Africa. Some of these lessons may apply to the general study of conflict resolution as well.

Conflict resolution became possible when the actors' fear of continued conflict exceeded their fear of settlement. Two considerations are pertinent here: (1) the costs of continued conflict and (2) the protection that settlement terms afford the warring parties. Settlement in Zimbabwe and between Angola and South Africa came only when the military costs of continued conflict became untenable for at least some of the participants. By the time of the Lancaster House conference in 1979, the

TABLE 4-1. *Conflict Resolution Efforts in Southern Africa, 1975–92*

Country	Adversaries	Mediator	Name (date) of negotiating effort	Result
Angola	UNITA, FNLA, MPLA	Portugal	Alvor agreement (January 1975)	Settlement not implemented; divisions deepened
	Angola, South Africa	United States	Lusaka Accords (February 1984)	Cease-fire reached but no political settlement; divisions deepened
	Angola, Cuba, South Africa	United States	Tripartite agreement (December 1988)	Settlement reached among Cuba, South Africa, and Angola; war between South Africa and Angola ended; civil war in Angola not addressed
	MPLA, UNITA	Zaire, Front Line States	Gbadolite mediation (1989)	No settlement; divisions deepened
	MPLA, UNITA	Portugal, United States, Soviet Union	Bicesse agreement (May 1991)	Settlement reached but not implemented; divisions deepened
Mozambique	Mozambique, South Africa	None	Nkomati Accord (March 1984)	Settlement reached but not implemented; divisions deepened
	FRELIMO, RENAMO (originally known as MNR)	Italy,[a] Portugal, United States, Front Line States	Rome agreement (October 1992)	Settlement reached; implementation incomplete
Namibia	SWAPO, South Africa	United Nations, United States and other Contact Group members,[b] Front Line States	Contact Group mediation (1977–83)	Parties brought closer to settlement

	Parties	Mediators	Process	Outcome
	SWAPO, South Africa	United States	Tripartite agreement (December 1988)c	Negotiated settlement successfully implemented
Zimbabwe	Zimbabwean nationalists, Rhodesian Front	South Africa, Front Line States	Victoria Falls (August 1975)	No settlement; divisions deepened
	Patriotic Front, Abel Muzorewa, Ndabaningi Sithole, Rhodesian Front	United States, Great Britain	Kissinger-Geneva (October 1976)	No settlement; divisions deepened, but some problem solving
	Patriotic Front, Abel Muzorewa, Ndabaningi Sithole, Rhodesian Front	United States, Great Britain	Anglo-American process (1977–78)	Parties brought closer to settlement
	Patriotic Front, Zimbabwe-Rhodesia	Great Britain	Lancaster House (September–November 1979)	Negotiated settlement successfully implemented
	ZANU-PF, ZAPU	None	Zimbabwe unity agreement (December 1987)	Negotiated settlement successfully implemented

Source: Authors' compilation.

a. Representatives of the Italian government and representatives from the Church of San Egidio acted as mediators.

b. The Contact Group consists of Canada, France, Germany, Great Britain, and the United States.

c. The three parties to the tripartite agreement are Angola, Cuba, and South Africa. The agreement tied Namibian independence to the withdrawal of Cuban and South African troops from Angola.

TABLE 4-2. *Results of Conflict Resolution Efforts, 1975–92*

Year	Successfully implemented	Negotiated settlements reached — Failed or incomplete implementation	Failed negotiations	Effect
1992		Rome agreement		Implementation still in progress
1991		Bicesse agreement		Divisions deepened
1989			Gbadolite mediation	Divisions deepened
1988	Tripartite agreement			Namibian independence
1987	Zimbabwe unity agreement			Prevented civil war; de facto one-party state
1984		Lusaka Accords		Divisions deepened
		Nkomati Accord		Divisions deepened
1983			Contact Group (1977–83)	Brought parties closer to settlement
1979	Lancaster House			Zimbabwean independence
1978			Anglo-American process	Brought parties closer to settlement
1976			Kissinger-Geneva	Divisions deepened
1975		Alvor agreement		Divisions deepened
			Victoria Falls	Divisions deepened

Source: Authors' compilation.

white security forces faced a desperate military situation and needed a settlement. In the case of Angola, the costs of continued conflict drove the MPLA and South Africa to reach a partial agreement in 1984, but the resultant cease-fire relieved the parties of their urgency to resolve the conflict fully. In 1988 Cuban escalation pushed the South African government into bargaining in good faith and provided a sense of crisis that heightened South African fear of continuing conflict. The devastating drought in Mozambique in 1992 accomplished what the Mozambican army could not, raising the costs of war for RENAMO and prompting it to finally sign a peace agreement. As for the Bicesse agreement, nothing stands out as a clear, compelling force for settlement. The sixteen-month cease-fire that preceded the 1992 elections seemed to strip away any fear of renewed conflict among the UNITA leadership. Its army intact and disciplined, UNITA returned to civil war. A similar danger now faces Mozambique, where a prolonged cease-fire may remove the antagonists' fear of war.[59]

The other side of the fear equation is that the security of the participants in the conflict must be protected. Under the best of circumstances, peacemaking is a highly contingent and indeterminate process. It involves risks for those willing to mediate and risks for those leaders who choose to pursue peace. First, it is risky for leaders to pursue peace because of the possibility that they will be branded as sellouts by hard-liners within their party. Second, a pledge to mutual security exposes one's party to the possibility of betrayal by the opponent. Third, even if an opposition leader negotiates in good faith, that leader may be unable to deliver his or her side in an agreement.

Problem solving must lessen such risks. Thus negotiations for a cease-fire and transition in Zimbabwe centered on the difficult process of protecting combatants who apply for amnesty, candidates who compete for election, and ordinary citizens who support one party or another. Whites wanted guarantees that ZANU would not eliminate them if it came to power. Similar concerns dominated the search for a settlement in Namibia. In the tripartite agreement made by Angola, Cuba, and South Africa, much time was spent hammering out precise timetables for withdrawal of troops so that no party would feel insecure during the peace process.

59. The Southern African experience with termination of civil war shows that the search for a cease-fire as a good in and of itself is counterproductive to terminating war. Solutions to the vexing conflict issues came while war continued to rage—indeed, at times threatened to escalate. Cease-fires relaxed the sense of tension necessary for war termination. This point seems to have gone unnoticed by mediators in the recent wars in the Balkans, who spent a year and a half insisting on a cease-fire instead of comprehensive negotiations.

Such concerns could not be addressed quickly. The military aspects of the tripartite agreement took about five months to resolve. In Zimbabwe the search for security measures took the better part of three years of intensive talks with all parties. In Mozambique security talks lasted nearly two years. The only case where problem solving seemed deficient was in the Bicesse negotiations, in which the parties were apparently more concerned with measures that would bring them to power than with those that would provide protection before, during, and after elections.

Details mattered and learning was important. This point grows out of the previous one. In the Zimbabwean case, participants seemed to believe at the beginning of the peace process that the conflict would be quickly settled if the parties all agreed on majority rule. Negotiations at Geneva dashed that belief. The details of a settlement posed real problems for an array of issues—security, a constitution, transition, cease-fire. Especially when the parties fear settlement more than they fear continued conflict, they need to know how specific concerns will be addressed. Moreover, because some proposals and solutions might confer benefits—however slight—on one or the other party, their implications need to be fully analyzed. Thus peacemaking must have an active problem-solving component. In the end at Lancaster House, the ability of the mediator to learn from the problems with past proposals made settlement possible. Similar learning by the Contact Group took place regarding Namibia.

The successful resolution of conflicts in Southern Africa demanded prolonged, intense attention from the international community. The Zimbabwean and Namibian cases commanded a large amount of international attention. In the former case, six years of international mediation had created a bank of knowledge about the participants and settlement terms from which the British could draw at Lancaster House. Moreover, the fact that there was always an outside party working for a settlement helped prevent the war from escalating into a regional or larger conflict. As for Namibia, first the Contact Group and then Chester Crocker worked continually for almost twelve years to reach a negotiated settlement. Even as the participants pursued unilateral options, a negotiated settlement was always available to them. In the case of Mozambique, it took over two years of talks to bring the parties to sign a formal agreement, and it was only when international participation intensified that progress was made. In the Bicesse agreement, settlement resulted first from Portuguese involvement and then from intensive U.S. and Soviet intervention.

The only instance in which international involvement did *not* play a key role in conflict resolution was the ZANU-ZAPU unity talks in Zimbabwe. In that case participants themselves could defuse tensions because conflict had not yet escalated to large-scale civil war. International factors did play a lesser, but still significant, part in pushing the opponents toward settlement. By drawing attention to ZANU-PF coercion in Matabeleland, international human rights groups raised the costs to the ruling party of a unilaterally imposed solution.

Successful implementation of agreements demanded international participation in monitoring and regulating the settlement. Both the Lancaster House agreement and the Namibian settlement involved an international presence in the form of cease-fire monitors and election observers. On the other hand, the Alvor agreement—which failed to end conflict in Angola—never drew an international commitment from either the patrons of the combatants or the United Nations. Likewise, the Nkomati Accord, which was not honored by the South African government, omitted provisions for international supervision.

The importance of the international component is best seen by comparing the international attention and commitment to the Lancaster House agreement and the Namibian settlement with international involvement in supervising the Bicesse agreement. In the latter case, the United Nations sought to minimize its commitment and failed to provide an adequate number of troops and personnel to supervise the peace process. While a large international presence cannot by itself ensure successful implementation of a peace accord, it can help enormously in establishing an environment for a settlement to succeed. Peace agreements will always have to be the product of antagonists' self-restraint and goodwill toward meeting commitments. International supervision is no substitute, but it can help the actors work together and provide a sense of security, allowing antagonists to take the risky steps necessary for peace.

Processes internal to the involved parties were crucial in terminating conflicts. In the Zimbabwean case, it was only at Lancaster House that Robert Mugabe had the kind of organizational control that enabled ZANU to choose peace. On the Rhodesian side, a settlement could take place only when the Rhodesian military had pushed aside Ian Smith as the negotiator for white Rhodesia. In the Angolan–South African peace talks, both the MPLA and the South African government were divided over the value of negotiation. For both sides the factions that wanted peace had to overcome intransigence from hard-liners. At one point in the conflict, immediately after the Lusaka Accords were signed, the warring parties were progressing to a broader settlement of their differences, only to have the process derailed by a hard-line faction in the South African military.

Some leaders defined the conflict in all-or-nothing terms and were unwilling to compromise for peace. Negotiated settlements are possible only if such leaders are marginalized. Two examples from Southern Africa suggest that individual leaders can play an independent role in preventing resolution of conflicts. In the case of Rhodesia, most participants felt—and comparison of the different negotiating episodes supports the belief—that peace could not be reached as along as Ian Smith negotiated for the white population. In Angola, Jonas Savimbi's behavior after the September 1992 elections revealed his intentions to win power outright. His commitment to peace was purely tactical.

The difficulty for a mediator—and for antagonists in civil war—is in gauging the sincerity of claims for peace. As civil wars rage, many leaders employ rhetoric suggesting that they will accept nothing less than complete victory and total power, yet when negotiations are under way, such leaders may profess that they would compromise if their security needs were met. But the consequences of a mistaken judgment about an adversary's sincerity can be disastrous, as in Europe in the 1930s when governments sought to appease Hitler. The mere signing of a peace agreement is not evidence of willingness to compromise. The best test of sincerity that the international community has developed for ending civil wars peacefully is a supervised election. When Savimbi refused to abide by the results of the Angolan elections, he failed that test.

The goals of the mediator placed limits on any settlement. Lancaster House succeeded because Britain was willing to live with Robert Mugabe as leader of an independent Zimbabwe. Twice before, peacemaking efforts had faltered because South Africa was an essential part of the mediation attempt, and what South Africa wanted in Zimbabwe—a friendly black regime—did not coincide with what could have ended the conflict. In the case of Namibia, the goal of the Contact Group—avoiding the imposition of sanctions—prevented the mediators from using the only leverage that might have pressed South Africa into accepting settlement.

It was extremely important to have the support and acquiescence of important regional actors. The Lancaster House settlement would not have been possible without the active support of Zambia and Mozambique, which pressured the Patriotic Front to compromise. Nor would it have been possible without the resignation of South Africa. The Front Line States were essential in assisting the formulation of proposals for Namibian independence and played an important role in pressuring SWAPO to comply with the tripartite agreement after the fiasco of the April 1989 cease-fire. The Front Line States also played a key role during the summer of 1992 in bringing together Chissano and Dhlakama of Mozambique to seal a peace agreement.

There were different paths and sequences to resolution of intense conflicts. While there are important similarities among the successful cases that differentiate them from the failures, there are also important differences. For example, Britain as mediator in Zimbabwe insisted that the parties work out an agreement on a constitution before holding elections. Lord Carrington reasoned that since constitutional issues were part of the cause of the conflict, those issues had to be addressed before a new government could come to power. In the Namibian case, broad constitutional principles were set out before elections were held, but the details themselves were worked out after elections. In both Zimbabwe and Namibia, demobilization and integration of armies took place after elections. In Angola they were to take place before elections. Even though the Angolan peace process failed, the United Nations believes that the Angola formula is the correct one for Mozambique and asserts that elections will not take place there until both armies comply with demobilization.

Legacies of Conflict Resolution in Southern Africa

In addition to the various lessons from the Southern African cases, there are also legacies that will most likely influence the course of future conflict and its resolution in the region.

Having terms dictated by a mediator had costs. Britain was able to impose a settlement on the participants in the Lancaster House negotiations, but by doing so it reduced the normative commitment of the participants to the agreement. In the Lusaka Accords and the tripartite agreement, one of the main participants in the conflict was omitted from the bargaining table. In both instances SWAPO's exclusion had ramifications that led to problems in implementing the agreements.

Successful conflict resolution in Southern Africa has taken the form of partial solutions. The Lancaster House settlement resolved the conflicts over white political domination and institutionalized racism, but it did so at the expense of leaving unresolved the land distribution conflict. The tripartite agreement ended the interstate conflict between Angola and South Africa, but it did not address the internal war between the MPLA and UNITA. In Namibia the independence conflict was resolved by postponing the resolution of important distributional questions. In the Zimbabwe unity agreement, the conflict between ZANU and ZAPU over ZAPU's political status was resolved at the cost of multiparty democracy in the country. The accomplishments of these agreements should not be denigrated—perhaps in all of these cases only partial solutions were possible. Nonetheless, it is important to point out that conflict is not fully resolved when agreements are signed or implemented.

Concessions in conflict resolution did not spring from political goodwill or moral reassessment; instead, they were a consequence of shrinking maneuvering space resulting from various pressures and leverages wielded by opponents and third parties. Violence has been used successfully in Southern Africa to force opponents to reach agreements. In many cases aggrieved parties first attempted nonviolent strategies of conflict resolution, only to be met with coercion and violence. In other cases actors sought security through the preemptive use of coercion and violence. The ugly outcome is that violence has become an acceptable method for trying to resolve conflicts. The tools of that violence are still plentiful and available in the region.

Although violence has been a central aspect of conflict resolution in Southern Africa, the region's leaders have also displayed a large degree of pragmatism in ending their conflicts. A positive legacy of Southern Africa's recent experience with conflict resolution is the development of a regional norm of pragmatism. As deadly as Southern Africa's wars have been, antagonists have repeatedly proved willing to engage in negotiations and to make peace. For Zimbabwe, Namibia, Mozambique, and South Africa peacemaking has demanded that leaders eschew ideological commitment, reconcile with former adversaries, and recognize the legitimacy of opponents' claims. When internal leaders have found it difficult to make peace with their enemies at home, regional colleagues have lent a hand. Samora Machel urged Robert Mugabe to pursue a policy of racial reconciliation. The Front Line presidents counseled

SWAPO to rule democratically. And to further the hopes of peace in Mozambique, the leaders of Zimbabwe and Botswana brought Chissano and Dhlakama together. Whereas most civil wars end in the elimination or surrender of one side, the rule in Southern Africa has been negotiated settlement. Indeed, the Angolan case, in which Jonas Savimbi evidenced a commitment only to total victory or defeat, is a regional anomaly.

Such pragmatism aside, the overall legacies of conflict and conflict resolution in Southern Africa suggest that the ending of South Africa's war of destabilization and the triumph of majority rule in South Africa will not by themselves lead to stable peace in the region. Too many loose ends still exist, as well as too many partial solutions to problems. Too many outstanding conflict issues were swept under the table by dint of the dominant regional conflict. Even as old conflicts are re-solved, new ones will come to the fore. Southern Africa in the future must find a way to resolve conflict that does not rely on ad hoc negoti-ations and mediations and the use of force. The challenge for the region on the national and regional levels is to build new institutions that can bound conflict and resolve it without the resort to violence.

Can the nations of the region, and the region as a whole, build such institutions? The next section of the book looks at conflict issues that are salient today—and at those that may become salient tomorrow—within the countries of Southern Africa and examines the capabilities of those countries to resolve them.

PART 2

National Conflict in Southern Africa

Chapter 5

South Africa's Second Interregnum

Many people hoped that Nelson Mandela's release from prison and the unbanning of the African National Congress in February 1990 portended a quick march to new democratic institutions for South Africa. Instead, it took four years and nearly 13,000 deaths to bring South Africa to its first one-person, one-vote election. Writing in 1993, Max du Preez, editor of the Afrikaans alternative newsmagazine *Vrye Weekblad*, captured the folly of South Africans' early optimism: "Anyone who thought we would be able to change 300 years of white domination and 45 years of apartheid into a liberal democracy in a flash and without releasing considerable energy was naive."[1]

Domestic and international circumstances brought the parties to recognize that negotiation was necessary to make peace in South Africa. Apartheid had bequeathed charged, nearly intractable conflicts that required creative, intensive problem solving, yet in 1990 the main parties put forward slogans as solutions—"one person, one vote" versus "group rights" and "economic nationalization" versus "free markets." Decades of combat—political and otherwise—complicated the hard work of problem solving. Each party suspected its adversary (and now companion in negotiations) of pursuing a hidden agenda for political victory.

As one analyst insists, the ANC and the National Party "entered into negotiations to achieve original, as opposed to compromised, objectives."[2] Since compromise was essential to progress in negotiations, leaders of both parties had to overcome several roadblocks. First, al-

---

1. Quoted in *Cape Times*, July 2, 1993.
2. Susan Booysen, "Changing Relations of Political Power in South Africa's Transition: The Politics of Conquering in Conditions of Stalemate," *Politikon*, vol. 19 (December 1992), p. 64.

though both sides stood to gain from a new political order, they also desired arrangements that would maximize their side's advantage. The transition in South Africa seemed alternately a love fest and a "grim struggle for ascendancy."[3]

Second, trade-offs between leaders at the top of the ANC and the NP alienated important constituencies within the parties, who viewed any compromise as a betrayal of fundamental principles. Third, important groups in South African society feared being left behind whenever the ANC and the NP did come to agreement between themselves. Throughout the negotiations in South Africa the exclusivity necessary for reaching agreement between the two most powerful parties has been at odds with the inclusiveness necessary for accommodating smaller parties, which, if left out, could—and often did—use violence to undermine new political arrangements.

Nonetheless, by April 1994 conflict resolution had achieved a series of important but partial successes in South Africa. An agreement among the ANC, NP, and various small parties set the stage for South Africa's first nonracial elections. A settlement among those same parties established the mechanisms for a gradual transition to democracy. Business, labor, and government formed a National Economic Forum to consult and propose solutions to South Africa's economic crisis. And one of the most troubling issues for both South Africa and the rest of the region—security—had begun to be addressed. Some progress registered in bringing accountability and reform to the South African Police and defense forces.

BACKGROUND TO NEGOTIATIONS

As described in chapter 3, by the late 1980s the National Party's policies of limited reform and repression had, in F. W. de Klerk's words, reached a dead end. De Klerk's accession to power in 1989 coincided with great changes in the world that emboldened him to seek a new direction. The collapse of communist regimes in Eastern Europe and the Soviet Union released the ideological stranglehold that anticommunism held on the South African state. The *political* defeat of South African

3. Fatima Meer, quoted in Timothy Sisk, *Democratization in South Africa: The Elusive Social Contract* (Princeton University Press, forthcoming 1994).

militarism in Angola and Namibia weakened those forces in the government most opposed to substantive change in South Africa. The continuing weakness of the South African economy led more and more business people to urge face-to-face negotiations with the ANC. Many of them had met with the ANC in exile and felt confident that a political solution could be reached that would address the fears of the white community. Afrikanerdom itself had gone through major changes: the major elite Afrikaner organization, the Broederbond, circulated a secret document in 1989 arguing that "the exclusion of effective black sharing in the political processes at the highest level had become a 'threat to the survival of the white man.' There could no longer be a white government and the head of government did not necessarily have to be white."[4]

When de Klerk released Nelson Mandela and unbanned the ANC and the South African Communist Party, he did so as the head of a deeply fractured state and political party. The South African state contained military and police elements who had been involved in domestic and regional terrorism and were opposed to a settlement with the ANC. The National Party itself contained advocates and opponents of negotiation. Even among those party members who favored negotiation, there was a wide range of opinion concerning optimal and minimal settlement terms.

The ANC's willingness to negotiate a settlement was rooted in its long advocacy of racial reconciliation and the creation of a nonracial nation. A combination of liberal strands in the party's heritage, a strong degree of legalism in its makeup, and a history of linking armed struggle to negotiation created an organization disposed to a negotiated transition.[5] Indeed, it was Nelson Mandela, writing from prison in 1986, who put forward proposals to meet with P. W. Botha to find a peaceful method of resolving South Africa's crisis. This disposition, combined with an increasing consensus within the party that armed struggle was not likely to bring down the regime in the short run, the loss of allies such as the Soviet Union and some Eastern European countries, and the

4. Hermann Giliomee, "Broedertwis: Intra-Afrikaner Conflicts in the Transition from Apartheid," *African Affairs*, vol. 91 (July 1992), p. 360.

5. Tom Lodge, "Perspectives on Conflict Resolution in South Africa," in Francis Deng and I. William Zartman, eds., *Conflict Resolution in Africa* (Brookings, 1991), pp. 125–30.

positive responses by the international community to de Klerk's initiatives, diminished the ANC's range of alternatives away from the bargaining table.

The ANC also contained deep divisions, exacerbated by the different experiences of so many of its members: in 1990 the ANC leadership consisted of long-term political prisoners in South Africa, exiles at their headquarters in Lusaka and elsewhere across the world, and civic association leaders who remained in South Africa and fought the regime as part of the United Democratic Front (UDF) and Mass Democratic Movement (MDM).[6] While the older leaders of the ANC were unified in their belief that armed struggle could not bring victory, younger rank-and-file members who had made the townships ungovernable felt mass action could topple the regime. Deeply distrustful of the South African government, the youth remained vigilant to any sign that their leadership might abandon them.

Not just the ANC and the NP were divided in 1990. All of South Africa was riven by multiple, deep chasms forged by centuries of white domination, forty-two years of apartheid, and more than a decade of war. Negotiators would have to replace a constitution that entrenched white political and economic power, but to do so they would have to confront a state bureaucracy with a vested interest in perpetuating its privilege. The stability of any agreement would depend on redressing deep-seated gaps between blacks and whites in wealth, income, land, and access to social services, but the ability of policymakers to narrow such gaps was constrained by a poorly performing economy. Nation building would have to overcome the centrifugal pull of narrow identities, a task made difficult by high levels of political and social violence which induce fear and breed mistrust. Reducing violence itself was a daunting task because of endemic poverty, the lack of professional police, and the presence of groups in society who had a stake in perpetuating violence. And if democracy was to take root as a solution to South Africa's multiple conflicts, leaders would have to create a climate of tolerance in the aftermath of what some whites and blacks saw as a total war.

6. For a perceptive analysis of the ANC in 1990–91, see Tom Lodge, "The African National Congress in the 1990s," in Glenn Moss and Ingrid Obery, eds., *South African Review 6: From "Red Friday" to Codesa* (Johannesburg: Ravan Press, 1992), pp. 44–78.

The Captured State and its Legacies

The capture of the South African state by Afrikaners in 1948 and their relentless hold on that state for over forty years posed major impediments to conflict resolution. First, in addition to creating a class of office holders with a vested interest in opposing reforms, Afrikaner dominance led to a connection in the minds of Afrikaners between ethnicity and power. As Giliomee observes, "By the mid-1980s the Afrikaners had come to consider the state as an Afrikaner state or Boereplaas. Furthermore they had come to value power not for purely instrumental reasons but as an end in itself and as confirmation of ethnic status."[7]

Second, the architects of apartheid acted out their belief that the security of white South Africans depended on the insecurity of black South Africans. As described earlier, the use of brute state power and coercion reached its zenith in the 1980s when the restructuring of the South African state under P. W. Botha gave an inordinate amount of autonomy to the security forces. The National Security Management System and the State Security Council constituted a state within a state, which lacked accountability and was deeply involved in assassination and terror within South Africa and in the region. The militarization of the state extended downward into society; all white South Africans were called to play their parts in defeating what was portrayed as a total onslaught of black nationalists, supposedly supported and abetted by forces of communism.[8] Although the Botha regime had set up the state to facilitate a unified response to threats, personal fiefdoms eventually arose in the security forces out of a combination of ideological zeal, corrupted power, and absence of accountability; bitter factional disputes broke out among leaders when they had to face hard choices on negotiations in the region and at home.

Third, the use of the state to foster insecurity among blacks extended into the police and judiciary, which are known in South Africa for arbitrariness, coercion, amateurishness, and injustice toward blacks. Because blacks view the police and judiciary as illegitimate forces of oppression, their attitudes toward "law and order" are a complete

7. Hermann Giliomee, "The Last Trek? Afrikaners in the Transition to Democracy," *South Africa International*, vol. 22 (January 1992), p. 118.
8. Jacklyn Cock, *Colonels and Cadres: War and Gender in South Africa* (Oxford University Press, 1991).

reversal of Western norms: time in prison is a badge of honor, not disgrace;[9] cooperation with the police to fight crime is a betrayal of community; if protection must be sought from police or criminals, township dwellers choose criminals;[10] if police brutality against criminals is alleged, a priori the criminals are victims.[11]

Fourth, apartheid spawned bureaucratic bloat. Because it insisted on ethnic separation, the South African state created multiple ministries and departments to provide each societal group with its own administration for functional areas such as education and health. For example, in 1990

9. This attitude in fact predates apartheid, as shown in Belinda Bozzoli's oral history of black South African women in the twentieth century, *The Women of Phokeng: Consciousness, Life Strategy, and Migrancy in South Africa, 1900–1983* (Johannesburg: Ravan Press, 1991) p. 164.

10. Vivid depictions of township attitudes toward the police can be found in Bloke Modisane's memoir, *Blame Me on History* (Simon and Schuster, 1990), pp. 59–64.

11. As late as 1993, a British television documentary based on the files of the noted South African coroner, Jonathan Gluckman, concluded that "Any black man risks death in police custody" in South Africa; *Weekend Argus*, February 25, 1993, p. 3. See also Gavin Cawthra, *Policing South Africa: The SAP and the Transition from Apartheid* (London: Zed Books, 1993), pp. 139–40. The common official explanation for black deaths in police custody is suicide. A famous South African poem, "In Detention," by Christopher van Wyk, in Andre Brink and J. M. Coetzee, eds., *A Land Apart* (Viking, 1987), p. 50, is a chilling satire of such explanations:

> He fell from the ninth floor
> He hanged himself
> He slipped on a piece of soap while washing
> He hanged himself
> He slipped on a piece of soap while washing
> He fell from the ninth floor
> He hanged himself while washing
> He slipped from the ninth floor
> He hung from the ninth floor
> He slipped on the ninth floor while washing
> He fell from a piece of soap while slipping
> He hung from the ninth floor
> He washed from the ninth floor while slipping
> He hung from a piece of soap while washing

there were eighteen departments of housing and education, each with jurisdiction over different geographical areas and racial groups.[12]

Fifth, the establishment of the homelands as "sovereign entities" created nominally independent bureaucracies and defense forces throughout South African territory. In 1990 one homeland, Transkei, explicitly rejected South Africa's divide-and-rule strategy and welcomed incorporation into a new South Africa. But in Ciskei and Bophuthatswana, dictators and other administrators who had profited from apartheid opposed reincorporation. Even in those homelands that resisted independence, such as KwaZulu and Gazankulu, black leaders with regional power bases depended on funds from the South African state to survive and were threatened by a unitary, democratic South Africa.

Economic Legacy: Distribution Conflict and the Crisis of Production

Apartheid as an economic system produced a massive distribution conflict with great disparities between whites and blacks in wealth, income, health, education, housing, and land. In few countries is the gap between rich and poor so wide as in South Africa. South Africa's Gini coefficient, a measure of income inequality, is between 0.55 and 0.66, a figure among the highest in the world.[13] With the estimated annual per capita income of whites in 1989 at $4,775.70, South Africa would rank among the upper-income countries of the world. The per capita yearly income of black South Africans—$417.80—would put South Africa into the category of "low-income" countries, however.[14] The South African government itself estimated that 45 percent of South Africans, most of them black, live below a "minimum living level."[15]

12. Desmond Lachman and Kenneth Bercuson, eds., *Economic Policies for a New South Africa* (Washington: International Monetary Fund, 1992), p. 19; and Gavin Maasdorp, "Meeting Expectations: The Policy Environment Facing the Post-Apartheid Government," in Robert Schrire, ed., *Wealth or Poverty? Critical Choices for South Africa* (Oxford University Press, 1992), p. 600.

13. Francis Wilson and Mamphela Ramphele, *Uprooting Poverty: The South African Challenge* (Cape Town: David Philip, 1989), pp. 17–18; and Bob Tucker and Bruce R. Scott, eds., *South Africa: Prospects for a Successful Transition: Nedcor–Old Mutual Scenarios* (Kenwyn, South Africa: Juta, 1992), p. 53.

14. William F. Moses and Meg Vorhees, *Corporate Responsibility in Changing South Africa* (Washington: Investor Responsibility Research Center, 1991), p. 32.

15. Andrew Donaldson, "Basic Needs and Social Policy: The Role of the State in Education, Health and Welfare," in Merle Lipton and Charles Simkins, eds.,

Wealth and land follow the same pattern. Four South African corporations, Anglo-American, Old Mutual, Rembrandt, and Sanlam, control companies that possess more than 80 percent of the assets of the Johannesburg Stock Exchange; Anglo-American alone controls companies that own 45.3 percent.[16] Land legislation in South Africa in 1913 and 1936 gave 87 percent of the land to white farmers, relegating blacks to overcrowded reserves that were farmed to death by the 1930s. Such legislation, combined with the establishment of the homelands in the most arid areas, left a large African rural population barely able to eke out a living. Some researchers describe as conservative an estimate that between 15,000 and 27,000 children under five years of age die from malnutrition every year; one source argues that "several hundred thousand children" are at risk annually from malnutrition and malnutrition-related diseases.[17]

The inadequate carrying capacity of the homelands forced illegal black migration to the cities in the 1970s and 1980s. The abolition of pass laws and the Group Areas Act further intensified urbanization and created a housing crisis of monumental proportions for poor blacks.[18] Estimates of the housing backlog for black families range from 1.1

State and Market in Post Apartheid South Africa (Witwatersrand University Press, 1993), p. 273.

16. Jos Gerson, "Should the State Attempt to Reshape South Africa's Corporate and Financial Structures?" in Lipton and Simkins, eds., *State and Market*, pp. 164–65.

17. Peter Moll, "A Food Stamp Programme for South Africa," Carnegie Conference Paper #223, cited in Wilson and Ramphele, *Uprooting Poverty*, p. 101.

18. The Urban Foundation estimates that between 1985 and 1990 the population of South Africa's urban and metropolitan areas grew by 3,400,000. See Charles Simkins, "State, Market, and Urban Development in South Africa," in Lipton and Simkins, eds., *State and Market*, p. 335. Typical of such urbanization is the growth of Khayelitsha, a black township of Cape Town. In 1988 there were 110,000 to 189,000 residents; in 1989, 305,323 official residents; and in 1990, an estimated 450,000 residents. Only 14 percent now live in formal housing; unemployment is said to be around 80 percent. See Gillian P. Cook, "Khayelitsha: New Settlement Forms in the Cape Peninsula," in David M. Smith, ed., *The Apartheid City and Beyond: Urbanization and Social Change in South Africa* (London: Routledge, 1992), p. 130.

million to 3.4 million.[19] In 1991 the average number of blacks per housing unit exceeded 16.[20]

State expenses for education also reveal a large gap between services provided to white and to black children. In 1988–89 per capita expenditure for white pupils was R 3,082, for Indians R 2,227, for Coloureds R 1,360. Spending for African children ranged from R 765 in the cities to R 481 in the homelands. While blacks average forty pupils to the teacher and more than fifty pupils per classroom, whites average under twenty pupils per teacher and fewer than fifteen per classroom. There are about 250,000 vacancies in white schools in South Africa, and there are 400,000 more African students than spaces provided.[21] The same unequal system rules in the health sector. Infant mortality for Africans is eight to ten times higher than for whites and significantly higher than in Zimbabwe, Zambia, and Botswana.[22] Tuberculosis strikes 780 of 10,000 black Africans, 13.5 of 10,000 whites.[23]

If the South African economy were healthy and growing at a steady rate, the distribution conflict would be more easily resolved, since "it is easier to deal with difficult distributive issues . . . if the total size of the cake is increasing."[24] But by 1990 South Africa's economy had been in a prolonged slump. Although apartheid economic policies contributed to rapid economic growth in the 1950s and 1960s, they became more and more counterproductive in the early 1970s because of the rigidity of the labor market, massive state subsidies to white business, and protection of the manufacturing sector and commercial agriculture. Between 1975

19. Lawrence Schlemmer, "Distribution and Redistribution Trade-offs," in Schrire, ed., *Wealth or Poverty?* p. 572. The low estimate comes from the South African government; the high estimate comes from the independent South African Housing Trust.

20. Ronnie Bethlehem, "The Sensible Thing to Do," *The Watershed Years: A Leadership Publication, 1991* (Johannesburg: Leadership Publication, 1991), pp. 102–06.

21. Spending numbers are from South African Institute of Race Relations; class and teacher ratios and vacancies are from *Watershed Years*, p. 139, "South Africa: Growth Crisis . . . or Development Challenge?"

22. Wilson and Ramphele, *Uprooting Poverty*, p. 108.

23. Colin Bundy, "Development and Inequality in Historical Perspective," in Schrire, ed., *Wealth or Poverty?* p. 25.

24. Stephen R. Lewis, Jr., *The Economics of Apartheid* (New York: Council on Foreign Relations, 1990), p. 136.

and 1990 South Africa's economic performance was on a par with the least developed countries in the world. Gross domestic product (GDP) growth averaged 1.3 percent per year from 1980 through 1989.[25] Real GDP per capita declined 2 percent each year during that period.[26] The decline in per capita GDP coincided with a sharp drop in fixed investment, from nearly 29 percent of GDP in 1980 to around 21 percent in 1990.[27] A black South African worker succinctly summarized the problem: "The bosses are on strike. Their duty is to invest capital and they are just not investing any capital right now."[28]

The economic decline produced massive unemployment. From 3.1 million in 1980, unemployment increased to 5.4 million in 1989, based on measures that broadly define as employed "anyone who was working for as little as five hours in a week."[29] Between 1986 and 1991 less than 13 percent of 400,000 first-time job seekers in South Africa found employment.[30] Unemployment disproportionately struck black youth: approximately 90 percent of those unemployed were under the age of 30.[31]

Mental Legacies

The political and economic legacies of apartheid have a corresponding set of mental legacies. These legacies include issues of identity, attitudes toward political and economic institutions, an absence of tolerance, and the psychological effects of violence.

AFRIKANER IDENTITY. The Afrikaner renegade poet Breyten Breytenbach once commented that apartheid reflected "a warped kind of identity crisis. It was in terms of so-called Afrikaner identity that all

25. Bobby Godsell and Jim Buys, "Growth and Poverty," in Schrire, ed., *Wealth or Poverty?* p. 640.

26. Barry Standish, "Public Works Programmes and Economic Development," in Schrire, ed., *Wealth or Poverty?* p. 261.

27. Nicoli Nattrass, *Profits and Wages: The South African Economic Challenge* (Penguin, 1992), p. 4.

28. Francis Wilson, "Poverty and Development," *Monitor*, October 1991, p. 58.

29. Tucker and Scott, eds., *Prospects for a Successful Transition*, p. 52.

30. Colin Bundy, "At War with the Future? Black South African Youth in the 1990s," in Stephen John Stedman, ed., *South Africa: The Political Economy of Transformation* (Boulder: Lynne Rienner Publishers, 1994), p. 53.

31. Bundy, "At War with the Future?" p. 53.

the horrible laws were constructed to make everybody else non-Afrikaners."[32] Because of the apartheid state's rigid categorization of peoples in South Africa, conflicts over who people are and who they should be are both pervasive and explosive.

Breytenbach's quote implies that the successful construction of a postapartheid South Africa would rest on the alleviation of the Afrikaner identity crisis. Some argue that apartheid's success in lifting the living standards of Afrikaners weakened the hold of Afrikaner identity. They contend that the prosperity of Afrikaners has diminished their parochial outlook, weakened their religious fundamentalism, and eroded their racism. Afrikaners, having benefited materially from 1950 to 1990, want to preserve those benefits, even if it means conceding on issues of cultural identity. In the words of Heribert Adam, "It has yet to be proven anywhere that a BMW-owning bureaucratic bourgeoisie with swimming pools and servants readily sacrifices the good life for psychologically gratifying ethnic affinities."[33]

Others reject these arguments and insist that Afrikaners continue to adhere to a coherent identity and feel intense fears for their cultural survival. They argue that a high degree of racism and racial fear remain in the minds of Afrikaner opinion leaders.[34]

Racism, fear, religiousness, and concern over ethnic identity may abide in Afrikaner attitudes, but for at least the last fifteen years Afrikaners have seriously differed on how to maintain their identity

32. Quoted in Kate Manzo and Pat McGowan, "Afrikaner Fears and the Politics of Despair: Understanding Change in South Africa," *International Studies Quarterly*, vol. 36 (1992), p. 1.

33. Quoted in Giliomee, "Broedertwis," p. 340.

34. Manzo and McGowan, "Afrikaner Fears," pp. 1–24; and Pierre Hugo, "Towards Darkness and Death: Racial Demonology in South Africa," *Journal of Modern African Studies*, vol. 26 (1988), pp. 567–90. Fears for survival are particularly intense among those Afrikaners who are members of the security and police forces. Laurie Nathan and Mark Phillips cite a BBC television documentary in which "members of the SAP's Western Cape riot unit claimed that '99% of [white] police do not trust the government.' They feared that they would be made 'political prisoners' under an ANC government and tried for 'riot crimes like the Nazis were in court for war crimes.' " See Laurie Nathan and Mark Phillips, " 'Cross-Currents': Security Developments under F. W. De Klerk," in Moss and Obery, eds., *South Africa Review*, vol. 6, p. 123.

and what core elements of their identity to protect.[35] Indeed, it was in the spirit of preserving Afrikaner identity that the Broederbond, the Afrikaner secret society composed of leading elites, argued for drastic reforms of South African politics.[36] Conflicts have erupted among Afrikaners over whether skin color or language defines Afrikaner ethnicity.[37]

BLACK POLITICAL IDENTITY. Since apartheid divided South Africa's people by race and ethnic affiliations, many South Africans believed that to use such classifications as the basis of political identity was to legitimize apartheid. Indeed, Patrick McAllister and John Sharp go so far as to argue that the mere discussion of ethnicity was a taboo.[38]

Nonetheless, four decades of white domination might have been expected to enshrine race as the prime determinant of political identity for blacks, as it was for whites. It is especially noteworthy, then, that the main liberation group in South Africa, the ANC, has steadfastly pledged to build a nonracial South African nation. The ANC project conflicts with some groups in the African community, such as AZAPO, that believe the struggle to be one of race and press color over nonracialism. The ANC also conflicts with groups like Inkatha that hold ethnic identity as their organizing principle. Finally, the self-identity of some within the ANC alliance is bound up with groups such as the South African Communist Party and COSATU (the largest association of black trade unions), which define themselves in terms of economic relationships with other groups. Different identities did not prevent

35. Giliomee, "Broedertwis," pp. 339–64.

36. Symbolic of the transformation of at least part of Afrikanerdom is that the Broederbond, for seventy years a white male bastion, now admits nonwhites and women.

37. The debate over language versus race in constituting Afrikaner ethnicity is directly related to the attempts of the National Party to attract Coloured voters in the Western Cape.

38. Patrick McAllister and John Sharp, "The Ethnic Taboo," *Indicator South Africa*, vol. 10 (Winter 1993), p. 7. For the ANC and its affiliates, the UDF and MDM, the taboo extended to any political institutions for a new South Africa that lessened central control in a unitary state. In 1989 Donald Horowitz, for example, found strong resistance to the idea of federalism among UDF leaders, who were convinced that the concept was "a cleaned-up version of the homelands policy." Donald L. Horowitz, *A Democratic South Africa? Constitutional Engineering in a Divided Society* (University of California Press, 1991), p. 243.

blacks from joining forces to fight apartheid, but conflict could arise if class identity clashes with national identity in the future.

LIBERATION AS IDENTITY. The struggle to overcome apartheid gave birth to an ideology of liberation which some see as more appropriate to the politics of revolution than to the politics of democracy. Khehla Shubane, a former political prisoner in South Africa, argues that because so many in South Africa saw the struggle as an anticolonialist war, the conflict took on many aspects of other independence struggles in Africa. Liberation movements that "arise to represent the interests of all the dominated and oppressed people," however, "tend to take an undifferentiated view of all the various interests that exist within the oppressed community."[39] Liberation as political identity, Shubane contends, prevents the development of civil society, which depends on diversity of interests and the free pursuit of those interests to thrive. Political movements that lead a fight for liberation tend to reject other parties or organizations as illegitimate, which not only throttles diversity but can propel political violence; this strain was evident at different times in the 1980s between the Mass Democratic Movement and supporters of AZAPO.

VIOLENCE AS IDENTITY. Apartheid's central core was violence against individuals on the basis of their skin color. That violence begat violence against the South African state and those who supported it. One of apartheid's most devastating legacies is the creation of two cultures of violence, one among state police and security forces and the other among marginalized black youths. Members of both cultures define themselves by their ability to inflict pain and terror, and their sense of self-worth comes from the barrel of a gun.

Some analysts explicitly link the militarization of South African society over the last twenty years to the white right wing's fascination with violence as a central element of their identity. And the white right-wingers are numerous: 100,000 whites belong to extremist groups, and thousands of those have paramilitary training. In December 1993 alone, white right-wing terrorist groups were believed to be responsible for thirty bombings in protest of negotiations with the ANC.[40]

39. Khehla Shubane, "Civil Society in South Africa," *Journal of Democracy*, vol. 2 (Summer 1991), p. 53.

40. South African Institute of Race Relations, *Watchdog on the South African Election: 5*, February 28, 1994.

Just as apartheid created a culture of violence among right-wing Afrikaners, the fight against apartheid created a generation of black youths who embrace violence as an integral part of their identity. As Mamphela Ramphele observes, in the 1980s the role of enforcement of antiapartheid activities was given to the youth of the townships: "The politics of making South Africa ungovernable . . . embedded in them a strong element of coercion and intimidation of those unwilling to participate. . . . Most of the responsibility for enforcing those campaigns rested on the youth. Young people thus assumed enormous powers, including the power to kill."[41]

CONFLICT RESOLUTION: 1990–94

The leaders of South Africa faced multiple challenges in 1990. South Africa needed new political institutions that would provide participation for the disenfranchised majority and that would be seen as legitimate by them. At the same time, these institutions had to alleviate the fears of racial and ethnic minorities without crippling the ability of the state to confront the economic and social problems of the country. South Africa also needed policies and institutions to eliminate violence at its core by incorporating marginalized groups for which violence had become a part of their identity. Finally, South Africa needed economic policies that could meet the housing, employment, and education needs of the majority and yet be compatible with policies promoting domestic and foreign investment to better the possibilities of economic growth.

Conflict resolution in a complex society like South Africa depends on much more than formal agreement among political leaders. Political leaders cannot reach agreement on such weighty issues as constitutional reform and economic policies without first reducing the distance that separates them, which calls for debate, exchange, interaction, and information sharing among groups and individuals in society. In South Africa parties have had to move beyond slogans to spelling out the details of achieving their goals. The following pages examine attempts between 1990 and 1994 to resolve three problems that stand in the way of attaining a new, democratic South Africa: (1) the lack of political

---

41. Mamphela Ramphele, "Social Disintegration in the Black Community: Implications for Transition," *Monitor*, October 1991, p. 12.

participation for the vast majority of South Africans; (2) violence and insecurity; and (3) economic inequality and stagnation.[42]

The Participation Conflict

The eighteen months following the release of Nelson Mandela were spent laying the foundation for substantive negotiations over the future of South Africa. In May and August 1990 two formal summits were held between the ANC and the South African government. The protocols of these summits, the Groote Schuur and Pretoria minutes, committed the parties to peaceful negotiation and resulted in the ANC's formal suspension of its campaign of armed struggle.[43] The purpose of the meetings was to address what are in some sense war termination issues: conditions for substantive negotiations, release of political prisoners, and formal cessation of violence.

While progress was made on establishing the preconditions for substantive talks, South Africa suffered from levels of political violence higher than those of the states of emergency in the 1980s. A low-intensity civil war between supporters of the ANC and Mangosuthu Buthelezi's Inkatha movement had been going on for almost five years in the province of Natal; that conflict spread to the townships of the Vaal triangle surrounding Johannesburg as Inkatha tried to establish a national presence. Some of the violence was between Inkatha-affiliated migrant workers from Natal who lived in hostels in the townships and ANC-affiliated township dwellers, but commuter train passengers also were massacred, murders that were designed to terrorize blacks. A

---

42. Obviously these three issues are not the only conflicts in South Africa, but we chose to examine negotiations in these areas because of their centrality in the South African transition. A full investigation of all of the conflicts in South Africa—including land, gender inequality, local governance, and urban management—would fill another entire book.

43. It is important to point out that Mandela was released and formal talks begun between the ANC and the government before the ANC renounced violence as a tool for political change. Some commentators in the West have mistakenly asserted that Mandela's release was conditional on rejection of violence. Moreover, the ANC's suspension of armed violence was not a permanent repudiation; it was expressly conditional on progress in resolving the constitutional crisis in South Africa.

pattern soon became evident: indiscriminate violence correlated with progress in negotiations between the ANC and the government.

Suspicious that the government was instigating violence and impatient at the government's dilatory pace in granting indemnity to political exiles and releasing political prisoners, the ANC suspended negotiations in May 1991. Some within the ANC disagreed with that decision, believing that the government's strategy was to delay negotiations. If that were the case, then a decision to boycott talks with the government signified victory for those committed to a protracted—or permanent—delay.

Evidence of collusion between the government and the Inkatha Freedom Party came in July 1991, when newspapers revealed that the government had funded IFP political rallies, tried to strengthen labor unions affiliated with Inkatha, and provided training to police officers in the KwaZulu homeland, the power base of Buthelezi and Inkatha. Those revelations weakened the government's credibility at a crucial time and gave ANC the opportunity to return to negotiations in a strengthened position. But the ANC decision to reopen talks with the government was not unanimous. Some ANC members felt that further negotiations would be a mockery in light of the fact that the government was not bargaining in good faith. Advocates of negotiation had to convince them that only through negotiations could the government be swayed to hand over power. The advocates of negotiation won a temporary reprieve, but their influence within the ANC waned as violence continued and new revelations of government hit-squad activity and police complicity in township attacks came forward.

Concerned private citizens, church associations, and business organizations expressed concern lest violence undermine negotiations. With their prodding, the government, ANC, and Inkatha signed a National Peace Accord in September 1991. The accord committed some of the main protagonists in South Africa to controlling violence by their followers. The accord also created mechanisms for monitoring political violence. Although violence continued, the peace accord mobilized hundreds of South Africans to engage in dialogue with enemies and attempt to resolve conflicts nonviolently.

Progress was also made on the negotiating front. The NP and ANC both issued proposals for the transition to a new constitution. And the two parties also put forward proposals for the constitution itself.

In April 1991 the ANC published its desired constitutional principles and structures. The constitution would be based on universal suffrage and a unified, nonracial, nonsexist nation. It would establish a far-reaching, justiciable bill of rights that would "acknowledge the importance of securing minimum conditions of decent and dignified living for all South Africans" and include "basic human rights in relation to nutrition, shelter, education, health, employment and welfare." Constitutional structures would include a strong presidency (limited to two terms of office) and a two-house legislature (one for national representation, the other for regional representation) elected through proportional representation. An independent judiciary and constitutional court would interpret and rule on the constitutionality of proposed legislation.[44]

The ANC national congress of July 2, 1991, hammered out proposals to guide the transition to democracy. The proposals addressed preconditions for constitutional negotiations, including the unconditional release of all political prisoners, removal of troops from the townships, cessation of political trials, and the ending of violence in the townships. After agreement with the government over cessation of hostilities, an all-party conference would be held to establish broad constitutional principles and agreements on an interim government, a mechanism to write a new constitution, and steps for the legalization of agreements from the conference. The ANC wanted a transitional government of national unity to rule for two to three years, during which time an elected constitutional assembly would draft the new constitution. When the new constitution was agreed upon, elections would be held and a new, legitimate South African government would rule.[45]

The ANC's constitutional and transitional proposals differed dramatically from those of the NP. Although the NP did not specify its preferred plan for transition, members of its constitutional committee spoke of a ten-year transition period. F. W. de Klerk expressed interest

---

44. Quotes from this paragraph as well as the description of proposals are based on African National Congress Constitutional Committee, *Discussion Document: Constitutional Principles and Structures for a Democratic South Africa* (Bellville, South Africa: Centre for Development Studies, University of the Western Cape, April 1991), pp. 15, 19.

45. "The 48th National Conference of the African National Congress," *Monitor*, June 1991, p. 82.

in an all-party negotiating conference, but he did not flesh out its purpose or process. The National Party wanted the parties themselves—not an elected assembly—to negotiate the substance and details of a new constitution. The National Party's constitutional proposals envisioned an extremely weak central government ruled by consociational principles, that is, by a committee of political parties, each with a veto power over central decisions. One legislative house would be based on proportional representation; another would consist of equal representation among parties that attained a low threshold of voter support. The latter house would also have veto power over legislation. At subnational levels, regions and communities would have their own tax bases and could curtail voting rights through property qualifications. The constitution would include a "charter of fundamental rights," but it would be limited to property rights and individual protections from government power, what are known in constitutional law as first-generation rights.[46]

The fundamental concerns of the two main parties in South Africa were clear. The ANC, believing it would gain a majority in a one-person, one-vote election, wanted a strong central government in order to redress societal and political inequalities forged by apartheid. The National Party wanted arrangements that would protect the economic and political interests of the white population. Fearing the results of majority rule, the NP wanted "to dilute the strong drink of democracy." As Roger Southall wrote at the time, "The NP's conversion to constitutional democracy is highly situational. . . . Its present proposals are designed to 'non-racially' entrench the existing disparities of property, wealth and power."[47] Ensconcing property rights and group veto power would forestall economic redistributive measures. A long transition would extend the careers of white bureaucrats and politicians and better ensure that their pensions would be honored.

CODESA. The only real accord between the major parties was that all-parties talks should negotiate the path to and principles of a new

46. Federal Council of the National Party's Outline of its Views Concerning a Constitution for a New South Africa, "Constitutional Rule in a Participatory Democracy," mimeo, no date; obtained through the South African embassy in Washington, D.C.

47. Roger Southall, "The Contradictory State! The Proposals of the National Party for a New Constitution," *Monitor*, October 1991, pp. 90–92.

South Africa. This slim reed of agreement led to the Convention for a Democratic South Africa (CODESA) on December 21 and 22, 1991, which established a broad declaration of intent to guide the search for a new constitution and created five working groups. The working groups were to establish a climate for free and fair political competition; devise constitutional principles and mechanisms; develop proposals for an interim government; plan the reincorporation of the homelands; and set a timetable for transition to a new government.[48]

CODESA provided first evidence of the difficulty of resolving South Africa's participation conflict. In terms of power the two most important players in the country were the ANC and the government. Any settlement would have to have their active support. The two parties combined, however, did not represent all of South Africa. Indeed, since blacks had never voted in South Africa, no party (not even the ANC) could claim to represent anyone other than its own members. CODESA therefore incorporated all of the various claimants to authority in South Africa, including all of the homeland governments and any political party that demanded participation, nineteen organizations in all.

The sheer size of the negotiating forum caused problems. The ANC feared CODESA would never agree on anything if decisions were taken by strict consensus. On the other hand, if decisions were taken by majority vote, small parties might sell their votes to larger parties in exchange for special considerations or promises. Moreover, majority rule would give equal weight to all CODESA participants, and not all organizations were equal at CODESA. To acknowledge the need for inclusion and the relative strength of the ANC and the NP, CODESA invented a decision rule called "sufficient consensus": if no agreement had been reached after prolonged debate, then a judge would determine whether there was at least enough agreement to take a decision. The inherent ambiguity of the concept effectively gave the ANC and the NP veto power over any decision.

Progress toward agreements varied by working group. Working Group 1 discussed the continued problems of amnesty for political prisoners, the repeal of discriminatory laws, the integration of security

48. The discussion of CODESA draws from Steven Friedman, ed., *The Long Journey: South Africa's Quest for a Negotiated Settlement* (Johannesburg: Ravan Press, 1993). Although this book is an excellent compendium of details about CODESA, we disagree with the thrust of its analysis, as we make clear.

forces, the strengthening of the national peace accord, and the reform of the South African Broadcasting Corporation (SABC). With the exception of an agreement on changing the composition of the SABC oversight board, the group never went further than broad statements of principle. Working Group 4, on reincorporation of the homelands, established the principle that all residents would take part in South Africa's first nonracial election. Because Working Group 5, which was to devise a timetable for the transition, depended on the progress of groups 2 and 3 toward devising constitutional principles and proposals for an interim government, it remained dormant.

Working Group 2 addressed what were the key issues of CODESA: where the parties were headed and how they would get there. The NP worried that an assembly elected by a majority of South Africans would dictate constitutional terms unacceptable to the rest of the country. Those fears could be addressed in two ways: through binding the assembly to previously established agreements or by setting a high voting threshold for passage of a new constitution (for example, 66 percent).

Room for agreement seemed possible. The ANC's transition proposals stated that constitutional principles could be negotiated beforehand and made binding on the elected constitutional assembly. The NP reasoned that its concerns could be met: it only had to win agreement from the ANC on its constitutional proposals. The ANC insisted, however, that since the constitutional assembly was a sovereign body, it could be bound by principles but not by details imposed through prior negotiation. The key question then was the difference between a "principle" and a "detail." On the issue of the voting threshold, too, there was possibility for compromise. The ANC's constitutional document of April 1991 did not specify what percentage of votes the constitutional assembly needed to pass proposals. It did mention, however, that once a constitution was in place, it could be amended only by a two-thirds vote.

The NP's initial strategy was to try to engage the ANC in a debate over constitutional principles and use CODESA as a de facto constitution-writing forum. The NP presented its proposal for a "presidency by committee"; the ANC rejected it, calling the proposal a detail of a constitution, not a broad principle. The NP then turned to distribution of power between regions and the national center, and to the protection of minority interests under a new constitution. Neither issue was resolved. The NP tried a different tack: it claimed that any interim government should be bound by a transitional constitution. A constitutional assembly would take time to write a new document, the NP insisted, and during that time the interim government would have to be bound by law or else rule by decree.

The dilemma was obvious. The ANC understood the need for some kind of law to be in place during the interim rule, and it did not want that law to be the constitution then in place. On the other hand, the ANC feared that if the constitution-writing process dragged on indefinitely or reached deadlock, "the interim might become permanent."[49] Such fears grew when the NP put forward its draft constitution as the proposed interim constitution. If the ANC accepted the need for an interim document, it would have to accept the added delay of negotiating it. The question of vote threshold for passing the permanent constitution would take on added meaning: the higher the percentage of votes needed to create the document, the greater the odds for deadlock.

The NP proposals for an interim constitution came immediately after the March 17 referendum asking white voters whether F. W. de Klerk should continue his reforms "aimed at a new constitution through negotiation." After an intense campaign of three weeks, marked by nearly 300 deaths, bombing of an NP headquarters, and physical attacks on de Klerk, the whites of South Africa turned out in massive numbers (86 percent) to vote overwhelmingly (68.7 percent) for continuing negotiations.

The referendum posed another dilemma for the ANC. It had a vested interest in seeing the referendum pass, but de Klerk could use a positive result to strengthen his hand at the negotiating table at CODESA. Most observers and many participants assert that in fact some NP negotiators did return to CODESA in a triumphal, nonconciliatory mood.

May 15 was the deadline for presenting the reports of the working groups at a second plenary of heads of parties and organizations (CODESA II). Between the March referendum and the beginning of May, important progress seemed to be made. Working Group 3, tasked with working out the substantial details of interim arrangements, reached agreements that acknowledged the "need for a multiparty transitional executive structure to function in conjunction with existing legislative and executive structures." The structure would consist of a transitional executive council (TEC), comprising representatives of all

49. Friedman, ed., *Long Journey*, p. 70.

parties of CODESA, with the mandate to "level the political playing field" and establish "a climate of free political participation." The TEC would preside over subcouncils to address local and regional government, finance, security and law and order, foreign affairs, and elections. Any issues in the TEC that failed to generate an 80 percent majority would be judged by an independent election commission (IEC), consisting of respected citizens vetted by CODESA and appointed by the president. Finally, following up on Working Group 1, an independent media commission would be established.[50]

Implementation of the third group's agreement depended on resolution in Working Group 2. By the beginning of May the ANC accepted that an interim constitution would be negotiated at CODESA and agreed that simple majority rule was inadequate for passage of the final constitution. The main sticking point became the percentage of votes that would be needed to pass the final constitution. The NP proposed a 66.7 percent threshold for ordinary legislation; legislation concerning regional and local powers and the bill of rights would have to meet a 75 percent threshold, a figure sure to give the NP a veto. The ANC grudgingly countered with 70 percent, but the NP did not budge: it insisted on 75 percent. Deadlock ensued and CODESA II failed to produce agreement.

EVALUATING CODESA. Analysts disagree on CODESA's accomplishments and why it failed. Some argue that much progress was made and that the parties were on the verge of a major agreement, only to be stymied by NP intransigence.[51] Others argue that only the semblance of agreement was achieved in April and May, and that neither side was truly prepared to make the concessions necessary to reach a settlement.[52] While the latter interpretation rightly observes that there was an enormous amount of fuzziness in the tentative settlement proposals, the former correctly identifies the National Party as the chief obstacle to resolution.

The agreement that might have come out of CODESA would have contained a lot of ambiguity. For example, the division of powers

---

50. Quotations are from proposals of Working Group 3, cited in Friedman, ed., *Long Journey*, pp. 93–94.

51. See, for example, the view of Colin Eglin, Democratic Party participant at CODESA, in Friedman, ed., *Long Journey*, p. 80.

52. Friedman, ed., *Long Journey*, passim.

between the TEC and the existing executive and legislative structures was obscure. CODESA left much unsettled, especially concerning the status of the homelands and how and when they would be incorporated. Even on its own terms, the tentative agreement would have required more negotiation (for example, to write an interim constitution). Indeed, top ANC negotiators themselves expressed confusion in May about the precise content of the proposed agreement.[53]

Lack of clarity, unresolved problems, and ambiguity need not doom an agreement to failure. In fact, the agreement finally reached in 1993, which led to the elections and transition of 1994, contained many of the flaws noted above: the roles of the TEC and the existing government were not precisely stated; the incorporation of the homelands was haphazard, not a result of negotiation; and the parties spent months drafting and revising the interim constitution.

An incomplete agreement can be the basis for conflict resolution, if sufficient trust, goodwill, and desire for settlement exist in both parties. Were such attributes present in May 1992? That the parties distrusted each other was self-evident, but this was true in 1993, too. At CODESA the ANC did make important concessions and clearly signaled a willingness to compromise.[54] It accepted that a constitution would be passed by more than a simple majority; it also accepted the need for an interim constitution. And critically important during this period was what the ANC did away from the negotiating table: it signaled a will-

53. David Ottaway, *Chained Together: Mandela, de Klerk, and the Struggle to Remake South Africa* (Times Books, 1993), p. 210.

54. Steven Friedman in *Long Journey*, pp. 80–84, argues that neither side desired a compromise settlement at that time. He argues that the ANC was still committed to mass protest aimed at harming the government, regardless of whether an agreement was attained at CODESA. He reaches his conclusion, however, through a misinterpretation of an ANC policy statement that called for mass action if CODESA failed and mass mobilization if CODESA succeeded. Friedman, believing this to be a smoking gun, accuses the ANC of unwillingness to settle at CODESA. The key then is whether mass action is the same as mass mobilization. But the two are not synonymous. Mass action refers to protest activities to increase the ungovernability of the state; mass mobilization refers simply to preparing one's supporters for a given task. Clearly, if an agreement had been reached at CODESA that put elections in the near future, a tremendous amount of organization would be needed and supporters would have to mobilize for everything from voter education to campaigning.

ingness to consider "sunset clauses" for minorities that would provide special constitutional protections (such as entrenched seats in parliament for whites or regulations prohibiting radical transformation of the civil service) for a specified period.[55]

The failure of CODESA to produce a settlement in South Africa rests squarely with the National Party. In the aftermath of its referendum victory in March 1992, the NP faced a classic choice between gaining mutual benefits through agreement with an adversary or pushing for the lion's share of those benefits, with the risk of attaining no agreement. The NP opted for the latter course and took an extremely hard line at CODESA. The ANC, rightly suspecting an NP trap, refused to become ensnared in a process designed to perpetuate NP rule.

It would be easy to denigrate CODESA's accomplishments, since it failed to provide a lasting agreement for transition. But CODESA did achieve partial breakthroughs that formed the basis for the settlement between the ANC and NP that led to elections in 1994. Indeed, the transitional arrangements were lifted almost completely from the proposals of Working Group 3. The basis for settlement—a constituent assembly to meet ANC demands and binding constitutional principles for the NP—resulted from CODESA. Many of the proposals that the ANC made in late 1992 and early 1993 stemmed from learning the demands and needs of the NP at CODESA.

The failure of CODESA did have costs for South Africa. In the short term the NP hard line alienated the ANC, weakened those within the ANC in favor of concessions, destroyed any modicum of trust between the parties, and paved the way for a campaign of confrontation and mass action by the ANC. CODESA also distanced the South African people from the negotiating process. The participants at CODESA raised expectations about an impending settlement and never fully kept the public informed about compromises that might be necessary or the lack of substantive progress on some issues.[56]

FROM CODESA TO THE MULTIPARTY NEGOTIATING FORUM. Direct talks between the ANC and NP broke down in June 1992 after Inkatha-affiliated hostel dwellers near the township of Boipatong went on a

---

55. The ANC acknowledged the need for sunset clauses in its party journal *Mayibuye* in March 1992.

56. Indeed, CODESA has become a verb in the black townships, which means "to talk endlessly and pointlessly."

rampage, killing forty-nine people, including twenty-four women and children. Nelson Mandela charged the government with complicity in the massacre, declaring, "I can no longer explain to our people why we continue to talk to a government that is killing our people." The ANC issued a set of demands that had to be met before negotiations could resume.

In August 1992 the ANC embarked on a campaign of rolling mass action that crippled the country. Strikes and labor stay-aways exacted a high cost from an already weak economy. The success of mass action led some ANC strategists to believe the government could be laid low through the "Leipzig option," named after the German city where mass protests and confrontations ended Erich Honecker's rule in 1989.

The first target was the Ciskei homeland, ruled by the unpopular dictator Oupa Gqozo. The ANC had negotiated permission to march to a stadium in the Ciskei capital of Bisho to hold a rally. In a spur-of-the-moment decision, some ANC leaders diverted the march toward the city center. Troops from the Ciskei opened fire on the marchers, killing twenty-eight and wounding two hundred.

South Africa's stalemate was confirmed. Bisho reminded the ANC that the government and its homeland minions controlled heavy lethal force, but the mass action campaign proved the strength of the ANC. Direct negotiations between the ANC and the NP resumed. On September 26, the two parties reached a "record of understanding" committing them to the principle of majority rule and binding the government to its prior commitment to release political prisoners. The most controversial aspect of the record was the provision that the government would undertake to seal hostels from townships and criminalize the carrying of Zulu weapons. Although the government did neither, the record infuriated IFP leader Mangosuthu Buthelezi and signaled that some within the NP recognized that a larger settlement could mean jettisoning Inkatha for the ANC.

Away from the negotiating table, an important debate was under way among ANC strategists. Joe Slovo, member of the ANC executive council and former head of the South African Communist Party, argued that the ANC would have to make substantial concessions to enable negotiations to succeed. He reasoned that the entrenchment of the NP within the state bureaucracy and security forces would undermine any settlement that did not address white fears and interests. Moreover, he stated that the ANC could not gain power through armed struggle or mass action; its only alternative was compromise on fundamental issues such as job security, retrenchment packages for the present administration, and general amnesty as part of a negotiated settlement. Slovo pushed forward ideas originally broached by the ANC in February concerning sunset clauses that would enshrine power sharing for a fixed number of years.[57]

Toward the end of 1992 and in January 1993, ANC and NP leaders participated in a series of private meetings to discuss a way out of their impasse. The ANC and the NP agreed that an election would produce a constitutional assembly which would write a new constitution and act as an interim government of national unity for five years; the assembly would elect a national president, and any party that received over 5 percent of the vote would place members in the cabinet. The party with the second largest vote total would select a deputy vice president. The ANC relented on the point that the constitutional assembly could be bound by arrangements established by prior negotiation. The ANC refused the NP demand for a collective presidency, but agreed that a new constitution must establish regional and local governments with some powers devolved to them. The new constitution would be ratified by a two-thirds vote of the assembly. The NP accepted that if the constitutional assembly could not agree on a new constitution in two years, there would be need for a deadlock-breaking mechanism, such as a referendum. The ANC wanted an election date set within a year; during the run-up to the election, an interim constitution would be drafted and a transitional election council and an independent election council put in place. The ANC and NP would return to a CODESA-like forum, which would involve as many parties as possible in the transition, to draft the interim constitution and constitutional principles.

In February 1993 the NP and the ANC went public with their agreement. They set multiparty negotiations for a date in March and started the hard sell of the agreement to their own constituencies and to the parties that had not been privy to their deliberations.[58]

57. Joe Slovo, "Negotiations: What Room for Compromise?" *African Communist*, no. 130 (Third Quarter, 1992), pp. 36–40.
58. It soon became apparent that the negotiators had not learned how to protect each other. When the ANC-NP deal was announced, the NP spokesman claimed that the ANC had finally accepted "powersharing," an explosive word with highly negative connotations for ANC supporters. ANC negotiators im-

The ANC encountered tough opposition from militants within the organization such as Winnie Mandela, Harry Gwala, and Peter Mokoba, then head of the ANC Youth League. All these partisans accused the top negotiators, in particular Cyril Ramaphosa, of selling out the revolution. Three years of violence and dashed expectations had embittered a corps within the ANC, especially among the youth. Mokaba warned the leadership that if it didn't bring along the youth, they could destroy any settlement. Throughout 1993 the ANC learned that its dictates would not be embraced automatically by angry young blacks.[59]

The NP was also beset by factionalism. A group of pro-reform members coalesced around Roelf Meyer, the chief negotiator for the party. As an architect of the compromise with the ANC, he bore the brunt of charges that the NP had abandoned a veto over policy in a new regime. Some NP officials turned to bureaucratic sabotage to undermine Meyer. Others contemplated quitting the NP to join the IFP.

The convergence of the ANC and the NP on constitutional proposals raised the issue of how to bring parties like the IFP into negotiations. The problem was compounded by the formation of an alliance (the Concerned South Africans Group, or COSAG) between Inkatha, the homeland governments of Ciskei and Bophuthatswana, and the Conservative Party and other representatives of the Afrikaner right. These parties, which objected to an ANC-NP deal and the loss of power in a new South Africa, put forward radical proposals for a new constitution. Inkatha demanded an essentially confederal state that would vest nearly total power in the regions and grant them autonomy. Some within the Afrikaner right demanded a sovereign white homeland.

---

mediately attacked the NP description of the agreement and came under heated attack from its own supporters, who suspected a "sell-out."

59. In February 1993 students defied ANC, PAC, and AZAPO demands for them to end class boycotts and return to school; *Cape Times*, February 25, 1993. A typical response to ANC calls for an end to school disruptions was a statement by COSAS (the Congress of South African Students): "We are an autonomous organization and the ANC does not have the right to decide for us." *Argus*, February 25, 1993. In March and May 1993, ANC officials repeatedly urged an end to striking students' use of violence, only to be rebuffed. See, for example, "Outraged ANC Calls Pupils Hooligans," *Argus*, March 25, 1993; and "We're in Charge, Say Defiant Student Leaders," *Weekly Mail*, May 14–20, 1993.

Although the members of the alliance differed on the endpoint of negotiations, they all insisted that a new constitution should not be written by an elected assembly.

The Multiparty Negotiating Forum

The ANC and the NP invited interested parties back to the negotiating table and promised to hear all of their concerns. The new multiparty negotiating forum began on March 5, 1993; it looked a lot like CODESA. Twenty-six parties met, sufficient consensus was still the decision rule, and hours were spent in tedious debate. This time, however, ANC and NP negotiators, Ramaphosa and Meyer, hoped that their common front could win over recalcitrant parties and produce an all-inclusive agreement.

The ANC strategy was to win confirmation of an election date and then build agreement, with the election as a deadline. COSAG members were adamantly opposed, and insisted that since the parties had not agreed to an endpoint, it made no sense to hold an election. Deadlock ensued; no one was willing to give ground. What soon changed, however, was the sense of urgency with which the ANC approached the question. On April 19, Chris Hani, former head of MK (the ANC armed wing) and leader of the South African Communist Party, was assassinated by a Polish emigrant to South Africa with ties to the Conservative Party. Hani, who figured prominently in liberation circles, was revered by the most militant factions of the ANC, yet he had supported the ANC-NP deal of February.

During the week after his death, youth violence erupted throughout the country. The crisis revealed how dramatically South African politics had shifted. Nelson Mandela, not F. W. de Klerk, appeared on SABC and appealed for calm. The ANC, working with the South African Police, took responsibility for keeping order among the enraged youth. At the same time, however, ANC radicals used Hani's death as an opportunity to try to mobilize the youth against political compromise. South African students went on strike in May and ignored ANC demands to return to school. Some feared that South Africa's interregnum had reached the point where the only party capable of restoring order—the ANC—might lose the power to control its own supporters.

On July 3 the ANC and the NP insisted that a date be set for South Africa's first nonracial election. Not surprisingly, COSAG objected, but the presiding judge at the forum declared that sufficient consensus existed to set the election for April 27, 1994. Delegations from Inkatha, KwaZulu, and the Conservative Party walked out but reserved the right to return when talks resumed in two weeks.

On July 26 a committee of constitutional experts chosen by the forum offered the first draft of an interim constitution. The draft established twenty-seven principles to bind the elected constitutional assembly. Among those binding principles were multiparty democracy; proportional representation; an independent judiciary; fundamental human rights; due process before the law; a two-house parliament, of which one would represent provincial interests; and strong local and regional governments, which would have some concurrent and exclusive powers vis-à-vis the central government.[60]

For the National Party, the issue of regions was crucial. Since the NP had abandoned its proposal for a "presidency by committee," it had placed its hopes in strong regional government as a means of checking central power. The initial draft signified an important concession and fundamental change in ANC thinking. Only three years before, the ANC had believed that any kind of federalism would perpetuate apartheid. The NP negotiators shrewdly chose not to use the term "federalism," but instead focused on regional governments and regional powers. The draft constitution established nine regional governments, put forward twelve different functional areas for which those governments would have competence (including taxation within the region, housing, education, traditional law, and health and welfare). The final demarcation of central and regional powers would be established by a commission on regional government. Regions would be allowed to have their own constitutions, so long as those were not at odds with the national constitution.

The draft constitution thus conceded the principle of regional government, established a mechanism for determining the power of regions, and listed those powers that regional governments should command. The constitution was therefore federal in intent and substance, if not in name. Moreover, the negotiating process left room for any party to bargain on the explicit powers of the regions.

60. The description of the constitution is from *Constitution of the Republic of South Africa, 1993* (draft outline, July 21, 1993).

Inkatha and right-wing white parties rejected the draft constitution upon its release. Radical Afrikaners insisted that a new constitution should provide for a "white homeland." Buthelezi and Inkatha, as well as the homeland governments of Ciskei and Bophuthatswana, labeled the document antifederal and demanded constitutional autonomy for the regions. Their insistence that their own proposals were "federal" was misleading: a central government that is an umbrella over regions with constitutional autonomy is not federal, but *confederal*. The ANC believed that if a central government in South Africa were beholden to regions with their own constitutions, then apartheid could be continued. If Inkatha won on this principle, it could win an election in KwaZulu, Buthelezi's homeland, and write a regional constitution that would perpetuate its authoritarian rule. Likewise, if a white party won a regional election, it could erect an apartheid constitution. The ANC insisted that a single national constitution would establish rights and obligations for every South African.

Constitutional negotiators continued to revise the draft by strengthening the powers of regions. A draft was finally accepted in November 1993, at which time a Transitional Executive Council was also established to guide the country to the April elections. Even after the interim constitution was accepted, the ANC and NP continued to make concessions to bring Inkatha and right-wing whites into the process. In March the ANC agreed to a dual ballot—one for regional government and one for the national government—in the April elections.

All four groups that promised to boycott the elections weakened. In Bophuthatswana, the dictatorship of Lucas Mangope fell on March 11 after homeland civil servants, police, and defense force personnel went on strike in support of a popular uprising for reincorporation into South Africa. Afrikaner militants rallied to support Mangope, only to find themselves under attack from the Bophuthatswana police. Mandela and de Klerk ordered the SADF into the homeland to replace Mangope and restore order. In the aftermath of the Afrikaner debacle, the white right wing split; one faction, led by retired SADF general Constand Viljoen, pledged to contest the April election. Within weeks a similar strike by civil servants brought down the government of Oupa Gqozo in Ciskei. By April the only spoilers were the most militant of the Afrikaners, including the AWB (*Afrikaner Weerstandsbeweging*, or the Afrikaner Resistance Movement) and Buthelezi's Inkatha Freedom Party, which drew support from Zulus in the KwaZulu/Natal region.

Between March 1993 and March 1994, Inkatha did not make a single concession in the negotiations. Two different messages emanated from the party. One insisted that Inkatha would join the negotiations if more powers were granted to the regions. The other maintained that Inkatha would not participate if there were a constitutional assembly, elections before a constitution, or an interim power-sharing agreement. The implication of the second course was that the ANC and the NP had to renounce all progress they had made and start again from ground zero.

ANC and NP negotiators sensed that a split had developed within the IFP between advisers of Buthelezi, who counseled him to hold out in the possibility of breaking the ANC-NP coalition, and those who advised him to participate in the negotiations and work for the best deal that the IFP could get under the circumstances. The ANC and NP proceeded under the assumption that the latter counselors would sway Buthelezi, and the two parties made several concessions to bring him back into the process.

Buthelezi, however, followed the first course of action. While at first his hard-line stance did win him some adherents from the National Party, he was unable to break the fragile coalition between the ANC and the NP. His strategy backfired. Buthelezi's alliance with conservative whites alienated much of his support among blacks in KwaZulu. His insistence on boycotting the election also lost him support among his followers. But as Buthelezi's support dwindled in KwaZulu, he had even less reason to join the negotiation process: in August 1993 observers believed that he could still win the region of KwaZulu/Natal in an election, but by March 1994 most analysts believed that he would lose.[61] Buthelezi's self-imposed marginalization left him with one option, to incite ethnic hatred and violence in the hope that his supporters could derail South Africa's first one-person, one-vote election.[62]

A crucial aspect of Buthelezi's strategy was his cultivation of the Zulu king, Goodwill Zwelithini. Part of Buthelezi's public renounce-

---

61. Opinion polls in Natal in January 1994 showed the IFP with 19 percent support as opposed to the ANC's 46 percent. "South Africa's Partners in Policing," *Africa Confidential*, vol. 35 (January 21, 1994).

62. Buthelezi also established a camp where former SADF officers commanded over 5,000 Inkatha cadres in paramilitary training. See Bill Keller, "Zulu Men Train for a Battle South Africa Hopes to Avoid," *New York Times*, April 2, 1994, p. 1.

ment of the new constitution was its lack of protections for traditional authority and institutions in KwaZulu. Buthelezi's demand for a constitutional monarchy within the province of KwaZulu led to one last negotiating effort between Mandela, de Klerk, Buthelezi, and Zwelithini on April 19, less than three weeks before the scheduled election dates. At that meeting Mandela promised constitutional protections and continued state funding for the Zulu monarchy. Buthelezi and Zwelithini rejected the offer, but agreed that a proposed mediation effort by Henry Kissinger and Lord Peter Carrington should go forward before the election.

Kissinger and Carrington arrived in Johannesburg the week of April 11 and quickly discovered that the parties had not agreed on an agenda or terms of reference for the mediation. After consultation with NP negotiator Roelf Meyer, the mediators agreed that the election date would not be included as a subject for negotiation. This prompted Buthelezi to refuse to participate in formal talks. Kissinger and Carrington left South Africa on Thursday, April 14.

The weekend of April 16–17 brought successive pressures on Buthelezi to join the elections. An aide to the Kissinger team, Kenyan opposition politician Washington Okumu, stayed in South Africa and met privately with Buthelezi. Okumu warned that if Inkatha continued its electoral boycott, Buthelezi would be out of power in less than a week; his only options at that point would be complete capitulation or protracted guerrilla war with no international support. While Okumu kept IFP hard-line advisers like Walter Felgate and Mario Ambrosini away from Buthelezi, King Zwelithini informed Buthelezi that he was considering accepting Mandela's offer of constitutional protections. IFP moderates also pledged to quit the party if Inkatha did not end the boycott.

By April 19, Buthelezi had capitulated. For a promise that the position of the Zulu monarchy would be considered in the new constitution—less than had been offered two weeks earlier—and a pledge by the Independent Electoral Commission to place Inkatha on the electoral ballot, Buthelezi and Inkatha joined the election.

The elections of April 26–28 brought a close to South Africa's long-standing conflict over political participation. The weeks before, during, and after the election were remarkably free of violence. Radical right-wing whites killed several people in bombing attacks in the greater Johannesburg area and destroyed twelve polling stations in the country, but such attacks stopped immediately after the South African Police arrested thirty-one Afrikaner militants and declared several locations in the Orange Free State and Northern Traansvaal as unrest areas.

Myriad logistical foul-ups created much confusion, but for the most part the election proceded in a free and fair manner. The major exception was in KwaZulu/Natal, where both the IFP and the ANC engaged in ballot fraud; numerous episodes of intimidation occurred in the Inkatha rural strongholds of KwaZulu. The provincial staff of the IEC refused to certify the election as "free and fair," only to be overruled by IEC chairman Richard Kriegler. The potential for violence to erupt in the region prompted the national leadership of the ANC, Inkatha, and the National Party to "cook" the results for the region. The parties agreed in the interest of national stability that Inkatha would win a bare majority and form the provincial government in KwaZulu/Natal.[63] In essence, the ANC national leadership sold out its most militant factions in Natal who had fought against Buthelezi for almost ten years. IFP and ANC leaders gambled that representatives of their moderate wings in the region could create a middle coalition against extremists on both sides and end the provincial civil war.

On May 6 the IEC announced what some observers called "the designer result." The ANC had won the national election with 62.6 percent of the vote, which was enough to form the new government but short of the two-thirds threshold that would have enabled the party to write the constitution by itself. The NP and IFP, with 20.4 percent and 10.5 percent, respectively, performed well enough to win seats in the

63. A major story of the South African election, the negotiated IFP "victory" in KwaZulu/Natal, received relatively little press attention in the United States. For coverage see Chris McGreal and others, "Natal Poll Fraud Hidden"; Chris McGreal, "ANC Seeks Deal with Inkatha on Disputed Ballots," *Guardian*, May 5, 1994; Chris McGreal, "Inkatha Deal—The Price of Peace in Blood-Soaked Land," *Guardian*, May 7, 1994; Karl Maier, " 'Free and Fair' KwaZulu Poll Stuns the ANC," *The Independent*, May 7, 1994; Mark Suzman and others, "South African Election Results Halted," *Financial Times*, May 4, 1994; Mark Suzman and others, "S. African Parties Barter for 'Lost' Votes," *Financial Times*, May 5, 1994; Patty Waldmeir, "The Horse-Trading Begins," *Financial Times*, May 6, 1994; Patty Waldmeir and Michael Holman, "Spirit of Reconciliation Sweeps Aside Letter of Vote," *Financial Times*, May 7–8, 1994; and Bob Drogin, "Ballot Fraud Casts Shadow on S. Africa Vote," *Los Angeles Times*, May 6, 1994.

new cabinet, and the NP's performance also assured F. W. de Klerk one of the two deputy presidencies. Both parties also maintained regional bases of support, with the NP winning the Western Cape province and IFP taking KwaZulu/Natal. No other party did well enough to secure representation in the cabinet, though the Freedom Front of Constand Viljoen, the PAC, and Democractic Party placed representatives in parliament.

Although we can only speculate at this point, it is likely that the national results were also a partially negotiated result among the major parties. The ANC, fearing that a two-thirds total would alienate major constituencies in the country and detract from national stability, accepted less than their real percentage of votes.[64]

The two main parties to the participation conflict, the ANC and the NP, sacrificed much for a bargain. Although the ANC won its demand for a constituent assembly, it compromised on the principles that would guide the writing of a new constitution. It gained its insistence that a single president would rule a new government, but it conceded much power to regional and local government. The ANC also agreed to a much longer interim arrangement than it wanted and accepted a five-year government of national unity. The National Party abandoned the idea of an executive by committee and a white veto on policy. In return it won a commitment to strong regionalism, limited power sharing for the first five years, guarantees for civil servant pensions and jobs, and the enshrinement of property rights in a new constitution.

64. The most telling piece of evidence so far, other than speculations of officials affiliated with the IEC, is that the IEC announced on May 5 that the ANC had 65.4 percent of the vote with an estimated 70 percent of the overall vote counted; *Financial Times*, May 6, 1994. At that time, the NP's and IFP's strongest regions had already been counted; ANC strongholds in the Durban area and PWV had not been counted. When the final results were released on May 6, the remaining national vote actually *reduced* the ANC percentage to 62.6 percent. Two of the most telling quotes of the counting week came from the chairman of the IEC, Richard Kriegler, who stated, "The [IEC] has never been asked to certify that the result is accurate. We have been asked to certify that the particular process is substantially free and fair," in Drogin, "Ballot Fraud." When asked about the rectitude of results being negotiated by the parties, Kriegler responded, "Come now, come now, let's not get purist. If the objector and the objectee come to terms, that is universally accepted as legitimate in the politicial game. . . . Let's not get overly squeamish." Suzman and others, "S. African Parties Barter."

The terms of the agreement hold potential problems. A new government will have to take dramatic action to deal with South Africa's crises of economic growth and distribution and insecurity. Although some feel that the forced government by coalition will lead to better policies through consensus building, others worry that the government will be too divided to make policies.[65] If new policies do not begin to address the needs of South Africa's majority, then radical parties may diminish the ANC's base of support, or militants within the ANC may push aside the negotiators. Others worry that bureaucratic sabotage could undermine the implementation of new policies. The potential for coalition partners to disagree and undercut each other will most likely increase as new elections approach.

Although the potential of any of these concerns could be realized, the negotiated compromise has already produced a corps of leaders under Mandela and de Klerk who have proven that they can work together to solve problems. Also encouraging is that the settlement has added legitimacy because it emerged from the actors themselves and not from international mediation, as in other cases in Southern Africa.

VIOLENCE AND SECURITY

Although the period 1990–94 saw dramatic progress in political negotiation, those years also saw high levels of violence and insecurity for most of the South African population. Phillip van Niekerk, a South African journalist, captured the juxtaposition of peacemaking and unprecedented levels of violence: "There is a new apartheid, two new South Africas: the South Africa of negotiations, where progress beyond the wildest imaginings of five years ago is being achieved, and a terrible South Africa of dust, decay, death and disillusion."[66]

An estimated 13,000 South Africans died in political violence between February 1990 and December 1993. But as Colin Bundy urges, South Africa's political violence must be put in the context of extraordinary overall societal violence. In the same period, nearly eight times

65. See the exchange between Eugene Nyati and Robert Schrire in "Will There Be Political Stability in South Africa after the April 1994 Elections?" *CQ Researcher*, vol. 4 (January 14, 1994), p. 41.

66. Phillip van Niekerk, "Meanwhile Back at the World Trade Centre," *Weekly Mail*, July 9–15, 1993, p. 17.

more people died from criminal violence. South African cities have the highest homicide rates in the world. Between 1984 and 1992, nearly two million South African women were raped; "statistically, one of every two women is likely to be raped in her lifetime."[67]

Violence can be thought of as an axis with political violence at one end and criminal violence at the other. Political violence in South Africa has four purposes: (1) to derail progress at reaching a settlement by those opposed to peace; (2) to ensure inclusion in negotiations by signaling the costs of marginalization by parties who fear being omitted from settlement; (3) to destabilize opponents in order to weaken their positions at the negotiating table; and (4) to control local territory as a means of garnering support and gaining control of scarce resources.[68]

At the other end of the axis, violence is criminal in nature and lacks political intent. In black communities high rates of violence can be explained by crushing poverty, overcrowding in urban squatter settlements, and scarcity of housing, water, and sanitation, combined with the nonexistence of legitimate police and judicial institutions. The lack of legitimate structures that can maintain law and order and support peaceful values and norms, in combination with overall socioeconomic distress, fuels the development of a culture of violence. Increasingly, violence is seen not only as a legitimate means of resolving conflicts and securing material advantages but as the *only* legitimate means of achieving these objectives.

Between the two endpoints of political and criminal violence, the types blend together. Groups that purport to fight for political ends engage in criminal activity and vigilantism; criminals try to legitimate their offenses by suggesting that their behavior is politically motivated. South Africans have even developed a word for such behavior—*com-*

---

67. Bundy, "At War with the Future?" p. 56. The alternative weekly newspaper of Cape Town, *South*, reported that girls as young as ten have been brought to family planning clinics in Cape Town for contraceptives, because their mothers fear that they will be raped. "Rape Terror: 10-year-olds on the Pill," *South*, July 17–21, 1993, p. 3.

68. The first three kinds of violence are derived from Timothy Sisk, "The Violence-Negotiation Nexus: South Africa in Transition and the Politics of Uncertainty," *Negotiation Journal*, vol. 9 (January 1993), p. 84. The fourth kind of political violence is derived from Graham Howe, "The Trojan Horse: Natal's Civil War, 1987–1993," *Indicator South Africa*, vol. 10 (Autumn 1993), p. 40.

tsotsi—derived from comrade (a political identity) and *tsotsi* (gangster). Although *comtsotsi* describes those youths who mouth the slogans of political liberation while engaging in gang-related crime, many others blur the distinction between political and criminal violence. In Natal, for instance, some Inkatha leaders have earned the epithet "warlords," and they justify criminal activity as a struggle against the ANC.[69] Some of the police officers who were implicated in the destabilization of black townships did so for the lucrative profits of gunrunning.[70] Similarly, members of the SADF involved in regional destabilization have been involved in illegal ivory smuggling.[71]

In South Africa approximately 93 percent of all politically related violence occurs in two regions, Natal and the townships of the Pretoria-Witwatersrand-Vereeniging (PWV) triangle surrounding Johannesburg.[72] In both regions there is intense competition between the ANC and IFP, but the violence is a result of more than ANC-IFP rivalry. The South African Police (SAP) and security forces have aided and abetted—even instigated—violence against the ANC.

The violence in Natal has its roots in the 1980s when the UDF and MDM attempted to render South Africa ungovernable. UDF members identified Mangosuthu Buthelezi and his Inkatha supporters in KwaZulu as "puppets of the white regime" and attempted to organize against them. Buthelezi and the KwaZulu police, with assistance from the SAP and the army, tried to physically eliminate all challengers to his authoritarian rule. The result has been a protracted civil war in KwaZulu/Natal that claimed nearly 7,000 lives between 1986 and 1993.

69. Anthony Minnaar, " 'Undisputed Kings': Warlordism in Natal," in Anthony Minnaar, ed., *Patterns of Violence: Case Studies of Conflict in Natal* (Pretoria: Human Sciences Research Council, 1992), pp. 61–94.

70. Thus the Goldstone Commission report of March 18, 1994, inferred that police instigated violence because they opposed majority rule, but the report also stated that involved officers "skimmed large sums of money" from selling guns to Inkatha. See "Inquest Finds South Africa Aided in Terror Campaign," *New York Times*, March 19, 1994, p. 7.

71. Hugh McCullum, "From Destruction to Recovery," in Mamphela Ramphele and Chris McDowell, eds., *Restoring the Land: Environment and Change in Post-Apartheid South Africa* (London: Panos, 1991), p. 170.

72. This is the estimate of the South African Human Rights Commission, based on political deaths in 1992. Cited in "South Africa Called 'The Most Violent Country in the World,' " *Weekend Argus*, March 20–21, 1993, p. 11.

In 1990 Inkatha exported the civil war in Natal to the townships in the PWV triangle in an attempt to portray itself as a national political movement. Inkatha found eager support among Zulu migrant workers who lived in all-male hostels in the townships. These hostels were socially and politically isolated from the larger communities that surrounded them, and many of their residents felt threatened as rumors circulated that the ANC planned to eliminate the hostels. Tensions exploded in mid-1990 in attacks by hostel dwellers upon nearby township residents. Many of these clashes took place under the eye of South African Police, who intervened only when hostel dwellers fell under counterattacks. In several confrontations, police escorted Inkatha members to safety and failed to prosecute those responsible for the attacks.

Terrorist massacres, which often coincided with progress in negotiations at the national level, and attacks on townships by perpetrators outside the community bred suspicion that a "third force" was behind the violence. Those suspicions were borne out in 1994 when the independent Goldstone Commission revealed evidence of SAP aid to Inkatha. Such aid included military training, supply of weapons, protection of Inkatha cadres, and assassination of ANC leaders and supporters.[73]

Both regions now contain "no-go" areas for opposing factions. Because no legitimate authority can impose order, many of these areas are now run by local warlords and young vigilantes distant from grand political and ideological concerns. These vigilantes are often beyond the

73. The official disclosure of such activities came on March 18, 1994, from the Goldstone Commission in South Africa; *New York Times*, March 19, 1994, p. 1. For articles describing the role of the South African Police in aiding Inkatha in Natal, see Roy Ainslee, "The North Coast: Natal's Silent Rural War"; Deneys Coombe, " 'Of Murder and Deceit': The Trust Feed Killings"; and Tim Smith, "Trust Feed Wasn't a One-Off Massacre," in Minnaar, ed., *Patterns of Violence*. For a larger discussion of police and security force complicity in South Africa's violence, see Paulus Zulu, "Behind the Mask: South Africa's Third Force," *Indicator South Africa*, vol. 10 (Summer 1992), pp. 8–14; and George Ellis, " 'Third Force': What Is the Weight of Evidence?" South African Institute of Race Relations, Cape Western Region, Regional Topic Paper 93/1 (May 1993). The role of the police and security forces in instigating violence, the inability of the police to capture the perpetrators of the violence, and the role of apartheid in establishing the context for township violence are what anger black South Africans who hear such violence described as "black-on-black" violence.

control of national leadership.[74] In some areas people fear the gangs more than the police or defense forces.[75]

Some have argued that the violence in Natal and the Vaal triangle is primarily a manifestation of a Zulu-Xhosa ethnic power struggle. Yet in Natal, where the civil war began, fighting has been mostly among Zulus. Those who see the ANC-IFP confrontation as a hidden ethnic struggle cannot explain why more than 80,000 residents of Natal are ANC members and no more than 40 percent of blacks there support Inkatha.

While the violence in the Vaal triangle has been between the ANC and Inkatha, it apparently fed on ethnic fears incited by rumors and forged documents that gave the appearance of a planned ANC pogrom against Zulu hostel dwellers.[76] Inkatha then exploited the anxiety of the hostel dwellers to intensify the conflict. Within months of the eruption of violence in 1990, many combatants described their motivation in ethnic terms; to them, the ANC equaled "Xhosa" and the IFP equaled "Zulu."[77] As violence continued, Zulu speakers in the PWV region

74. This point has been admitted by ANC officials on several occasions. See, for example, Chris Hani's remarks to the South African business community: "Some of the political violence is the result of ill discipline on our side, of political intolerance, of comrades turning into *tsotsis,* of the legitimate right to self-defence being hijacked for personal ends." Reprinted as "Just How Possible is Peace?" in *African Communist* (Third Quarter, 1992), p. 11. See also Nelson Mandela's remarks in "Mandela: ANC is Also Guilty," *Cape Times,* August 6, 1993, p. 1.

75. A study of township residents near Merafe Hostel in Soweto found that 75 percent expressed fear that people's self-defense units established by the ANC "prolonged the violence and worked against the creation of a culture of political tolerance"; see Jacklyn Cock, "The Dynamics of Transforming South Africa's Defense Forces," in Stedman, ed., *South Africa,* pp. 149–50. The problem of undisciplined self-defense units led Chris Hani to call for transforming them into a youth peace corps. See "Hani Wants Peace Corps," *New Nation,* April 8–15, 1993, p. 1.

76. Lauren Segal, "The Human Face of Violence: Hostel Dwellers Speak," *Journal of Southern African Studies,* vol. 18 (March 1991), p. 223; and Anthony Minnaar, "Hostels on the Reef: The Goldstone Report," *Indicator South Africa,* vol. 10 (Autumn 1993), p. 65.

77. Segal, "Human Face," pp. 213–25; Minnaar, "Hostels on the Reef," pp. 65–71; and Hilary Sapire, "Politics and Protest in Shack Settlements of the

came under verbal and physical assault because residents assumed they had to be either Inkatha supporters or troublemakers.[78]

Another explanation for the violence in Natal and the Vaal triangle is that rapid urbanization has spawned a struggle between insiders who have access and claim to resources and outsiders who are "have-nots." Thus in the Vaal triangle the violence reflects a social disconnection between hostel dwellers and their neighborhoods; in Natal, the violence reflects intense competition for scarce resources.[79]

But if the disparity between the "haves" and "have-nots" were the main cause of South Africa's political violence, then violence would be thriving in *every* urban area.[80] In Cape Town, where urbanization is high and squatter communities proliferate, there has been sporadic political violence between township factions of the ANC, but the fighting there does not approach the magnitude of that of Natal or the Vaal triangle. Nor have the hostels of the townships of Cape Town led to the amounts or kinds of violence associated with those two regions.

Although poverty, urbanization, and shortages of essential resources are not sufficient explanations for the political violence in South Africa, they do supply the context for such violence. As one civic leader put it, "You just have to throw in a match from outside, and then the fire spreads on its own momentum."[81] Moreover, the absence of legitimate police and courts makes it difficult to extinguish such a fire. As Laurie Nathan observes, "In democratic societies, central government, local authorities, the courts and the police provide meaningful avenues for people to raise grievances and settle disputes. In South African townships these institutions lack the will, the legitimacy and the capacity to

Pretoria-Witwatersrand-Vereeniging Region, South Africa, 1980–1990," *Journal of Southern African Studies*, vol. 18 (September 1992), pp. 694–97.

78. See "Outsiders Turn Daveyton into Killing Fields," *Weekly Mail and Guardian*, July 30–August 5, 1993; and " 'His Sin Is That He Speaks Proper Zulu—in Jo'burg,' " *Weekly Mail*, June 18–24, 1993.

79. See, for example, Heribert Adam and Kogila Moodley, *The Negotiated Revolution: Society and Politics in Post-Apartheid South Africa* (Johannesburg: Jonathan Ball, 1993), pp. 142–46.

80. Peter Gastrow, member of the National Peace Accord secretariat in South Africa, suggested this point to Stephen Stedman.

81. Private communication.

do so."[82] Between 1990 and April 1993 there were thousands of politically motivated murders in South Africa; eleven convictions were returned.[83]

Yet some progress is evident. South African political and community leaders have established monitoring and investigative commissions to establish responsibility for acts of violence and to work with communities to reduce violence. The Goldstone Commission, for example, has a mandate to examine past cases of violence, especially in order to weigh the culpability of state actors in carrying out attacks. The commission used to be criticized for avoiding particularly difficult or sensitive cases and for not having an independent investigative capacity, but it established its bona fides in the fall of 1992 with reports that led F. W. de Klerk to sack twenty-three senior SADF officers for their involvement in political dirty tricks—including assassination—against political opponents of the state.[84] The most dramatic findings of the commission were published in March 1994; the report revealed that a network inside the South African Police had colluded with Inkatha in assassination, massacres of civilians, and illegal gunrunning.[85]

The National Peace Accord (NPA) in 1991 established societal institutions for ameliorating violence, including a National Peace Committee and a National Peace Secretariat. These bodies, consisting of representatives of the major political parties and church groups in South Africa, monitor ongoing violence, mediate conflicts, and attempt to prevent future violence. For that purpose, eleven Regional Dispute Resolution Committees (RDRCs) and eighty-seven Local Peace Committees (LPCs) have been set up. The LPCs are tasked with bringing "local parties together to foster cooperation and a 'culture of tolerance,'" creating conditions for and monitoring "public gatherings which have the po-

82. Laurie Nathan, "An Imperfect Bridge: Crossing to Democracy on the Peace Accord," *Track Two*, vol. 2 (May 1993), p. 4. (*Track Two* is the monthly newsletter of the Centre for Intergroup Studies at the University of Cape Town.) A similar point is made in Sapire, "Politics and Protest," p. 696.

83. Paula Cardoso, monitoring coordinator for Black Sash, a South African women's organization, in *Cape Times*, April 1, 1993.

84. For a description of the events leading up to the firing of the officers, see Rich Mkhondo, *Reporting South Africa* (New York: Heinemann, 1993), pp. 85–88.

85. *Interim Report on Criminal Political Violence by Elements within the South African Police, the KwaZulu Police and the Inkatha Freedom Party* (copy received by electronic mail).

tential for violence," and promoting development initiatives at the local level.[86]

The National Peace Accord is a remarkable experiment in using civil society to resolve political and social conflicts, but, if judged by overall levels of violence in South Africa, it has not succeeded. This begs the question, however, of whether violence would have been greater in the absence of the NPA. For instance, the NPA is credited with negotiating and monitoring the conditions of hundreds of peaceful political marches in the Vaal triangle, one of the most highly charged areas of the country. Steven Goldblatt, advocate for the Thokoza Civic Association, credits the NPA for saving "many thousands of lives."[87] In areas with little political violence, the NPA has "allowed LPC members to overcome their mutual mistrust and build sound working relations."[88] Unfortunately, the RDRCs and LPCs have been unable to translate occasional successes into stable peace in areas where political violence has been intense. Often the bitterness and suspicions of the antagonists prove too deep to overcome for long.[89]

As one writer observes, the NPA structures "cannot resolve the crisis of governance. They cannot conceivably become substitutes for the police, the courts and the government."[90] The April 1994 elections will go a long way toward addressing South Africa's political legitimacy crisis. A new government, however, will take over institutions com-

---

86. Mark Shaw, "War and Peace: Resolving Local Conflict," *Indicator South Africa*, vol. 10 (Winter 1993), p. 63.

87. Quoted in Stephen Laufer, "The Secret to Peace Isn't Accords and Commissions," *Weekly Mail*, July 2–8, 1993, p. 11. While the title of this article would lead one to believe that the author dismisses the value of the NPA, in fact Laufer recognizes several key contributions that it has made to peace in South Africa.

88. Both quotes in this paragraph are from Nathan, "Imperfect Bridge," p. 4. For other evaluations of the National Peace Accord, see Timothy Sisk, "South Africa's National Peace Accord," *Peace and Change*, vol. 19 (January 1994), pp. 50–70; Laufer, "Secret to Peace"; and Shaw, "War and Peace."

89. Dan Mofokeng, director general of the Civic Association of Southern Transvaal, noted that by late 1991 civics had withdrawn from all RDRCs in Southern Transvaal because "it is untenable to sit and discuss security issues with SAP generals and Inkatha members in the day-time, if these people use the occasion to target you as a victim for night-time assassinations." (Private interview, Johannesburg, November 17, 1992.)

90. Nathan, "Imperfect Bridge," p. 4.

posed of members of the old regime, such as the South African Police and the South African Defence Force. A successful transition to security and democracy rests on the transformation of these institutions into ones that can effectively provide protection and security for all of the peoples of the country, and thereby command confidence from them.

The last four years have brought both troubling and positive signs in the transformation of the police and defense forces. On the positive side is the December 1992 purge of defense force officers who had a part in provoking violence, carrying out murder, and destabilizing South Africa. Some felt, however, that de Klerk should have disclosed more information about the officers' misdeeds and opened the SADF to further public scrutiny. Many felt also that the purges did not go far enough; they thought other individuals involved in the "total strategy of the 1980s" (such as General Joffel van der Westhuizen, head of the military intelligence department) should have been fired. Others believed that forced retirement was far too lenient—the officers should have been forced to account for their actions publicly.

Many of the problematic aspects of the Goldstone revelations into the military hold true for the investigation of the South African Police. Officers charged with complicity in fomenting violence were not arrested; they were temporarily suspended, pending further investigation. And while Goldstone praised de Klerk for cooperating in the investigation and raised no questions about his involvement, important evidence in the report pointed to direct cabinet involvement in the SAP-Inkatha terror network. For example, the report charges that when several high-ranking SAP officers came under suspicion of wrongdoing, the cabinet offered them retirement and in one case "authorized an unusual $340,000 pay out to the commander of a secret police unit when he was discharged."[91]

The official discovery of SAP and SADF complicity in political violence is a triumph of conflict resolution in South Africa, but it is an incomplete triumph and one that generates difficult questions about political reconciliation. Most South African leaders entered negotiations with a preference for a liberal, forward-looking peace; few, if any, have demanded prosecution of individuals involved in political crimes. Even when the government forced through a bill in October 1992 grant-

91. Bill Keller, "Inquest Finds South Africa Police Aided Zulus in Terror Campaign," *New York Times,* March 19, 1994, p. 7.

ing amnesty for political crimes, the ANC did not object on substance, but said only that such amnesty should emerge through mutual negotiation. Some ANC members want a peace commission to investigate war crimes committed by individuals on all sides, not as a vehicle for prosecution, they say, but as a way to allow South Africans to heal.

But the war crimes did not end in 1992. The latest report of the Goldstone Commission reveals that state officials were purposefully using violence to further their own programs and interests in 1994. In fact, the commission announced its findings publicly because it feared that the SAP-Inkatha network would attempt to destabilize the April 1994 elections. How should such individuals be treated? Should they benefit from a liberal amnesty program? At what point does individual accountability for actions begin? *Can* South Africans heal unless individuals are forced to assume accountability for their actions?

The evidence of the Goldstone Commission establishes that a hard-core clique of individuals who are opposed to majority rule used the police to undermine negotiations and continue the oppression of South African blacks. That is the bad news. The good news is that an investigation took place at all. The other good news is that over the last four years the ANC has found some members of the SADF and SAP who will help build a new South Africa. Some police have begun training programs in community policing; indeed, an ex-MK commander has responsibility for teaching some police officers new norms of justice and law and order. The SADF, MK, and the homelands armies together established a national peacekeeping force, which will eventually join the larger SADF as part of a reformed national army. The SADF and MK have been exploring since 1991 ways to create such an army.

The hope is that change in the police and defense forces will be met by change in black South African attitudes toward these institutions. Hatred of the South African Police runs deep, however; it will not dissipate easily.[92] Another hope is that the election of a new government in South Africa and the reform of the police and defense forces

---

92. From January to June 1993 alone, 109 police were killed, 1,720 injured, and the homes of 516 police were attacked; "Toll Rises after Township Killings," *Cape Times*, July 12, 1993, p. 2. Both the ANC and the PAC appealed to their followers to stop indiscriminate attacks on officers, as both movements claimed that many police had joined their organizations. See "ANC and PAC Call for End to Killing of Police," *Argus*, June 30, 1993.

will reduce political violence in South Africa. Yet another is that the establishment of effective, legitimate police and courts will reduce criminal violence. Ultimately, however, significant, sustained reduction of violence in South Africa depends on alleviating poverty, creating jobs, reducing inequalities in society, and establishing a "culture of learning" in black schools.

Many black youths who were instrumental in rendering South Africa ungovernable remain mired in a culture of violence, cut off from the politics of negotiation although their political action boosted the ANC to national power. One survey of South African black youth concluded that 5 percent (about a half million people) were "lost—that is, ejected by society, with no hope for the future and frequently involved in criminality and/or violence," 27 percent were marginalized and could slip into the "lost" category, and a further 43 percent were "at risk" and showed signs of alienation.[93]

The stakes are too high to let marginalized and at-risk youth slip into criminality and violence. Ungovernability in South Africa will persist and violence and insecurity will increase unless a new government can capture their attention and new programs can address their needs. Here again South Africans have embarked on a search for solutions: the ANC and business leaders have proposed a youth job corps and peace corps, and educators have put forward ideas on improving the content and delivery of education.

Militant youths have already shown their independence from and impatience with the ANC. If their needs are not met, they will form a large pool of recruits for any party that outbids the ANC with radical, racist programs. The ending of formal apartheid may not end political rage in South Africa.

ECONOMIC PROBLEM SOLVING

Economic reconstruction is crucial to restoring order and providing security to South Africans. As stated earlier, South Africans in 1990 inherited an economy with a dual crisis: (1) inequality between blacks and whites, with crushing poverty among blacks; and (2) stagnation and decline in industry, mining, and agriculture. Between 1990 and

93. Bundy, "At War with the Future?" p. 58.

1994 leaders from business, labor, government, and the ANC moved the debate on economic policy beyond slogans to a broad consensus on how best to address deep-seated poverty and inequalities and yet generate and sustain growth in South Africa.[94]

In terms of diagnosis, consensus has it that South Africa's economic woes are structural in nature and far exceed any temporary damage caused by international sanctions in the 1980s. Decades of protectionism destroyed South African industrial competitiveness in world markets, while apartheid prevented the development of South Africa's human capital and imposed heavy costs on black labor. Because black unions have been able to organize legally since 1981, wage levels for workers have increased dramatically, but higher wages have not led to increased productivity. The situation is paradoxical: black workers are paid much less than their counterparts in Europe, the United States, and the industrialized countries of Asia, but they get higher wages than counterparts in most less-developed countries; at the same time, South African workers still suffer from poverty and are less productive than similarly paid workers elsewhere.

In terms of prescription, the consensus holds that any comprehensive economic strategy in South Africa must address the high levels of unemployment, counter the adverse effects of apartheid on the black work force, and deliver immediate improvements in the living conditions of the African population—all while the new government practices fiscal responsibility. Most participants in the debate agree that (1) government will have to play an active economic role in South Africa; (2) populist economic programs must be avoided; (3) large-scale nationalization is not a viable economic tool; (4) redistribution should not take place at the expense of economic growth; and (5) South Africa's export competitiveness must be restored.

Although some important constituencies question the consensus and many policy recommendations have not been implemented, the progress of the last four years has laid the foundation for confronting South Africa's two-pronged economic crisis. That a consensus emerged at all

94. For a summary of the sterile economic debate of 1990, see Robin Lee and others, "Speaking or Listening? Observers or Agents of Change? Business and Public Policy: 1989/90," in Robin Lee and Lawrence Schlemmer, eds., *Transition to Democracy: Policy Perspectives, 1991* (Oxford University Press, 1991), pp. 118–24.

signifies progress, since it took intensive problem solving and cooperation among representatives of business, labor, and political parties to undertake research on South Africa's economy, debate policy alternatives, and exchange information concerning national, regional, and global economic trends.

The first attempt at economic problem solving took place in 1990–91 when two South African companies, Nedcor and Old Mutual, brought together a team of senior economists and analysts from other fields of academic expertise (including some with links to the government, ANC, Inkatha, and big business) to develop a comprehensive strategy for South Africa to meet its economic crises.[95] The economists argued that although apartheid economic policies contributed to rapid economic growth in the 1950s and 1960s, they became more and more counterproductive in the early 1970s because of the rigidity of the labor market, massive state subsidies to white business, and protection of the manufacturing sector and commercial agriculture. They concluded that South Africa must radically reorient its economy toward export promotion. Such a change, they contended, is the only hope for "growth with redistribution." Their final report outlines an ambitious program for industrial reorientation, combined with immediate redistributive measures to alleviate the exigency of blacks.

The economists pointed out that the South African economy suffers from structural weaknesses in manufacturing and mining. Manufacturing is the largest production sector in South Africa, contributing about 22 percent of the GDP. With strong government support, it expanded rapidly from the 1920s until the late 1960s. The apartheid regime channeled surplus from mining and agriculture into the manufacturing sector under an import substitution strategy. As happened in so many other countries, the inward-looking orientation produced good results in the beginning but later led to high production costs, which hurt international competitiveness and necessitated strong protection.

The economists further noted that South Africa's foreign trade resembles that of a typical third-world country. Exports are dominated by minerals, metals, and agricultural products, and are therefore vulnerable to external factors such as world market prices and business cycles in the industrialized countries. Gold, with its strong vulnerability to

95. The final report from this scenario exercise was published in 1992. See Tucker and Scott, eds., *Prospects for a Successful Transition.*

world market price, still provides around 30 percent of total export earnings. But because of new foreign competition, new technology, and the increase in labor costs, the economists warned, South Africa can no longer live off its gold.[96]

In looking toward the future, the report argued that the annual growth rate necessary to reduce unemployment is 5–6 percent. When the authors modeled South African short-term growth in 1990–91, however, their most optimistic forecast predicted real GDP growth rates of 3 percent, which would increase unemployment by 1.3 million, to a total of 6.7 million in 1995. The authors' pessimistic forecast of zero real GDP growth per year yielded an added half million jobless, for a total of 7.2 million.[97]

Short of major structural changes in the economy, the report concluded, South Africa would continue its precipitous decline. The authors formulated a plan to deal with the economic crisis and dubbed it the "kick-start program." The first component of the plan calls for an outward-looking, export economy. To restructure the manufacturing base to compete in the international economy, South Africa would have to reduce its elaborate, extensive protectionism, and work together with industry to locate international market niches that South African industry could fill. The second component of the program recommends immediate state subsidies and business cooperation in providing plots of land, housing, electrification, and skills training to South Africa's black citizens. The program rests on a series of social compacts among citizens, business, government, and workers. At the community level the compact spells out the obligations of all of these actors in local development; a social contract at the elite national level would create a supportive context for local agreements. The plan—both its redistributive components and the reorientation of industry—demands a heavy role for government.

---

96. Indeed, between 1987 and 1993, 140,000 jobs were lost in the gold mining industry. Bobby Godsell, Chamber of Mines president, in "140,000 Mining Jobs Lost," *Cape Times*, June 9, 1993.

97. As it turned out, their pessimistic forecast was optimistic: in 1991 real GDP growth declined by 0.6 percent, and in 1992 it fell 2.1 percent more. See Mike McGrath and Merle Holden, "Economic Outlook: The 1993–1994 Budget," *Indicator South Africa*, vol. 10 (Autumn 1993), p. 19.

Although the kick-start program was put forward in 1991, none of its recommendations had been implemented by 1994. The Nedcor/Old Mutual exercise was not a failure, however, because it has influenced the thinking of all major participants in the South African economic debate, who largely accept the analysis and prescriptions concerning export promotion and immediate community development.[98] Perhaps the most important contribution of the exercise was to serve as a model for economic consultation among political and economic adversaries. Following the Nedcor/Old Mutual effort, three other forums were established to assist economic problem-solving in South Africa: the Mont Fleur Team, the Professional Economic Panel, and the National Economic Forum.

In 1992 the Mont Fleur Team, consisting of economists, political scientists, and civic and business leaders, presented four possible political futures for South Africa.[99] In the "ostrich" scenario, a recalcitrant National Party chose to withdraw from negotiations and form a coalition without the ANC, resulting in further economic and political chaos in South Africa. In the "lame duck" scenario, negotiations led to a protracted transition and all-party coalition government. Because the government is all-inclusive, it is indecisive and unable to implement bold economic solutions to South Africa's problems. Because the transition is protracted and the endpoint uncertain, investors hold back from putting money into the economy. In the end, insufficient growth and the inability to address social problems lead to deeper crisis. In the "Icarus" scenario, a popularly elected government takes over in South Africa and goes on a populist spending binge. In the short run economic growth is high because of government inducement; but, like the mythical character the scenario is named for, the economy crashes, inflation rockets, and sovereignty is handed over to the International Monetary Fund and World Bank so they can mend the broken wings.

98. One aspect of the exercise that was not accepted concerned social development and the African community in South Africa. Based on a skewed reading of American race relations, the report warned against affirmative action because it created a "culture of entitlement." Economic advisers in the ANC expressed interest in and support of the economic program contained in the exercise, but felt that the warnings against a culture of entitlement were nonsense.

99. The four scenarios are found in "The Mont Fleur Scenarios," supplement to *Weekly Mail*, 1992, pp. 1–16.

Finally, in the "flight of the flamingos" scenario, a new democratic government leads to good macroeconomic policies, social reconstruction, investment, and sustained economic growth.

The net result of the Mont Fleur scenarios was to delegitimize economic populism as a strategy for confronting South Africa's problems. The economic message from the exercises was clear: a market-oriented society is necessary; a new government will have to practice monetary and fiscal discipline; an investment-friendly environment is essential; and exports must grow. Significantly, five ANC members were on the Mont Fleur Team. Within six months of the publication of the scenarios, key ANC officials Cyril Ramaphosa and Tito Mboweni warned against the pitfalls of populist government spending. As Jeffrey Herbst observes, "The ANC is probably the only liberation movement in history to speak of financial discipline before it assumes power."[100]

As a follow-up to the Old Mutual/Nedcor exercise, the companies established the Professional Economic Panel (PEP). PEP brought together a wider array of South Africans than the original exercise had, and included representatives from trade unions and small black businesses. PEP issued twenty-two specific proposals "which would stimulate growth and contribute to economic democracy."[101] Some of the proposals aimed at addressing the unemployment problem through public works programs and a youth job corps. Other proposals targeted ways of empowering and freeing small businesses in black communities from antiquated governmental regulations held over from the apartheid era. Still others put forward institutions to better the quality of economic policy-making itself, such as a Performance Auditor's Office "to combat mismanagement, gross wastage, and corruption," and an Industry and Trade Development Council "to spearhead the country's drive to become more internationally competitive." PEP also argued that the South African Reserve Bank should be independent from political control and that a Permanent Fiscal Commission be set up to advise on the formation and implementation of fiscal policy.

100. Jeffrey Herbst, "South Africa: Economic Crises and Distributional Imperative," in Stedman, ed., *South Africa*, p. 36. While Herbst commends the ANC's attitude, he is deeply skeptical of the party's ability to practice financial discipline when it takes office.

101. The proposals are in "Growing Together," a special section of *Argus*, February 26, 1993, p. 1. All quotes in this paragraph come from that document.

While the aim of the Nedcor/Old Mutual exercise, the Mont Fleur Team, and the Professional Economic Panel was to further public and elite debate over optimal economic policies for South Africa, the National Economic Forum (NEF), established in November 1992, sought to bring together business, labor, and government officials to engage in policy formulation. The NEF has established subcommittees to recommend specific policies on job creation, job security, and centralized bargaining. It has held plenary meetings at which top leaders debate agreements forged in working groups. In August 1993, NEF was given responsibility for administering a R 49 million job-creation project.[102]

The NEF has been useful in bridging the differing priorities of government, business, and labor. The South African government participated because it wanted to persuade the union movement that increased productivity and wage flexibility were needed to improve industrial competitiveness. COSATU joined the NEF so it could push for economic reconstruction and job creation. The goal of NEF, according to Finance Minister Derek Keys, is to "invent and then create an economy that answers more closely to the needs of our community."[103] Keys formally invited the NEF to participate in the writing of the next state budget in 1994.[104]

South Africa's enormous political uncertainty profoundly limits what can be accomplished in forums such as the NEF. The ANC has applauded the NEF's work, but it chose to observe rather than participate in the forum for fear of becoming locked into solutions before it even took office. Moreover, the ANC objected to the inclusion of the National Party in the forum, saying it gave a dying government power it doesn't deserve.[105] The government argued that the forum should be a consensus-building institution, and the trade unions want a forum that can make binding policy decisions.[106] On this point the ANC agrees

102. "NEF Jobs Scheme," *South*, August 7–11, 1993.

103. Quoted in van Niekerk, "Meanwhile Back at the World Trade Centre," p. 17.

104. Anthony Johnson, "Business, Labour Get New Role," *Cape Times*, March 27, 1993.

105. Paraphrase of a quote by Trevor Manuel, ANC head of economic planning, in "Moving Towards a People's Economy," *New Nation*, July 9–15, 1993, p. 8.

106. See, for example, the contrasting views of Derek Keys and Ebrahim Patel, COSATU representative on the NEF, in "A Wonderful Opportunity—Derek

with the government: the NEF can play an important role in recommending policies, but "the state has the ultimate responsibility for macro-economic policy."[107]

If one gauges success by specific policies that have been implemented, economic problem solving has failed so far in South Africa. The fate of the kick-start program is telling: big business resisted providing loans without government guarantees and questioned the desirability of reduced protectionism. Labor raised objections over the need to hold the line on wages. The ANC and the government were unwilling to work together to implement the program, and the government could not do so on its own.

Looking at economic performance during the 1990–94 period, one finds that South African economic woes intensified. Real GDP per capita declined every year and by the second quarter of 1993 was 13.5 percent lower than in the second quarter of 1988;[108] capital flight continued at an average of R 4 billion a year;[109] gross fixed investment fell to 16 percent of GDP;[110] the number of homeless people in South Africa increased to 7.7 million;[111] and a South African bank warned that less than 1 percent of those who left school would find formal employment in 1994.[112] Good news could be found in the lowering of inflation during that period, but as the finance minister himself explained, the decrease was due to the fact that "the

---

Keys," pp. 16–22; "Going in with Confidence—Ebrahim Patel," pp. 23–29; "Keys and Patel: The Economic Debate Continues," pp. 56–61; *South Africa Labour Bulletin*, vol. 17 (January–February 1993).

107. Reg Rumney, "Manuel's Changed Manifesto," *Weekly Mail*, July 2–8, 1993.

108. McGrath and Holden, "Economic Outlook," p. 19. The 13.5 percent figure is cited in Reg Rumney, "The Omens Are Good, but the Miracle Won't Happen," *Weekly Mail and Guardian*, August 27–September 2, 1993, p. 33.

109. Nineteen hundred ninety-two marked the eighth consecutive year that capital flight exceeded R 4 billion; Dr. Chris Stals, South African Reserve Bank governor, in Bruce Cameron, "Keys Role is Pivotal in Turning Economy Around," *Weekend Argus*, February 6–7, 1993, p. 3.

110. "The Flawed Inheritance," *The Economist: A Survey of South Africa*, March 20, 1993, p. 19.

111. "Housing Target Can't Be Attained," *New Nation*, July 16–30, 1993, p. 33.

112. "No Work for School Leavers," *Cape Times*, May 27, 1993, p. 6.

economy is buggered."[113] Only at the beginning of 1994 did it appear that South Africa had ended its four-year recession.

But policy implementation and economic performance do not fully measure the resolution of South Africa's economic conflicts. A focus on these indicators misses the polarity of opinion that existed in February 1990 and the context of profound uncertainty of the transition to democracy. The true test will come when a new government is elected in April 1994. Will that government reform South Africa's ailing economy to make it more internationally competitive? Will it embark on a thorough program of social and economic reconstruction to alleviate the poverty of black South Africans? Will it do so in a fiscally responsible way? Will labor hold down demands for wage increases? Will it place a high priority on job creation? Will South African business adapt to a changing global environment and embrace the need to be competitive? Will it act as a socially responsible corporate citizen and work to redress the inequalities in South Africa?

There are some who answer no. Jeffrey Herbst, for example, argues that an ANC-led government, under pressure from its diverse constituencies, will give in to popular demands and go on a populist spending spree. He also believes that the trade unions will be unable to moderate their demands for higher wages and to reduce their militancy.[114]

Both of these predictions merit concern. The ANC may find it difficult to bridge the gap between popular expectations and the resources available for redistribution. The ANC has comprised a mélange of constituencies, and, as long as it was on the outside fighting to create a new government, it was able to promise everything to everyone. Now that it forms the government, however, the ANC must make choices.

Some of those choices are the following: (1) constrict wage gains made by organized labor or give up a policy of increasing employment; (2) target urban development and housing or rural development; (3) maintain macroeconomic fiscal responsibility or attempt to redistribute resources immediately.

The likely behavior of South Africa's trade unions also deserves attention because an important conflict looms between organized labor in South Africa, which represents blacks who have jobs, and blacks

113. "Flawed Inheritance," p. 19.
114. Herbst, "Economic Crises," pp. 29–45.

without jobs.[115] While labor leaders have seemingly discovered that "what is good for South Africa's poor is good for South Africa," rank-and-file union members have resisted labor's inclusion in institutions like the National Economic Forum. The detailed, sophisticated proposals for industry restructuring come from equally detailed, sophisticated technical discussions, which exclude the rank and file. Consequently, many union members feel that their leadership has abandoned the democratic principle of consultation with the members.[116] And during the four-year transition, the inability of the ANC to explain its concessions to the NP has led many union members to question whether the ANC has abandoned them as well in its quest for power. In 1993 a powerful movement emerged in the mining unions to form a worker's party that would pressure the ANC to implement socialist programs and to nationalize key industries.[117]

Such concerns point to a key aspect of problem solving: political constraints must be addressed in creating workable solutions. Here lies a paradox. It takes time for elites who differ dramatically on end goals and strategies to debate, discuss, and share information in order to bridge their differences. At the same time, constituents become more and more frustrated as negotiations drag on, yet they are wary of their respective leaders' willingness to compromise.

Over the last four years there has been incredible progress at the elite level in forging a consensus about what needs to be done to resolve South Africa's economic conflicts. Evidence can be found in the detailed proposals put forward by ANC-affiliated economists[118] and in ANC insistence that social and economic change will not be rapid in a new

115. Lewis, Jr., *Economics of Apartheid*, p. 159.

116. "Concern in Unions as Democracy Shrivels," *New Nation*, July 2–8, 1993, p. 28.

117. Ray Hartley, "Workers' Discontent—A Timely Warning Sign," *New Nation*, July 16–30, 1993, p. 32; and "Unions at Odds over New Workers' Party," *Sunday Times*, July 11, 1993, p. 2. See also Jeremy Cronin, "Back to the Future? A Brazilian Workers' Party in SA?" *Work in Progress*, August–September, 1993, pp. 30–32.

118. See, for example, Avril Joffe and others, "Meeting the Global Challenge: A Framework for Industrial Revival in South Africa," in Pauline Baker, Alex Boraine, and Warren Krafchik, eds., *South Africa and the World Economy in the 1990s* (Brookings, 1993), pp. 91–126.

South Africa;[119] the willingness of labor to educate itself on international competitiveness and productivity and its concern over job creation;[120] and big business's attempts to think hard about addressing the wide gaps in South African society and the poverty of the majority of South Africans.[121] The debates and incipient consensus formed in institutions like the National Economic Forum are unprecedented in South African history and cannot be labeled rhetoric. They form a necessary—but insufficient—condition for the economic conflict to be resolved.

CONFLICT RESOLUTION IN SOUTH AFRICA: EXPLAINING PARTIAL SUCCESS

South Africa's first nonracial election held on April 26–28, 1994, culminated four years of intensive negotiations. Two trends characterize

119. A major concern expressed in Herbst, "Economic Crises," is that the ANC might make irresponsible promises during the election campaign in 1994. Instead, their campaign stressed that while ANC policies would address key issues, solutions would not come overnight. Mandela himself has spoken of the need to dampen expectations; see his comments in Mkhondo, *Reporting South Africa*, p. 142.

120. For instance, the Community Growth Fund, a mutual fund established by the trade unions for investing pensions, ranks possible investments above all on their commitment to job creation. The period 1992–93 also saw innovative negotiations between unions and management, including profit-sharing agreements in the mining industry in exchange for lower wage increases. Bobby Godsell cited such innovations as a way the South African mining industry might cope with its economic challenges; Erica Jankowitz, "Constructive Labour Relations the Key," *Cape Times*, June 9, 1993.

121. When ANC economist Tito Mboweni discussed a wealth tax as a means of funding social needs, some portions of the business community reacted surprisingly calmly. One leading businessman argued that redistribution "is not a matter of political expediency, but of economic survival. . . . Business can react in one of two ways: it can scream, deny, denounce—and be saddled with the inevitable, perhaps in a more damaging and disruptive form than necessary. Or it can give considered, serious input on how such a levy can be made to ensure minimum damage and provide maximum return." *Argus*, August 7, 1993, p. 1. In a survey of 500 industrial managers in 1993, 75 percent agreed with the concept of affirmative action; Mziwakhi Hlansani, "Absence of Long-Term Strategies Hurts Firms," *Business Day*, July 29, 1993, p. 12.

those years. First, political adversaries across the ideological spectrum have been engaged in intensive problem solving—debating, exchanging information, learning, and negotiating solutions to the myriad conflicts that rage in South Africa. South African political parties and interest groups, as well as individual South Africans, reduced the gaps among them on such issues as a future constitution, reduction of violence and insecurity, and an economic policy for achieving growth with redistribution.

At the same time, however, political parties have been engaged in a battle for primacy of power that led to a level of direct political violence unprecedented in recent South African history. Between February 1990 and December 1993, nearly 13,000 people died in massacres, assassinations, and other forms of political violence, mainly in black townships. During that time radical rhetoric escalated, the political positions of peacemakers weakened, and the economy—in desperate need of domestic and foreign investment—continued to plunge as joblessness and poverty, already high, increased.

For the National Party and the African National Congress, the incongruity of problem solving and the struggle for primacy translated into a double agenda. On the one hand, the government sought to portray itself as a responsible political actor that was seeking solutions to problems through dialogue and negotiation and that was preparing for a democratic and transparent political competition with the ANC over the future of the country. On the other hand, elements within the government, in collusion with revanchist whites and the Inkatha Freedom Party, sought to undermine the ANC as a credible and responsible political force through illegal, covert action.

For the ANC the incongruity produced internal conflict over the extent of compromise necessary to reach power. ANC leaders found themselves caught between the exigencies of negotiation and the need to be accountable to their diverse constituencies. Problem solving was therefore a balancing act: what must be shared to reach out to former enemies had to be weighed against what must be maintained to satisfy long-time friends.

The transition in South Africa became bogged down by a dilemma. Many South Africans agreed that new institutions had to be created if South Africa was to prosper in the future, but those same South Africans realized that new institutions would carry distributional consequences. Hence there was incentive for political actors to control the creation of those new institutions in order to maximize their share of benefits. The dilemma was simple, but vexing: most political actors in South Africa—the National Party, the ANC, the PAC, Inkatha, the labor unions, and the business community—all saw the need for new political arrangements in which everyone would be better off. At the same time, they knew that different possible arrangements would benefit some actors disproportionately. Deadlock arose because no actor was strong enough to impose a solution.

Deadlock can be broken in two ways: through changes in the power resources of the actors or through problem solving that prompts the antagonists to change their conceptions of their interests. In South Africa the balance of power between the ANC and the government seemed remarkably stable; each had the power to wreck any solution that ignored its interests. Moreover, their stalemate had the character of a grinding battle rather than one in which both sides perceived a cataclysm if talks failed.

Conflict resolution in South Africa has had to rely on cognitive change, or "enlightened self-interest," whereby groups "see the long-term superiority of social contracts over simple contracts."[122] That change came through learning and problem solving and established a corps of leaders in the ANC, NP, trade unions, and business committed to cooperative solutions to South Africa's most intractable problems.

Skeptics would reply that the progress South Africans have made toward conflict resolution is immensely fragile for at least three reasons. First, the solutions of the last four years have not been put into place. A social and economic contract among business, labor, and government does not exist. The ANC and the NP have not yet proved whether their period of power sharing will be a recipe for inaction and confrontation or a brave experiment in national reconstruction. Second, there are powerful incentives for all of the actors to resort to limited conceptions of self-interest. The ANC and the NP, although partners in government for the next five years, will be rivals in any forthcoming election. Each will have incentives to undercut the other. Trade unions and businesses, although learning how to cooperate, still differ on bottom lines

122. Horowitz, *A Democratic South Africa?* p. 151. For an in-depth discussion of various factors involved in problem solving in South Africa, see Stephen John Stedman, "South Africa: Transition and Transformation," in Stedman, ed., *South Africa*, pp. 19–24.

of profits and wages. Third, conflict resolution in South Africa has been an elite concern; it has not suffused society. Although this last statement is an exaggeration—problem solving indeed has extended into many communities on issues ranging from housing to sanitation—it is nonetheless true that many township youths remain angry about ANC cooperation with the NP; many union members are deeply suspicious of union collaboration with business; and many members of the government are wary of their new masters.

All of the skeptics' concerns are valid, but one must accept them as possible outcomes rather than givens. If the last four years have proven anything, it is that South Africa's peoples have remarkable, sustained resilience and imagination for trying to resolve their conflicts. The last four years have produced a wealth of social capital that did not exist in the South Africa of 1990: many adversaries have shown that they can work together, that they can trust one another, and that they share a vision of a peaceful, prosperous, democratic South Africa.[123]

Conflict resolution is far from complete in South Africa. In the short term extremist parties, in conjunction with rogue elements in the police and defense forces, may attempt to undermine the first government elected on a nonracial basis. Over the longer term, legacies inherited from apartheid and the war to end it—economic inequality, mass poverty for blacks, violence, intolerance, and distrust—will pose difficult barriers to the creation of a peaceful, democratic society. The challenge for the new South African government is to tap the impressive creativity that its peoples have shown thus far in grappling with the country's problems.

123. For a discussion of the importance of social capital (trust, norms of reciprocity, and networks of mutual support) for development, see Robert D. Putnam, *Making Democracy Work: Civic Traditions in Modern Italy* (Princeton University Press, 1993), pp. 163–85.

Chapter 6

The SADC States: Profiles in Conflict

As far as security is concerned, no nation in Southern Africa is an island. The major source of regional interstate insecurity during the last thirty years has been spillover violence from various domestic conflicts, primarily the struggles against colonialism in Angola, Mozambique, Namibia, and Zimbabwe and over apartheid in South Africa. The April 1994 elections in South Africa end one era of regional conflict. South Africa's struggle now is to build a stable, democratic nonracial nation, but even there progress toward resolving internal conflicts is affected by events throughout the region. The resumption of civil war in Angola, for instance, sobered many leaders in South Africa and prompted them to redouble their efforts at negotiation. Guns and refugees from Mozambique flood South Africa, placing a further burden on the task of making peace. This chapter identifies those internal conflicts that could spill over borders in Southern Africa, as other conflicts have in the past.

Whether Southern Africa can end its long period of insecurity rests on how these conflicts are—or are not—resolved. Efforts at resolution are complicated, however, by the acute, general economic stagnation that the entire region confronts. The last decade and a half has seen a steady decline of the region's economies. For example, with the exception of Botswana, Lesotho, and Swaziland, gross domestic product (GDP) per capita in the SADC states declined from $402 in 1980 to $380 in 1992.[1] Mozambique, Tanzania, and Zimbabwe have been particularly hard hit: GDP per capita in those countries fell in the period 1982–91 by 58 percent, 66.7 percent, and 28 percent, respectively.[2]

---

1. *Southern African Economist*, vol. 6 (February 1993), p. 3.
2. Figures are calculated from World Bank, *World Tables, 1993* (Johns Hopkins University Press, 1993).

Nor are standard-of-living data encouraging. The "index of human suffering" places Angola and Mozambique among the bottom five countries in the world in terms of quality of life; Mozambique is ranked the harshest country in the world, below even Somalia, Afghanistan, Bangladesh, and Ethiopia.[3] In the Mozambican capital of Maputo, the numbers of children dying from malnutrition "have risen from around 1.6 percent of child deaths in the city's hospitals in 1980 to 22 percent in 1992."[4] In 1992 all but three countries in Southern Africa suffered from outbreaks of cholera; the World Health Organization reported 45,217 cases.[5] The most devastating health problem is an epidemic of AIDS. Estimates of HIV-positive cases among the sexually active run as high as 20 percent in Angola, Malawi, Tanzania, Zambia, and Zimbabwe.[6]

The grim economic reality of Southern Africa has two important implications for conflict and conflict resolution in the countries surveyed in this chapter. First, economic crisis exacerbates already existing distribution conflicts and fans the flames of other conflict issues. Second, the lack of economic resources seriously hampers the conflict resolution capabilities of most of the members of the Southern African Development Community.

CONFLICT PROFILES

The following profiles describe present conflicts within the countries of Southern Africa, consider latent conflicts that could erupt in the near

---

3. International Human Suffering Index (Washington: Population Crisis Committee, 1992).

4. Rob Davies, "After the Euphoria: What is Happening to the Southern African Dream?" *Work in Progress*, March 1993, p. 26.

5. *Southern African Economist*, vol. 6 (February 1993), p. 3.

6. Alan Whiteside, "At Special Risk: AIDS in Southern Africa," *Indicator South Africa*, vol. 10 (Summer 1992), p. 67. Beyond the staggering cost in human life, AIDS will also devastate the economies of the region. For example, John T. Cuddington contends in one macroeconomic study that "without decisive policy action, AIDS may reduce Tanzanian GDP in the year 2010 by 15 to 25 percent in relation to a counterfactual no-AIDS scenario." See Cuddington, "Modeling the Macroeconomic Effects of AIDS, with an Application to Tanzania," *World Bank Economic Review*, vol. 7, no. 2 (1993), p. 173.

future, and assess the capabilities of the countries to resolve those conflicts.

Angola: Renewed Civil War

The resumption of civil war in Angola after the election of September 29–30, 1992, is a tragedy attributable to one person: Jonas Savimbi. Although flawed by scant international participation, the peace agreement that led to the election nonetheless gave the antagonists a chance to reveal their character and intentions. What Savimbi revealed was his unwillingness to accept anything less than complete power.

The election and subsequent civil war show the disjunction between the objective reality of a military situation and the subjective assessment of that reality. The election results showed strong support for Savimbi across the middle swath of Angola, known as the central highlands, and equally strong support for the MPLA elsewhere in the country, especially in Luanda. From an objective military point of view, neither force can conquer Angola. The people of Luanda hate UNITA and would resort to urban terrorism and partisan warfare to make the city ungovernable if UNITA took over. On the other hand, the MPLA cannot control the central highlands, where armed mobilization would make occupation untenable. Such a stalemate, combined with the staggering costs of the war, should surely suggest the need for compromise.[7] But Jonas Savimbi apparently did not view the situation objectively. Instead he gambled that UNITA—and he—could win all by resuming the war.

Savimbi's behavior raises another issue concerning negotiated settlement of civil war. Peacemaking can end a civil war only if both sides

---

7. Before the war resumed, it had already cost more than $30 billion in material damage alone; 300,000 people were killed, 50,000 children orphaned, and between 1,000,000 and 3,000,000 peasants displaced. See Victoria Brittain, "Peace under Threat," *Guardian Weekly*, April 4, 1992, quoting U.N. figures. The United Nations estimates that an additional 100,000 people have died since the return to war. In addition, Save the Children now believes that Angola's infant mortality rate, 300 per 1,000, is the highest in the world. See Cindy Shiner, "Angola: The World's Worst War," *Africa Report*, vol. 39 (January–February 1994), pp. 13–16. By January 1994, 3,000,000 Angolans were in need of food or emergency assistance; see David Hecht, "UN Battles to Bring Relief to War-torn Angola," *Africa Recovery Briefing Note*, January 1994.

define the war as something less than total. If just one side defines the war as an all-or-nothing conflict, then negotiation can address only terms of surrender. Jonas Savimbi has defined the war as total, and it is the people of Angola who must live with the consequences. The human and economic costs of the war will mount until the MPLA or UNITA surrenders, or until Savimbi is removed as leader of UNITA.

Given this situation, it makes little sense for the international community to attempt to mediate a settlement to the war. Negotiations have taken place sporadically since the resumption of war, however, and in March 1994 U.N. mediators reported that the two sides were close to agreement on a cease-fire. Observers of the talks argue that UNITA is once again using negotiations for tactical gain; Savimbi hopes that a cease-fire under U.N. protection will allow UNITA to consolidate possession of territory seized in the war.[8]

If Angola did reach another settlement, its leaders would still face the practical difficulties of creating a new army from the government's 100,000 soldiers and UNITA's 60,000, plus large numbers of paramilitary troops on both sides. Since the country would have to be demilitarized anew, many troops would have to be cashiered and employment found for them in order to prevent widespread social banditry. No one could expect the two parties to trust each other.

Angola would still need to reconstruct its economy, a process likely to engender conflicts over distribution. Angola faces a stagnant industrial sector, insignificant agricultural production, budget deficits, huge external debt, staggering costs to rebuild infrastructure, and a nonexistent internal tax base.

Finally, if the current round of civil war comes to an end, Angola will confront even more intense racial, ethnic, and regional polarization. Although UNITA and the MPLA did not have their roots in ethnic politics, the last fifteen years of war have reinforced ethnic tendencies in the two parties. UNITA has become identified with the Ovimbundu peoples of the central highlands. During the election Savimbi campaigned on the rhetoric of racial and ethnic hatred, and he accused the MPLA of discriminating against the rest of the country in favor of Luandans and against Africans in favor of *mestiços*. Election results

8. See "Angola: The Ruins of Rebellion," *The Economist*, February 26–March 4, 1994, pp. 44–45; and "Angola: The Militarists on Top," *Africa Confidential*, vol. 35 (February 18, 1994).

showed Savimbi with 60 percent to 84 percent of the vote in the areas he carried, and losing as heavily in MPLA strongholds.[9] When the civil war resumed after the election, both sides engaged in large-scale ethnic killing. MPLA troops and supporters massacred Ovimbundus in Luanda and attacked cities in the central highlands in indiscriminate air and artillery raids. UNITA indiscriminately killed *mestiço* civilians throughout the country.

The continuing war between the MPLA and UNITA has prevented Angola from fully resolving another serious conflict. Demands for independence of the oil-rich Cabinda enclave have been taken up by an armed movement, FLEC (Front for the Liberation of the Enclave of Cabinda), which, reportedly, is supported covertly by Zaire and the Congo. Cabinda produces 80 percent of Angola's oil, which accounts for about two-thirds of Angola's foreign exchange earnings. The Angolan government and UNITA therefore are opposed to independence. The government has agreed to negotiate some autonomy for Cabinda, however, and has promised that Cabinda will get 10 percent of oil revenues.

The civil war also raises anew interstate conflict over international support for UNITA. Zairian troops, South African supplies, and white mercenaries of unknown origin all assisted UNITA when the civil war resumed. The participation of Zairian soldiers in Angola's war, in particular, renews a long-standing conflict between Angola and Zaire. Zairian president Mobutu has often asserted that Angola gives sanctuary to rebels against his regime. On the other hand, Zairian forces invaded Angola in 1975 to assist the FNLA in its attempt to overthrow the MPLA, and UNITA had supply depots in Zairian territory throughout the 1980s.

9. Savimbi carried four provinces: Benguela (59.8 percent), Bie (84 percent), Huambo (81.4 percent), and Kuanda Kubango (76.3 percent). The MPLA candidate, Angolan president dos Santos, received a majority in twelve provinces, with a range from 53.1 percent to 81.5 percent. In Luanda, dos Santos outpolled Savimbi 70.9 percent to 22.9 percent. In two provinces (Uige and Zaire) neither presidential candidate won a majority of votes. Election results were obtained from the International Foundation for Electoral Systems in Washington, D.C., *Results of Presidential Elections*, October 14, 1992.

Mozambique: Unstable Peace

On October 4, 1992, just four days after the ill-fated elections in Angola, Mozambican president Chissano and RENAMO leader Dhlakama signed a peace agreement in Rome. In the capital Maputo and throughout the country, the much longed-for peace was received with controlled joy and a cautious wait-and-see attitude—twenty-eight years of uninterrupted war had bred an understandable skepticism among Mozambicans. Initially the skepticism seemed warranted. Several serious violations of the cease-fire were reported in the three weeks following the agreement. Yet, remarkably, the cease-fire has held. Land travel throughout most of the country became possible for the first time in a decade. Shipments of emergency food relief reached their destinations. Government and RENAMO soldiers were seen fraternizing on television, raising hopes that the end had truly come to a war described as "one of the most brutal holocausts against ordinary human beings since World War II."[10]

Whether or not the peace agreement leads to a stable settlement in Mozambique will hinge on tackling four problems of war termination. First, in order to discourage RENAMO from returning to war, the United Nations should prevent any renewal of external military support for RENAMO from South African territory. Reports from ex-RENAMO officials and RENAMO defectors, and eyewitness accounts of equipment deliveries, plane drops, and RENAMO troop movement to and from Mozambique from South Africa, all attest to cross-border support for RENAMO well into 1992. Covert external involvement could embolden Dhlakama to renounce the peace process, especially if RENAMO loses in elections scheduled for October 1994.

Second, RENAMO must be transformed from a proxy force—created only to destroy—into a political party. Even as RENAMO tried to project itself as a liberation movement, its behavior earned it the appellation of "Southern Africa's Khmer Rouge." In his report to the U.S. State Department on RENAMO, Robert Gersony writes: "[T]he relationship between RENAMO and the civilian population, according to the refugee accounts, revolves almost exclusively around a harsh ex-

10. Deputy Assistant Secretary of State for African Affairs Roy Stacy, speaking at a donors' conference in Maputo, quoted in James Brooke, "U.S. Assails 'Holocaust' by Mozambican Rebels," *International Herald Tribune*, April 26, 1988.

traction of labor and food. If these reports are accurate, it appears that the only reciprocity provided by RENAMO for the efforts of the civilians is the possibility of remaining alive."[11] In another passage he says that many "civilians in these [RENAMO] attacks and other contexts were reported to be victims of purposeful shooting deaths and executions, of axing, knifing, bayoneting, burning to death, forced drowning and asphyxiation, and other forms of murder where no meaningful resistance or defense is present. . . . Children, often together with mothers and elderly people, are also killed."[12]

Third, all of the parties in Mozambique must work to prevent outbursts of violence, which could destabilize the precarious cease-fire. Violence has become institutionalized in the Mozambican countryside; the entire society has been militarized. Many have concluded that living by the gun is preferable to dying without it. As one Mozambican said, "A gun is your money; it's a system."[13] The ready availability of weapons makes it easy for disgruntled actors—warlords and their recruits from the marginalized rural poor—to resort to violence and banditry. Even if aid is directed to those most in need and their violence is curbed, arms will flood over borders into South Africa, Malawi, and possibly into Zimbabwe, as they did into Namibia and South Africa during the Angolan cease-fire.[14]

Another roadblock to ending the violence in Mozambique is the threat of semi-independent militias. UNAMO, a RENAMO breakaway group led by a former RENAMO general, is one such force. The Napramas, spiritualist peasant forces who initially fought RENAMO in

11. Robert Gersony, *Summary of Mozambican Refugee Accounts of Principally Conflict-Related Experience in Mozambique*, report submitted to Ambassador Jonathan Moore, Director, Bureau for Refugee Programs, and Dr. Chester A. Crocker, Assistant Secretary of African Affairs, U.S. Department of State, April 1988, p. 25.

12. Gersony, *Summary of Mozambican Refugee Accounts*, p. 19.

13. Quoted in William Finnegan, *A Complicated War: The Harrowing of Mozambique* (University of California Press, 1992), p. 169.

14. Alex Vines, "The Unhappiest Nation on Earth," *Southern Africa Review of Books*, September–October 1992, p. 18. Indeed, the cross-border arms flow has already started. AK-47s from Mozambique are being sold illegally to Inkatha. In December 1993, there were rumors that the Malawian army had uncovered a cache of AK-47s and RENAMO uniforms at the headquarters of the ruling Malawi Congress Party. See *Africa Confidential*, vol. 34 (December 17, 1993).

the central and northern provinces but who now side with it against the government, are another. Independent warlords also hinder domestic stability.[15]

Fourth, an immediate imperative for ending the war—the repatriation and resettlement of Mozambique's 2 million refugees and 6 million internally displaced persons—contains the seeds of protracted conflict. Plans to provide land for these individuals have run into an array of intractable problems. Only 18 million of Mozambique's 80 million hectares of land are suitable for agriculture. Of these 18 million hectares, nearly half of the best land has already been acquired by large transnational agribusinesses. Conflicts have already broken out between returning smallholders and commercial interests.[16] Given the amount of displacement of Mozambicans in the last twenty years, it is extremely difficult to establish legal claims to ownership. In few areas, if any, can the state adjudicate conflicting land claims.

In the end, resolving the immediate problems of war termination and reconciliation can be only a prelude to addressing deep-seated political, economic, and social conflicts that will plague Mozambique well into the next century. Mozambique exists as a state because of international recognition and international aid. Ever since it gained political independence in 1975, Mozambique has been in a downward spiral of underdevelopment, insecurity, and violence. The state, monopolized by FRELIMO, had several objectives at independence. Among them were to make society more equitable and to reduce negative dependence on other countries; to strengthen the state and its institutions; to build a nation based on socialist principles; and to make the country less vulnerable to external and internal threats.

Successes in the areas of primary health care, vaccination, and literacy went hand in hand with mistakes in the development process. FRELIMO committed errors that helped undermine its legitimacy. It

15. For an extensive review of groups that have used violence in Mozambique, see K. B. Wilson, "Cults of Violence and Counter-Violence in Mozambique," *Journal of Southern African Studies*, vol. 18 (September 1992), pp. 527–82.

16. Figures for land tenure are from Gregory W. Myers, "Reintegration, Land Access and Tenure Security in Mozambique," *Confusion, Contradiction and Conflict: Land Access in Mozambique in the Post-Peace Period: Four Case Studies from Manica, Sofala, Gaza, and Inhambane Provinces*, University of Wisconsin, Land Tenure Center, September 1993, p. 36.

failed to involve traditional leaders in the process of state making. Nor did it address ethnically based demands from the nonsouthern provinces for greater representation in the upper echelons of party and government. FRELIMO also failed to consider the peasantry's expectations, demands, and needs following independence.

But any regime that came to power in 1975 would have found its ability to rule highly circumscribed, since Mozambique's colonial heritage presented its new rulers with an almost herculean task. Moreover, South Africa's destabilization policy never gave Mozambique the chance to learn from its developmental errors. As Joseph Hanlon has argued, without South African destabilization "the crisis would have been much less severe. No conceivable set of Frelimo errors could have resulted in a million dead and $18 billion in economic losses. To put the primary responsibility on Frelimo or socialism makes nonsense of history; it is blaming the victim."[17] Yet war weariness and economic hardship have caused many Mozambicans to blame FRELIMO for failing to deliver on promises. While RENAMO is embraced by few and hated by many, FRELIMO tends more and more to inspire either indifference or sullen resentment.[18]

FRELIMO's legitimacy has been undermined also by its economic policies, dictated in part by international lenders and aid organizations. It has pursued a structural adjustment program, but the lack of viable independent economic actors, functioning banks, and credit authorities

17. Joseph Hanlon, *Mozambique: Who Calls the Shots?* (London: James Currey, 1991), p. 5.

18. In June 1993, the National Democratic Institute for International Affairs in Washington, D.C., hired Louis Harris and Associates to conduct focus groups throughout Mozambique. The attitudes of people toward RENAMO and FRELIMO are telling: "FRELIMO was characterized as the nation's liberators who went wrong once they got into power, but have improved their behavior somewhat in the last several years. This improvement is not significant enough to have generated widespread enthusiasm for FRELIMO but has certainly improved their standing. . . . RENAMO is often described as brutal and violent, but it is also viewed as doing the nation a great service by forcing FRELIMO to reform and introduce democracy. One person said, 'they made us discover things, but their means were wrong. They fought through violence and killed many people.'" See Louis Harris and Associates, *Imagining Democracy: A Report on a Series of Focus Groups in Mozambique on Democracy and Voter Education*, June 1993, pp. 18–19.

makes the program difficult to implement. At the same time the program makes the rich richer and the poor poorer, which, combined with the effects of political uncertainty, drought, and a huge inflow of donor funds, fuels large-scale theft and corruption.[19]

The political legitimacy crisis in Mozambique coincides with a socioeconomic crisis of crushing proportions, as shown in the following data:

—The per capita GDP is around $80, making Mozambique the poorest country in the world.[20]

—External assistance has accounted for 70 percent of measured GDP since 1988.[21]

—At least one million Mozambicans died either in the war or from the indirect effects of war (mainly disease and starvation).[22]

—Nearly eight million Mozambicans are displaced, refugees in their own country or in neighboring countries.[23]

—Infant mortality (death before the age of one) is estimated at 149 per 1,000. Child mortality (death before the age of 5) is approximately 280 per 1,000.[24]

—About a quarter of a million children have been traumatized by war experiences, malnutrition, and disease.[25]

—Half of the primary schools in the country have been destroyed.[26]

Maputo has been one of the fastest growing cities in the world since the late 1980s, and the urban infrastructure—roads, water, sewage, electricity, and basic social services—is wholly inadequate to cope with

19. For evaluations of Mozambique's experience with structural adjustment, see Merle Bowen, "Beyond Reform: Adjustment and Political Power in Contemporary Mozambique," *Journal of Modern African Studies*, vol. 30, no. 2 (1992), pp. 255–79; and Hanlon, *Who Calls the Shots?* pp. 113–65.

20. World Bank, *World Development Report, 1993* (Washington, D.C., 1993), p. 238.

21. David N. Plank, "Aid, Debt, and the End of Sovereignty: Mozambique and Its Donors," Journal of Modern African Studies, vol. 31, no. 3 (1993), p. 411.

22. Ernest Harsch and Roy Laishley, "Mozambique: Out of the Ruins of War," *Africa Recovery Briefing Paper*, vol. 8 (May 1993), p. 13.

23. U.S. Committee on Refugees, "No Place Like Home: Mozambican Refugees Begin Africa's Largest Repatriation," draft, November 1993, p. 13.

24. *World Development Report*, p. 292.

25. Harsch and Laishley, "Mozambique," p. 3.

26. Harsch and Laishley, "Mozambique," p. 13.

the influx. The inflow of refugees from the countryside and the repatri-
ated miners and other migrant workers from South Africa add to already high levels of unemployment, social disturbance, and violent
crime. The situation is potentially explosive. Any government would
find it difficult to generate the means necessary to provide all of
Mozambique's citizens with even a minimal level of socioeconomic
welfare. Distribution of scarce economic goods is bound to be a major
source of conflict for the foreseeable future.

The political will of the Mozambican government to end the war and
to initiate national reconciliation is beyond question. By the end of the
1980s the government had identified three overriding concerns: to
guarantee individual survival by bringing the war to an end; to address
short-term emergency threats and needs arising out of the war; and to
restart the process of state making and nation building, thus paving the
way for stability and socioeconomic growth. It adopted a law on clem-
ency in 1987, directed toward RENAMO. That same year, in conjunction with the International Monetary Fund, it embarked upon a three-
year program for economic rehabilitation (PRE); PRE was succeeded in
1990 by a new three-year plan for structural adjustment. It created a
new constitution, adopted in November 1990, that abandoned Marxism-
Leninism; drastically reduced the role of the FRELIMO party; introduced clear divisions among the executive, legislative, and judicial
branches; enshrined political pluralism; supported a market economy;
guaranteed a free press and freedom of information; and ensured the
right to strike.

Yet, all these efforts notwithstanding, the Mozambican government
lacks the capabilities to address the problems of legitimacy and distribution. It cannot enforce laws; it cannot provide order; it cannot provide its citizens with minimal protection against life's hardships. What
is also missing in Mozambique is a convincing political opposition, a
civil society that joins the process as an independent actor, and a sensitive approach by international financial institutions and the donor community, which need to help Mozambique avoid further violence and
conflict.

Equally troubling is that the war has changed how Mozambicans,
both citizens and leaders, think about such things as identity, family,
kinship, race, and ethnicity. Many have traded in commitments to
nationalism and patriotism for more limited goods, often linked to
personal survival and aggrandizement. That prolonged warfare forces

modifications in the way people perceive their roles and functions is not particularly surprising. But the absence of a larger shared identity leaves the resolution to the national question in Mozambique—how the country should be organized, how the state apparatus should be configured, and so on—distinctly more conflictual today than it was in 1975.

Zimbabwe: Problems after Lancaster House

A political cartoon on the cover of a 1990 issue of the Zimbabwean magazine *Social Change and Development* artfully summarizes many of the conflicts that the country faces in the foreseeable future. The cartoon shows a prisoner, representing the country of Zimbabwe, escaping from a jail called Lancaster House. In front of the prisoner runs a river, and on the far bank lie democracy and socialism. Before the prisoner can ford the river, he must pass four wild animals that confront him. The animals—hyena, hippopotamus, lion, and elephant—represent dictatorship, the one-party state, bureaucracy, and the life presidency and corruption. The title on the cover is "After Lancaster House . . .?"

The negotiated settlement at Lancaster House left a number of basic conflicts unresolved in Zimbabwe. In particular, although the agreement settled the national struggle, it did so at the cost of leaving the land distribution issue unresolved. Although blacks and whites in Zimbabwe coexist peacefully, reconciliation has not taken place between them. Lancaster House did not foresee the violent conflicts among blacks that took place in the 1980s in Zimbabwe. Nor did the Lancaster House constitution provide protection against hegemonic parties that seek to dominate power. The ruling party, ZANU-PF, has used its political advantage to reduce the threat of organized opposition and has stirred a new conflict concerning political participation.

In part, as Kenneth Grundy asserts, Zimbabwe's record is an impressive one: "The old regime has been dismantled, despite a recognizable element of continuity. Parts of the economy have been reformed and others left largely intact. The most racist elements have been encouraged to leave. Two, and in some respects three, large armed forces have been integrated and then reduced in size."[27] Zimbabwe has also

27. Kenneth Grundy, "The Demilitarization of Southern Africa," in Harvey Glickman, ed., *Toward Peace and Security in Southern Africa* (New York: Gordon and Breach, 1990), p. 69.

made important strides in providing health care and education to the population.[28]

On the other hand, the limits of change since Zimbabwe gained independence in 1980 need to be addressed, as do the conflicts that are unresolved. First, racial reconciliation has been a limited affair. De jure apartheid has ended, but a concomitant change in the hearts and minds of many whites has not taken place. Jeffrey Herbst describes the whites in postindependence Zimbabwe as an enclave that benefits economically but does not contribute to the making of a new society.[29] The reconciliation that has occurred more resembles mere coexistence than racial harmony and integration.

Second, this coexistence comes at the price of continued inequalities of wealth and income. In 1993 the *Financial Gazette*, Harare's business journal, described a "silent apartheid" that still grips Zimbabwe: banks that proffer most of their loans to whites, industry monopolies that stifle black business, a formal economy that sentences blacks to the periphery of economic activity.[30] According to Christine Sylvester, little has changed economically for most blacks in Zimbabwe: "They face nagging continuities in their personal economic circumstances."[31] The biggest losers in the Lancaster House exchange were the landless poor, who have been abandoned by the new regime in large part. By 1992 only about 52,000 of the targeted 152,000 black families had been given land, mostly of poor quality.[32] In contrast, 6,700 farmers (less than 1

28. Between 1979 and 1985 primary school enrollment rose from 819,000 to 2,200,000. In those same years, attendance at secondary school increased from 79,000 to almost 500,000. Infant mortality was reduced from 120 per 1,000 in 1980 to 50 per 1,000 in 1989. See Jonathan N. Moyo, "State Politics and Social Domination in Zimbabwe," *Journal of Modern African Studies*, vol. 30, no. 2 (1992), pp. 316–17. Moyo, like many others, questions whether Zimbabwe can sustain such progress during its structural adjustment program.

29. Jeffrey Herbst, *State Politics in Zimbabwe* (University of California Press, 1990), pp. 221–27.

30. Cited in "White Privilege Again a Target as Austerity Bites in Zimbabwe," *Southern African Monthly Research Bulletin*, March 1993, p. 5.

31. Christine Sylvester, *Zimbabwe: The Terrain of Contradictory Development* (Boulder, Colo.: Westview Press, 1992), pp. 132, 140–43.

32. Moyo, "State Politics," p. 319. Those families who were granted land received few agricultural services to help them settle, and many are still desti-

percent of all Zimbabwean farmers), mostly white, still owned 47 percent of the arable land.[33]

Third, struggles among blacks did not stop after Lancaster House; they have been even more violent than during the civil war. The conflict peaked in 1984 and 1985 when President Mugabe sent Shona-speaking troops into Matabeleland, killing civilians and destroying property indiscriminately. The struggle took on ethnic overtones, but the conflict was predominantly one over power between elites. Two points are important. First, ZAPU, ZANU-PF's opposition, did not play by the rules set out at Lancaster House; instead, ZAPU cached arms. Second, at least some blacks opposed to the government sought clandestine support and cooperation from South Africa, thus prompting the government to fear a South African–led, RENAMO-like insurgency against Zimbabwe.

The unity agreement of 1987 between ZANU-PF and ZAPU ended the violence in Matabeleland and merged ZAPU into the ruling party. Reconciliation between the Ndebele, the region's predominant ethnic group, and the government apparently has progressed admirably.[34] But subsuming ZAPU prompted a conflict between the enlarged ruling party and those who want some formal opposition to ZANU-PF. Evidence of corruption in the highest rungs of government stoked this conflict.

President Mugabe has never favored multipartyism and has acted to restrict any political participation that might threaten ZANU-PF's rule. While Mugabe scrupulously obeyed the Lancaster House constitution, he also made clear his intention to transform Zimbabwe into a one-party state as soon as the Lancaster House sunset clauses expired in 1990. Although the government rescinded emergency security legislation in 1990, it used that legislation throughout the 1980s to harass, torture, and threaten opposition. ZANU-PF has battled extensively with the judiciary in an attempt to curb that branch's independence and

---

tute; see Sam Moyo, "Economic Nationalism and Land Reform in Zimbabwe," *Southern African Economic and Political Monthly*, June 1993, p. 40.

33. Moyo, "Economic Nationalism," p. 41.

34. Terence Ranger, "Matabeleland since the Amnesty," *African Affairs*, vol. 88 (April 1989), pp. 161–73.

domain; it has also been hostile to autonomous social organizations such as unions and the university.

Those who favor multipartyism are a strange amalgamation of traditional ZANU political opponents, students, the small emerging African bourgeoisie, and elements of the white commercial sector. In 1990, in conjunction with pressures from within ZANU-PF, they were able to force President Mugabe to back down from creating a de jure one-party state. But that same year ZANU-PF implemented laws restricting the autonomy of the university, organized labor, and the judiciary. To paraphrase one report, ZANU-PF laid the one-party state to rest but strengthened its own arbitrary authority.[35]

ZANU-PF's continuing attempt to monopolize political participation has undermined its legitimacy among important sectors of society. University students, in particular, reject the heavy-handedness and totalitarian tendencies of the party.[36] Such tendencies coincide with implementation of an ambitious, draconian liberalization program. Zimbabwe already suffers from a dramatic unemployment problem, which will only grow worse in the short run. Limiting participation and simultaneously embarking on economic reforms will most likely further reduce the party's legitimacy.[37]

35. Economist Intelligence Unit, *Zimbabwe: EIU Country Report*, no. 2, 1991 (London, 1991), p. 10.

36. Angela P. Cheater, "The University of Zimbabwe: University, National University, State University, or Party University?" *African Affairs*, vol. 90 (April 1991), pp. 189–205. Indicative of Robert Mugabe's sensitivity to any public criticism, in October 1992 the president lashed out at three ZANU-PF members of parliament who had questioned the need to raise government salaries. Mugabe's attack prompted the monthly journal *Moto* to ask, "What is ZANU-PF's concept of democracy, when intelligently critical MPs are accused of 'treasonous' behaviour?" See Donatus Bonde, "Revolt in Parliament," *Moto*, February–March 1993, p. 6.

37. Although ZANU-PF won two by-elections in March 1993, less than 10 percent of eligible voters participated; Lloyd Sachikonye, "Whither the Zimbabwe Opposition Movement?" *Southern African Political and Economic Monthly*, May 1993, p. 49. Jonathan Moyo predicts that grassroots opposition will reach a peak in 1995, when Zimbabwe's next presidential elections are scheduled, and believes that ZANU-PF could be voted out of office; see "State Politics," pp. 328–29.

The state in Zimbabwe has powerful capabilities, albeit capabilities that differ according to issue area.[38] The biggest problem facing the Zimbabwean state, however, is not its capabilities but its lack of norms of state autonomy. The Zimbabwean state is so thoroughly penetrated by ZANU-PF that it is assumed that what is good for ZANU-PF is good for the state. Moreover, Robert Mugabe's predominance in ZANU-PF leads to a corollary belief that what is good for Mugabe is good for the state. But ZANU-PF's capture of the state, and its monopolization of participation to protect its hold, weakens the ability of the state as an institution to reduce conflict. Its domination of government has reduced accountability to the people and increased corruption. Measures taken purportedly for the good of the state are increasingly perceived to be for the good of the party. The recent strengthening of arbitrary authority threatens to destroy the autonomy of the judiciary, the only remaining state institution with conflict resolution capability and norms. Finally, ZANU-PF's continued repression of unions, the university, and the media has eviscerated the conflict resolution capabilities of civil society.

Namibia: Reconciliation versus Redistribution

Conflict in Namibia stems from two intertwined processes: (1) the reconciliation of races and peoples after a protracted, bloody civil war; and (2) a highly inegalitarian distribution of wealth and income.

Namibia, like Zimbabwe, came to independence after a civil war that ended through negotiation. Unlike Lancaster House arrangements, however, Namibian independence called for creating a constitution after an election. SWAPO won the independence election but failed to attain the two-thirds vote that would have allowed it to dictate the terms of the constitution. Like Robert Mugabe in Zimbabwe in 1980, SWAPO leader Sam Nujoma put the reconciliation of peoples as one of his highest priorities. The process of writing the constitution for Namibia was not the acrimonious one that people had expected. During the negotiations SWAPO made several concessions to structure the government in ways that would check and balance the power of all parties. It accepted the advice of trade unions and churches in the formulation of an extensive bill of rights. Having learned from the Zimbabwean experience, the drafters of the Namibian constitution also restricted the

38. Herbst, *State Politics*, pp. 243–61.

government's ability to use emergency legislation to violate human rights. The final draft of the constitution has been praised throughout the world for its protections of individuals, including the outlawing of capital punishment, and Namibian political elites take pride in the constitution's provisions. Civic organizations have established an education campaign to inform the citizenry of the rights and obligations that the constitution provides.

The drafting of the constitution was only a first step toward national reconciliation. SWAPO agreed that former employees of the colonial government could keep their jobs. The government has successfully created one military out of the two contending armies, PLAN (People's Liberation Army of Namibia) and SWATF (South West African Territorial Forces). One analyst judges reconciliation to have been quite successful: "The positive effects of the policy have been considerable. It has been one of the main reasons for the relative absence of hostilities since independence and for the lack of antagonism among former adversaries in the army and police. It has also succeeded in promoting a sense of nationhood and increasing the confidence of foreign investors, the business sector and the white community."[39]

As in Zimbabwe, the policy of reconciliation implies shelving the distribution conflict, which in Namibia is severe. Ten years ago the ratio of white to black incomes was 25:1.[40] The 70,000 whites in the country live comfortably, with a per capita yearly income of $14,000. Blacks—about 75 percent of whom engage in subsistence farming—earn on average $663.[41] Unemployment and underemployment range from 30 percent to 50 percent.[42] Only 4,045 farmers, mostly white, own 74 percent of the arable land.[43] The shortage of land among blacks has led to

39. Laurie Nathan, "Marching to a Different Drum: A Description and Assessment of the Formation of the Namibian Police and Defence Force," *Southern African Perspectives*, Working Paper 4 (University of the Western Cape, Centre for Southern African Studies), February 1991, p. 34.

40. David Simon, "Independent Namibia: One Year On," *Conflict Studies* 239 (London: Research Institute for the Study of Conflict and Terrorism, 1991), p. 13.

41. Robert S. Jaster, The 1988 Peace Accords and the Future of South-Western Africa, Adelphi Papers 253 (London: Brassey's for the International Institute for Strategic Studies, 1990), p. 52.

42. Simon, "Independent Namibia," p. 14.

43. Chris Tapscott, "National Reconciliation, Social Equity and Class Formation," *Journal of Southern African Studies*, vol. 19 (March 1993), p. 36.

intense conflicts between poor and wealthy black farmers in historically communal areas.[44]

The bargain that produced Namibian independence opened up the political arena for blacks and at the same time froze existing economic inequalities. As Robert Jaster argues, "The most critical issue facing the SWAPO government is the tension between Namibia's limited employment opportunities and the people's expectations of immediate and substantial material benefits from independence."[45] The unemployment rate for returning Namibian exiles is about 90 percent.[46] The most disgruntled sector of the population seems to be ex-combatants who, having put their bodies on the line for the liberation struggle, found themselves extraneous after independence. As in Zimbabwe, the policy of reconciliation has "led to public charges that it is a one-sided process that is benefitting the white settler community far more than the poor majority."[47]

For the time being the participation conflict is solved in Namibia. The question now is whether SWAPO will become inclusive or exclusive. In the independence election SWAPO derived its strength mostly from Ovamboland in the north, where it gained 95 percent of the Ovambo vote, raising speculation about future ethnic polarization and conflict.[48] In local elections in November and December 1992, SWAPO temporarily ended such concerns by expanding its base of support nationally and making inroads into opposition strongholds in the south. SWAPO's consensus style of national decision making also has reduced fears that it would dominate Namibian politics.[49]

It is too early to address Namibia's institutional capacity for conflict resolution. The colonial past leaves Namibia with a ready-made administrative structure, thus providing state capability. But the independence bargain left intact the existing bureaucracy, which, because of South Africa's apartheid legacy of multiple offices for different ethnic

---

44. Tapscott, "National Reconciliation," p. 37.

45. Jaster, *1988 Peace Accords, p.* 53.

46. Simon, "Independent Namibia," p. 9.

47. Tapscott, "National Reconciliation," p. 35.

48. William A. Lindeke, "Democratization in Namibia: Soft State, Hard Choices," paper prepared for delivery at the 1993 annual meeting of the American Political Science Association, p. 27.

49. Lindeke, "Democratization in Namibia," pp. 11–13, 16–17.

groups, is larger than needed. Since the jobs of previous civil servants were guaranteed, many of the racial and ethnic biases of state officials remain. The surplus of staff inherited in 1989 has not permitted a vigorous affirmative action program to bring more blacks into government.

The new state's biggest weakness is that reconciliation has entrenched "the status quo by protecting the pre-independence gains of the minority and by legitimising patterns of social differentiation that had existed in the colonial era."[50] Its capacity to deal with the potentially explosive issues of inequality and race is circumscribed by economic and historical legacies of the past.[51]

Tanzania: Beyond the One-Party State

Tanzania suffers from two interrelated primary conflicts: political participation and identity. A fierce debate on democratization has been under way there since 1990. Under strong pressure both from outside (via IMF conditionalities to aid) and from within (especially from students and trade unions), the ruling party—Chama cha Mapinduzi (CCM)—has slowly liberalized and begun to dismantle its monopoly of power over the state.[52] In 1992 CCM legalized multiparty competition and called for elections in 1995. CCM has improved public accountability, attacked corruption, and improved its human rights record.

CCM's embrace of multipartyism has been a cautious one. State officials, harking back to arguments that Julius Nyerere made in the early 1960s, contend that multiparty competition and political liberalization could unleash ethnic violence that would threaten national unity. That line of reasoning could be simply a justification for authoritarianism, some critics feel. But the Tanzanian mainland alone has some 140 ethnic groups, many with their own language, and some CCM concern is probably prudent. Moreover, the violent ethnic rivalries that neighboring countries have experienced breed caution.

50. Tapscott, "National Reconciliation," p. 29.

51. Linda Freeman, "The Contradictions of Independence: Namibia in Transition," *International Journal*, vol. 46 (Autumn 1991) pp. 687–718.

52. Tanzania's one-party state was constitutionalized in 1965 after the union of Tanganyika (the mainland) and Zanzibar (the islands of Zanzibar and Pemba and several small islets). The CCM was formed in 1977, when the mainland party TANU (Tanganyika African National Union) merged with Zanzibar's Afro Shirazi Party (ASP).

Political liberalization in Tanzania coincides with a structural adjustment program to address the country's economic stagnation. The confluence of political openness with visible growing disparities of wealth has led to African resentment toward Tanzania's Asian community. That resentment has found a voice in one of the new parties, the Democratic Party of Reverend Christopher Mtikila. Mtikila has accused the Asian community of parasitism, and he has been equally vocal in condemning the Islamic religion.[53] This comes at a time when Islamic fundamentalism is growing on the island of Zanzibar and making inroads into Dar es Salaam.

Ethnic and religious tensions have also fueled speculations that Zanzibar will secede from Tanzania. Such speculations have arisen in the past, and demands for Zanzibar's independence are not new. What makes the issue different this time is that many mainlanders, influenced by the Democratic Party, now favor such a divorce.[54]

The Tanzanian state's greatest weakness in the past was its attempt to control political and economic life from the center. Its successes—the promotion of national identity through language, educational, cultural, and welfare policies—will be put to the test in a new pluralistic environment. Ironically, its failure—bureaucratic overreach, which led to general incompetence—may have given Tanzania the strength necessary to resolve the intense conflicts it will very likely face in the near future. The bureaucratic sclerosis of the 1980s prodded ordinary Tanzanians to form civil associations that provided everything from credit to security.[55] Tanzania will be a crucial test case for the proposition that civil society can augment rather than detract from the state's strength.

53. Ruth Evans, "Pride and Prejudice," *BBC Focus on Africa*, vol. 4 (July–September 1993), pp. 33–37.

54. "Seeking a Parting of the Ways," *Africa South&East*, April 1993, p. 18. Zanzibar already has its own assembly and an independent judiciary; it controls its own immigration rules and, in part, its economy. Integration with the mainland has been gradual: Zanzibar became independent in 1963, formed a union with the mainland in 1964, and merged ASP with TANU into CCM only in 1977.

55. Aili Mari Tripp, "Local Organizations, Participation, and the State in Urban Tanzania," in Goran Hyden and Michael Bratton, eds., *Governance and Politics in Africa* (Boulder, Colo.: Lynne Rienner Publishers, 1992), pp. 221–42.

Zambia: Multiparty Democracy and Multiple Challenges

Zambia had its first competitive elections in two decades in November 1991. Frederick Chiluba and his Mass Movement for Democracy (MMD) ousted long-term leader Kenneth Kaunda and inherited a three-pronged crisis: an economy that has ceased to produce, an economic reform program that will exacerbate hardships for the foreseeable future, and a state that lacks norms of autonomy and the capacity to provide services to its population.

Under former president Kenneth Kaunda's leadership, the Zambian government relied on revenues from its copper industry to establish a huge state bureaucracy, which created and implemented policies on the basis of political rather than economic logic.[56] In particular, policies were designed to keep Kaunda and his United National Independence Party (UNIP) in power. Offering jobs in the government helped UNIP get support; the number of state employees has increased sixfold since Zambia became independent. Kaunda consistently reshuffled and removed state ministers who put the interests of their bureaucracies ahead of UNIP interests.

The economic aspects of the crisis stem from price policies that undercut agricultural production while benefiting the urban masses and from the establishment of inefficient parastatal industries. The gradual decline of agriculture created the highest rate of urbanization in Africa, with the exception of South Africa; by 1986, the urban rate stood at 48 percent. The copper industry which created the country's wealth suffers from the overall decline in that commodity's global value.

Challenges to President Kaunda's "crony statism" came first from external sources. The International Monetary Fund prescribed a set of economic adjustments to nurse Zambia to economic health. The adjustments soon produced powerful political effects. Groups most hurt by economic reforms protested, and President Kaunda lost support among the urban sector and the powerful mining unions. With the government weakened, the political process accommodated more fundamental demands for change, including the push for Kaunda to step down, politi-

56. This discussion of Zambia draws from Thomas Callaghy, "Lost between State and Market: The Politics of Economic Adjustment in Ghana, Zambia, and Nigeria," in Joan Nelson, ed., *Fragile Coalitions: The Politics of Structural Adjustment* (Princeton University Press, 1990), pp. 257–320.

cal liberalization, elections, and multiparty competition. In the words of Thomas Callaghy, Kaunda became "hostage to an urban population he could neither subsidize nor control."[57]

Multipartyism is now legal in Zambia, and the elections of 1991 and the peaceful transfer of power have overcome, for now, Zambia's crisis of participation. A second set of conflict issues, however, concerns the complementarity of political and economic change. Will broadening political participation lead to resolution of the crisis of production and distribution? Chiluba's government must deal with the country's precipitous economic decline. To do so it must have the will to put in place a long-term program that will not show any dividends soon. It usually takes four to seven years for foreign investment to return to a country after it has implemented a structural adjustment program.[58]

Under Kaunda, every halfhearted attempt at economic liberalization was quickly thwarted by well-entrenched, powerful social opposition. Callaghy argues that success of economic adjustment is determined by the ability of a government "to insulate itself from the political logics, characteristics, and effects of the post-colonial syndrome."[59] The state apparatus must withstand societal pressure in order to make and execute decisions based on economic logic. The new government in Zambia may be thwarted, too. The Chiluba coalition is an unlikely alliance of technocratic reformers, business people, and those most likely to be hurt the worst by reform. The state remains controlled by former UNIP cadres who have hindered significant change.[60] Some MMD politicians have used the government as a feeding trough and have manipulated privatization to their own benefit.[61]

In his first three years in office, Chiluba has maintained his commitment to the adjustment program. His government has decontrolled prices, eliminated important food subsidies, laid off 20,000 civil servants, and reduced the budget deficit. The price of reforms for the

57. Callaghy, "Lost between State and Market," p. 302.
58. Tony Hawkins, "All Cards on the Table," *Southern African Economist*, vol. 6 (February 1993), p. 46.
59. Callaghy, "Lost between State and Market," pp. 262–63.
60. Carol Graham, *Safety Nets, Politics, and the Poor: Transitions to Market Economies* (Brookings, 1994), chap. 6.
61. "Zambia: Slipping through a Loophole," *Southern African Economist*, vol 6. (February 1993), p. 36.

people of Zambia has been staggering, however. The price of maize, the country's staple, has increased by 500 percent. Privatization has led to increased unemployment, to about 60 percent; plans call for 50,000 more civil servants to be fired. The Catholic church and the trade unions have criticized the program's harshness, its lack of safety nets, and its inequity.[62]

Rampant corruption and the inability of Chiluba's government to improve living standards have led to a new legitimacy crisis in Zambia. Chiluba pushed through emergency legislation in March 1993 to curtail press freedoms only to rescind it when confronted with massive international criticism. MMD has suffered thirteen resignations of members of parliament, some of whom established a new opposition party.[63] But the especial danger of the current legitimacy crisis is that Zambia's people may come to see democracy itself as the cause of their problems.[64]

Lesotho: Structural Instability

Richard Weisfelder in 1992 observed that "the reputation and legitimacy of the Basotho nation-state have been tarnished during Lesotho's quarter-century of independence."[65] In its short existence, Lesotho has experienced nearly twenty-five years of authoritarian rule; the refusal of one government to accept electoral defeat; a low-level insurgency; two military coups; and the exile of its monarch. In 1991 Lesotho's military rulers pledged to carry out multiparty elections. Their announcement met with much skepticism, but they kept their promise, and in March 1993 the victory of the Basutoland Congress Party (BCP) at the polls ended six years of military dictatorship.

62. Figures are from Richard Chidowore, "Zambia: More Challenges Facing MMD," *Southern Africa News Features*, February 1993, p. 2.

63. "Zambia: Defeats and Defections," *Africa Confidential*, vol. 34 (December 17, 1993).

64. There is some evidence that this may already be the case. Only 13 percent of 1.5 million registered voters participated in the local government elections of November 1992. See Chidowore, "Zambia: More Challenges," p. 1.

65. Richard F. Weisfelder, "Lesotho and the Inner Periphery in the New South Africa," *Journal of Modern African Studies*, vol. 30, no. 2 (1992), p. 651.

The BCP triumph raised hopes that Lesotho would achieve political stability. Those hopes were tempered, however, by long-standing problems of poverty, economic dependence on and political interdependence with South Africa, and an intrusive military.

Lesotho's economic fate has been tied inextricably to South Africa. Sixty percent of its male population works in South Africa's mines. Almost half of its families rely on wage remittances from South Africa for their main source of income. Retrenchments in South Africa reduced Lesotho migrant mine workers from 120,000 in 1989 to 75,000 in 1991, and unemployment rose in Lesotho from 21 percent to 41 percent over those same years.[66]

South Africa also kept a tight political leash on the country. When Lesotho's ruling Basotho National Party (BNP) strayed toward criticism of Pretoria, South Africa funded and armed the BCP. The coup that overthrew the BNP in 1985 was supported by South Africa. Now that majority rule is imminent in South Africa, Lesotho must redefine its relationship with its larger neighbor. Some politicians, with support from within South Africa, even broach possible incorporation.[67]

The first indication of trouble with Lesotho's transition to multipartyism came immediately after the March 1993 vote. Because the electoral results were not based on proportional representation, the BCP won every seat in parliament although the BNP garnered 23 percent of the vote.[68] The BNP ultimately accepted the result, but not until its protests were dismissed in court. The lack of parliamentary opposition bodes poorly for the legitimacy and acceptance of Lesotho's democracy, especially since most members of Lesotho's army are members of the BNP.[69]

In what could be a sign of things to come in Lesotho, fighting broke out in January 1994 between rival factions of the army. The motives behind the violence remain obscure. Some believe that the fighting stemmed from a revolt by soldiers over pay; others contend that it was a failed coup attempt. Regardless of the cause, the violence prompted

66. Figures in this paragraph are from "Sackings on SA Mines Bring Mass Unemployment," *Southern Africa Monthly Research Bulletin*, April 1992, p. 11.

67. Weisfelder, "Lesotho," passim.

68. "Lesotho: Military Goes Back to the Barracks," *Southern African Economist*, May 1993, p. 12.

69. "Lesotho: When Royal May Not Mean Loyal," *Africa Confidential*, vol. 35 (February 4, 1994), pp. 3–4.

an immediate meeting of Southern African states, which pledged support for the BCP and threatened to intervene militarily to restore order if the need arose. Some South African officials worried that militant South Africans opposed to the democratic transition might use Lesotho as a base and sanctuary if disorder continued there.[70]

Malawi: Transition or Implosion?

In another illustration of dramatic change in Southern Africa, Malawians will vote in multiparty elections for the first time in May 1994. The elections will culminate a two-year process of courageous protest against the regime of nonagenarian dictator Hastings Banda and his Malawi Congress Party (MCP). For more than thirty years Banda presided over a regime known first and foremost for its efficient, systematic elimination of political opposition.

In March 1992 the Catholic bishops of Malawi sent a pastoral letter criticizing Banda's human rights record and corruption, nepotism, and general inequalities in Malawian society. The regime immediately jailed some priests and expelled others. One month later, long-time exiled trade union leader Chakufwa Chihana ignored Banda's threat to feed dissidents to the crocodiles; he returned to Lilongwe, where he was imprisoned by government officials.[71] Following the suppression of mass protests against the regime, the Paris Club of Donors decided in May 1992 to suspend all but humanitarian aid to Malawi.

The suspension of international aid was a double blow—it hurt the economy at a time of economic adjustment and it emboldened further opposition. Many more Malawians began to protest against the government, and two groups—the United Democratic Front (UDF) and the Alliance for Democracy (Aford)—publicly announced their opposition to the MCP. In some cases the Malawian army protected the protesters, bringing their loyalty to the regime into question.

In response to the growing international and domestic pressures, Banda called for a referendum to test whether Malawians wanted an end to the one-party state. His hope was that disorganization in opposition ranks and government control of the media would ensure a vote in

70. "Lesotho: When Royal," p. 4.
71. Keith Somerville, "Banda Fighting to Keep Autocracy in Malawi," *Guardian*, April 11, 1992.

his favor. But in June 1993 Malawians voted 63 percent to 35 percent against the one-party state. After protracted negotiations between the MCP, UDF, and Aford, a National Executive Council (NEC) was established to rule alongside the government. The NEC eventually chose May 1994 for presidential elections.[72]

The interim period before elections has not been auspicious for Malawi's transition. Dual sovereignty exists as the MCP and NEC assert control over the levers of government. The Malawian army, which supports the NEC, has clashed with the Young Pioneers, a youth vigilante group of the MCP. The army killed several Young Pioneers in skirmishes in December 1993 and raided the headquarters of the MCP, where they allegedly found a stockpile of arms and RENAMO uniforms. The Young Pioneers have been accused of caching arms around the country.[73]

There is a real possibility that the May 1994 election will not produce an orderly turnover of government. The pattern of campaigning evident thus far suggests that the opposition parties might split the vote and allow MCP to triumph. The MCP, for its part, has made ethnic appeals to foment violence "as a means to fulfill its own predictions that a multi-party system would bring ethnic division."[74] Fragmented opposition and private armies could spur a descent into civil war or even a Somalia-like implosion in which central power collapses and no force in society is powerful enough to restore order.

Swaziland: The Politics of Anachronism

In Swaziland, as in Malawi, the main conflict issue is political participation. When King Sobhuza II repealed the independence constitution in 1978, he also declared a state of emergency that has been in force ever since. Political parties were banned, freedom of expression was denied, and legislation allowing detention without trial was introduced. The emerging opposition, most vocally represented by Pudemo (People's

72. For a discussion of the referendum and the formation of the NEC, see Keith Somerville, "Malawi Votes for Reform," *World Today*, vol. 49 (August–September 1993), pp. 150–51.

73. Richard Carver, "The Army Factor," *Africa Report*, vol. 39 (January–February 1994), pp. 56–58.

74. Carver, "Army Factor," p. 58.

United Democratic Movement), demands that emergency strictures be lifted and that the present *tinkhundla* electoral system be abandoned in favor of the multiparty system outlined in the constitution.[75]

The Swazi monarchy has fended off efforts to lessen its power. The committee it established to examine reform called for increased political liberalism, but it did not institutionalize party competition. The Swazi people have shown little support for the monarchy's reform efforts; they prefer a return to the multiparty constitution.[76] Pudemo continues its calls for democracy even though its cadres have been arrested and harassed.[77]

The participation conflict in Swaziland is compounded by economic challenges. The country must cope with burgeoning urbanization caused by population growth and loss of arable land, and it also has to consider the potential loss of jobs as industries relocate in South Africa.

Botswana: The End of Exceptionalism?

Botswana is exceptional in Southern Africa—indeed, it is exceptional within the third world. Between 1965 and 1985 it had the highest growth rate in the world. In 1966 its per capita gross national product was less than $100; it is now over $1,600. Its state bureaucracy has been praised for its efficiency. Stability, as measured by absence of violent domestic conflict, has been an intrinsic feature of Botswana's political life. Its human rights record for the last twenty-five years has been better than that of the United Kingdom.[78] And it has accomplished all this as a liberal democracy, albeit one dominated by one party.

75. The *tinkhundla* system involves public voting for district representatives. For more details on Swaziland, see Jabulane Matsebula, "Challenging the Royalty: Underground Politics in Swaziland," *SAPEM*, vol. 4 (May 1991), pp. 27–29; and Economist Intelligence Unit, *Swaziland: EIU Country Profile*, 1991–92, pp. 63–67; and Swaziland: EIU Country Report, no. 1, 1992, pp. 13–14.

76. Marieta Snyman, "Swaziland," in Larry Benjamin and Christopher Gregory, eds., *Southern Africa at the Crossroads?* (Rivonia, South Africa: Justified Press, 1992), p. 167.

77. Andrew Masina, "Swazi Democrats in Fear," *Africa South&East*, May 1993, p. 10.

78. Amnesty International's annual reports on human rights violations consistently condemn Great Britain for violating due process in arrests and trials involving Northern Ireland. The organization has also found fault with curbs

Botswana's exceptionalism demands explanation: Why has Botswana, in one of the most conflict-ridden regions of the world, been so free of violent conflict? What institutions have been able to mediate conflict and resolve it without individuals resorting to violence? Is Botswana's success a product of history, culture, or resources that cannot be replicated elsewhere? Or does Botswana's experience hold lessons for the rest of the region? Finally, what are the limits of Botswana's accomplishments? What likely problems and conflicts loom in the future?

Botswana gained independence in 1966 under extraordinarily difficult circumstances. Its economy was dependent on international aid, its cattle industry, and migrant labor to South Africa mines. Its date of independence coincided with the end of a drought that had killed more than a third of the cattle population.[79]

Botswana's chief assets were political leaders and their ethos of state action: "the primacy of commercial criteria, a high value placed upon compromise, stability, security, and the systematic accommodation of competing interests."[80] J. Stephen Morrison attributes the development of such norms to a crisis in the late 1950s when the Bechuanaland Protectorate faced the collapse of regional cattle markets. Faced with potential disaster, black and white cattle owners, colonial state authorities, and African leaders forged a compromise that ensured that economic decisions would address the business concerns of the cattle industry, but in ways that would strengthen state authority and national autonomy. When independence came in 1966 an elite consensus existed that the cattle industry was the new nation's only viable economic sector, that national survival depended on its performance, and that its development "needed bigger herds, more throughput, more exports, better water, better roads, and other infrastructure."[81]

---

placed on press freedom for reasons of state security. Botswana, on the other hand, has been criticized occasionally for its use of the death penalty and for forced repatriation of Zimbabwean refugees.

79. Stephen R. Lewis, Jr., "Policymaking and Economic Performance: Botswana in Comparative Perspective," in Stephen John Stedman, ed., *Botswana: The Political Economy of Democratic Development* (Boulder, Colo.: Lynne Rienner Publishers, 1993), p. 13.

80. J. Stephen Morrison, "Botswana's Formative Late Colonial Experiences," in Stedman, ed., *Botswana*, p. 27.

81. Morrison, "Botswana's Formative Late Colonial Experiences," p. 44.

Botswana's pragmatic leadership eschewed ideological formulas for development. As one researcher notes, "In many respects development has been Botswana's ideology."[82] Its first president, Seretse Khama, never developed a personal, charismatic style of leadership like that of Nyerere in Tanzania, Kaunda in Zambia, or Machel in Mozambique. Nor did the Botswana Democratic Party (BDP) portray itself as a party of liberation. Indeed, its ability to bring together white and black cattle interests and rural dwellers was enhanced by the threat posed by the more radical Botswana People's Party (BPP).[83]

Good fortune, international aid, and, most important, good policy-making led to outstanding economic performance. Luck came in the discovery of diamonds in 1969, a find that would play a key role in Botswana's development.[84] Mineral wealth in Africa, however, has proven more of a curse than a boon for economic growth: countries with such wealth "have generally done worse, not better, than those without."[85] And although Botswana has been one of the biggest recipients of international development aid, such assistance in other countries has often been squandered.

Stephen R. Lewis, Jr., who worked as an economic adviser to Botswana in the 1970s, observes that openness, debate, and learning have been at the heart of economic policy-making in Botswana. Intense consultation takes place among politicians and domestic and foreign economic advisers. Such consultation has been beneficial in two senses: politicians have become economically literate, and economists have learned the constraints under which the politicians operate. Botswana's leaders learned to anticipate future economic problems and plan for them. Occasional good policy choices are made elsewhere in Africa, but in

82. Lewis, Jr., "Policymaking and Economic Performance," p. 23.

83. Morrison, "Botswana's Formative Late Colonial Experiences," pp. 40, 44.

84. One aspect of the luck is that the diamonds were discovered after independence; had it been otherwise, Botswana probably would have fallen prey to massive white settlement or incorporation into South Africa.

85. Lewis, Jr., "Policymaking and Economic Performance," p. 14. See also Stephen R. Lewis, Jr., "Primary Exporting Countries," in H. Chenery and T. N. Srinivason, eds., *Handbook of Development Economics*, vol. 2 (Amsterdam: Elesevier Science, 1989). Bernard Weimer and Olaf Claus attribute the poor performance of mineral-producing countries to the pitfalls of rent-seeking behavior by state officials; see Bernhard Weimer and Olaf Claus, "A Changing Southern Africa: What Role for Botswana?" in Stedman, ed., *Botswana*, p. 189.

Botswana the process itself has become self-replicating. Botswana now has an able corps of trained economists and has been able to reduce gradually its reliance on outside advisers and expertise.[86]

Lewis argues that Botswana's democratic system has been crucial to its successful policy-making. The openness of debate and exchange of information has led to better policy decisions. And certain features of Botswana's democracy, in particular, its strong local government and reliance on traditional institutions such as the *kgotla* (or village meeting), ensure that the government consults its citizens at the local levels, learns their needs, and explains its actions. The combination of modern democratic practice with traditional institutions confers political legitimacy.[87]

Others note, however, that tensions exist between the bureaucracy in Botswana and democracy.[88] The bureaucracy, which prides itself on its excellent performance, bridles at political control by elected leaders. Bureaucrats worry that ceding decision making to politicians will endanger Botswana's developmental success and stability. Proponents of democracy in Botswana, on the other hand, acknowledge that the bureaucracy has been essential for the country's development but argue that it may become corrupt and arrogant if civil society does not develop to hold it accountable. They point to recent incidents of corruption in Botswana's Housing Commission as evidence of a decline in norms of good governance.[89]

Moreover, the relationship between Botswana's traditional institutions and modern government remains controversial. Some believe that the *kgotla* is a democratic institution, akin to the small town meetings of New England. The *kgotla* is said to show that Botswana's political culture is inherently democratic and that civic values form the basis of Botswana's modern political success. John Holm and Patrick Molutsi,

---

86. Lewis, Jr., "Policymaking and Economic Performance," pp. 18–23.

87. Lewis, Jr., "Policymaking and Economic Performance," pp. 21–23.

88. See for instance, Gloria Somolokae, "Bureaucracy and Democracy in Botswana: What Type of a Relationship?" in Stedman, ed., *Botswana*, pp. 113–22; and Mpho Molomo, "The Bureaucracy and Democracy in Botswana," in John Holm and Patrick Molutsi, eds., *Democracy in Botswana* (Macmillan, 1989), pp. 237–43.

89. Kenneth Good, "At the Ends of the Ladder: Radical Inequalities in Botswana," *Journal of Modern African Studies*, vol. 31, no.2 (1993), pp. 225–28.

however, reject the argument that the *kgotla* is inherently a democratic forum.[90] They contend that state leaders use the forum to control the political process as a means of gaining stability, and that leaders use the forum to inform citizens of decisions, not to consult with them about decisions. The *kgotla* itself is said to be antidemocratic: local chiefs can use the forum to silence dissidents, and women are rarely allowed to participate.

Some observers suggest that Botswana's ethnic composition—about 85 percent of its population are Tswana—has contributed to its political stability and openness. While such homogeneity is certainly helpful, it is not sufficient. After all, Botswana's ethnic makeup is roughly similar to that of Zimbabwe, which has not escaped violent ethnic conflict and instability.

But the glowing picture of developmental success should not obscure certain failures on Botswana's part. First, developmental success has come at the expense of marginalization of the San population.[91] Second, the cattle industry and its voice in the BDP have pursued policies that threaten dire ecological consequences.[92] Third, while economic growth has been spectacular and progress has been made in living standards and social services throughout the country, economic policy has failed to address the problems of urban housing, incomes policy, and inegalitarian distribution of wealth.[93]

Finally, as with every country in the region, there are some potential conflict issues. First, the ruling party, the BDP, has always won elections comfortably, but it may face stiff competition from its rivals in the mid-1990s. If it does, the stability of the multiparty system will be tested for the first time.[94]

Second, the ability of Botswana's democracy to mediate conflict has depended in part on economic growth and the successful channeling of that growth into development. Some analysts question whether

90. Patrick Molutsi and John Holm, "Developing Democracy When Civil Society Is Weak: The Case of Botswana," *African Affairs*, vol. 89 (July 1990).

91. Good, "At the Ends of the Ladder," pp. 205–21.

92. Rodger Yeager, "Governance and Environment in Botswana: The Ecological Price of Stability," in Stedman, ed., *Botswana*, pp. 123–37.

93. Good, "At the Ends of the Ladder," pp. 222–30.

94. Jack Parson, "Liberal Democracy, the Liberal State, and the 1989 General Elections in Botswana," in Stedman, ed., *Botswana*, pp. 65–90.

Botswana's democracy will prove resilient if economic performance lags in the future, as predicted.[95]

Third, as mentioned above, there is a growing conflict in Botswana between what might be called its two political cultures—one that values democracy and participation and the other that values bureaucratic autonomy. Political liberalism in Botswana has fostered a democratic culture that is antibureaucratic and demands more participation. If civil society grows, one may see conflict between state and society over bureaucratic accountability. As one scholar from Botswana notes, "The critical question is, and will remain for quite some time, 'How can Botswana build and maintain a strong and independent bureaucracy without jeopardizing its democracy?' "[96]

Fourth, there is concern over the growing power of the military in Botswana's politics. The military portion of the budget has increased annually since 1986, and the military has tried to exempt itself from the bureaucratic openness that characterizes other sectors of the state. Tensions over the military's rising role came to a head in 1992 and 1993 over the decision to build a multimillion-dollar air force base which is beyond Botswana's present needs. The base was controversial within Botswana and also prompted great mistrust among neighbors, who accused the Botswana government of establishing the base for the use of the American air force. Despite advice from junior military officers and politicians to confront the allegations, the Botswana military insisted upon confidentiality. Finally, in April 1993, after much regional suspicion, military leaders did publicly discuss the plans and rationale for the base.

Botswana suggests a number of lessons for conflict resolution for the other countries of Southern Africa: the importance of a strong state, the value of political openness, the need for the center to maintain connections to local politics, the advantages of effective state intervention in the economy, and the compatibility of multiparty democracy with economic growth. Botswana's example also holds a lesson for international economic institutions: the imperative of discussion, debate, and mutual learning for interaction between policymakers and foreign economists. But one must also keep in mind that Botswana had two advantages the

95. Keith Somerville, "Botswana at the Crossroads," *World Today*, vol. 50 (February 1994), pp. 22–24.
96. Somolokae, "Bureaucracy and Democracy," p. 120.

rest of the region did not. First, it discovered its mineral wealth *after* independence and therefore avoided incorporation into the regional economy on terms set by white settlers. Second, Botswana's path to decolonization—not only peaceful but carried out with close coopera- tion between British colonial agents and national politicians—was idio- syncratic. Elsewhere in the region, independence followed either civil war (as in Zimbabwe, Angola, Namibia, and Mozambique) or hostile relations between colonialists and nationalists (as in Zambia and Tan- zania). Unlike every other country in Southern Africa, Botswana came to independence with a stock of social capital derived from a record of effective cooperation between foreign experts and administrators and local politicians.

THE CASES COMPARED: DOMESTIC CONFLICT

As this chapter's country profiles show, domestic conflict issues in Southern Africa fall into four clusters.

Conflicts Associated with War Termination and Reconciliation

In Angola, Mozambique, South Africa, and now (to a much lesser extent) Namibia are several issues concerning war termination and reconciliation. These include technicalities such as signing cease-fires and peace accords, gathering soldiers and arms at assembly points, demobilizing armies, freeing war prisoners, and integrating former enemies in a joint military force. Other issues in this area concern objectives and attitudes of the parties, or, in other words, the commit- ment and sincerity of the parties toward the agreements they reach.

In Mozambique, FRELIMO and RENAMO now attempt to abide by a cease-fire, integrate their armed forces, and turn their competition into one of ballots instead of bullets. Eventually the parties will have to create a unified state. All of these processes call for the two parties, enemies on the battlefield for years and still rivals for power, to work together. Accusations of bad faith and misunderstandings are inevita- ble. The ability of the parties to cooperate will be put to the test con- stantly. Their cooperation will be tempered with awareness that how reconciliation is resolved, and how integration is carried out, will have

implications for distribution of goods and participation in future decision making. In Angola, the resurgence of civil war proves the immense
difficulties of the transition from peace treaty to actual peace, which is
complicated further in this case because one of the parties' commitment
to peace was purely tactical and made in bad faith. At the heart of the
present conflict in South Africa lie issues of integration of security
forces, the creation of trust between citizens and police, and reconciliation of peoples after decades of violence. In Namibia issues of reconciliation and war termination have been resolved remarkably well, but
even there resentment lingers among many ex-soldiers who were cashiered during military integration and general demilitarization.

Conflicts over Distribution

Conflicts over how a country's resources are distributed and over
demands for economic and political change generated by inegalitarian
structures of wealth fall into two groups in Southern Africa. First are the
cases in which governments pursue structural adjustment programs
with identifiable distributional consequences that prompt conflict, such
as in Mozambique, Tanzania, Zimbabwe, and Zambia. Second are the
conflicts over distribution that are tied to conflicts over reconciliation,
as in Namibia and Zimbabwe. The newly elected governments in those
countries struck a deal at independence to sustain a highly inegalitarian
distribution of wealth in exchange for gaining political participation for
blacks. Although the new black political elite may enjoy new economic
rewards and privileges, the economic power of the masses remains
limited. The same trade-off may be made in South Africa.

Conflicts over Political Participation

Fundamental conflicts over political participation rage in Southern
Africa. In almost every country groups and individuals are demanding
political rights, the institutionalization of democracy and an end to
one-party states, and more accountability from leaders. In Angola, Mozambique, Zambia, Lesotho, and South Africa, leaders opened the political process to multiparty elections. Promises to do the same were made
in Tanzania and Malawi. In Zimbabwe, ZANU-PF has stepped back
from its intended goal of establishing a one-party state, but it has also
become more authoritarian toward its people.

Conflicts over Political Identity

Many countries in the region face conflict now or in the near future over identity. In some cases the attempts to stabilize young nation-states clash with ethnic, tribal, religious, linguistic, and other subnational loyalties, because the state believes it needs, and it demands, dominance over such attachments. In other cases, ethnic or racial groups capture the state and use it to oppress others. Leaders who fear political change or stand to lose from it appeal to "traditional" identities in the hope of clinging to power. In Angola, Mozambique, Namibia, South Africa, Malawi, Tanzania, and Zimbabwe, various ethnic, racial, and religious groups have mobilized to fight or to demand political change.

CONCLUSION

Although the conflict issues covered in this chapter can be isolated for analytical purposes, in reality they interfuse. Conflicts over participation have implications for distribution. Conflicts over identity are often conflicts over participation and distribution. In their various manifestations, however, the conflicts all reflect the loss of popular legitimacy state apparatuses suffer when governments are unwilling or unable to meet the expectations of citizens. In many of the countries examined, the government failed to instill in its population the belief in the government's right to rule. In other countries, governments that once seemed to have overwhelming popular legitimacy lost it. In every case, the state has weakened relative to other actors.

The countries of Southern Africa face daunting tasks. Three of the countries are in various stages of armed conflict—South Africa, Angola, and Mozambique. Namibia, no longer at war, still grapples with issues of reconciliation. Autocratic rule in Swaziland has fostered demands for political participation and human rights. Zimbabwe, although still a de jure multiparty state, suffers from growing corruption and a near monopoly of power by its ruling party. Zambia's recent experiment in electoral democracy teeters, burdened by debt and the need to satisfy international lenders. Tanzania faces demands to broaden political participation and may soon confront a secessionist conflict over Zanzibar.

The countries of the region must solve their deep-rooted conflicts over reconciliation, distribution, participation, and identity during a crisis of economic productivity. Economic stagnation, and in some cases economic decline, limits the ability of the countries of Southern Africa to address their myriad conflicts. Recent drought and a rising regional epidemic of AIDS further burden already limited carrying capacities. All of these countries face a dual imperative to foster economic growth and to provide basic economic security for their peoples.

Various economic and political remedies have been suggested that might help resolve the basic domestic conflicts of Southern Africa. We turn to these in the next chapter.

Chapter 7

State Building for Conflict Resolution in Southern Africa

Even with good intentions and political will, Southern African governments will find it difficult to end ongoing wars and resolve conflicts over participation, distribution, and identity. Destabilization and war and crises of economic production put tremendous strain on the capabilities of the countries of the region to create new institutions to resolve societal conflicts. External political forces and international finance organizations add to the strain. Liberal doctrines now enjoy a monopoly among strategies of economic and political development. The United States, Great Britain, Germany, and Sweden all have endorsed economic liberalization and multiparty democracy as the only vehicles for achieving development; they have attached conditionalities to aid to ensure that countries in Africa will pursue those vehicles.

Between 1991 and 1994 eight regimes in Southern Africa initiated political reforms, including the legalization of opposition parties and moves toward competitive elections. If successful, these eight countries (Angola, Lesotho, Malawi, Mozambique, Namibia, South Africa, Tanzania, and Zambia) will join Botswana as multiparty democratic regimes, leaving Swaziland as the sole autocratically ruled country and Zimbabwe as something in between.[1] Already one of the eight, Angola, has been dealt a sharp setback and is once again immersed in civil war.

Like the newly independent countries of Eastern Europe and the former Soviet Union, most of the countries of Southern Africa are simultaneously implementing draconian economic structural adjustment programs and attempting to establish multiparty democratic pol-

1. Although opposition is legal in Zimbabwe and there is contestation for power, the ruling party has engaged in large-scale intimidation, violation of human rights, and harassment of the press and trade unions.

itics. In the long run, structural adjustment *may* relieve the economic problems that beset Southern Africa, but even that is in doubt. The United Nations has warned that not all less developed countries embarking on economic liberalization can succeed, simply because there are so many of them and they must compete for foreign capital.[2] The record of structural adjustment in Africa has been mixed and raises serious doubts about its effectiveness.[3] Foreign investment, a crucial aspect of structural adjustment, has not materialized.[4]

In the short run, the structural adjustment programs of the international lending organizations generate widespread criticism and even revolt among populations who lack belts to tighten further. Successful transitions to democracy, difficult at best under conditions of poverty, can thereby be undermined. Even more problematic than the sustainability of democratic politics under such programs is the provision of basic security for the peoples of Southern Africa. In much of the region, structural adjustment programs have cut safety nets and jobs, which has led to rising crime and banditry just when the state's ability to provide internal security is compromised. The result for a country like Zambia could easily be disintegration into Somalia-like chaos rather than the attainment of all good things. And in Mozambique, a country mired in civil war, with living standards poorer than in Somalia, economic liberalization has compounded internal disorder and insecurity.

The crisis of insecurity in Southern Africa is complex and multifaceted. Unfortunately, the economic demands that the international community has made on the countries of the region address only a single aspect of the crisis. Political demands for multiparty democracy likewise focus on one component of the problem. Each strategy may make sense for resolving parts of the crisis, although evidence suggests that

2. United Nations Center on Transnational Corporations, *World Investment Report, 1991: The Strategic Triad in Foreign Direct Investment* (New York, 1991).

3. United Nations Program of Action for African Economic Recovery and Development, *Economic Crisis in Africa: Final Review of the Implementation of UN-PAAERD* (New York, September 1991).

4. Thomas Callaghy, "Africa and the World Economy: Caught between a Rock and a Hard Place," in Donald Rothchild and John W. Harbeson, eds., *Africa in World Politics* (Boulder, Colo.: Westview Press, 1991), pp. 39–68.

both strategies may be deficient even in their limited realms and may not be complementary.[5]

If economic liberalization and multiparty democracy are insufficient by themselves to resolve present and future conflicts and provide security for the countries of Southern Africa, what capabilities must those countries develop to do the job? Is multiparty democracy compatible with building those capabilities, and, if so, what minimum conditions must be met for multiparty democracy to take root in Southern Africa? Can such conditions be met while implementing economic liberalization and structural adjustment programs? This chapter seeks answers to these questions.

PREREQUISITES FOR DOMESTIC CONFLICT RESOLUTION AND NATIONAL SECURITY IN SOUTHERN AFRICA

Conflict issues affecting Southern Africa involve war termination and reconciliation, distribution, participation, and identity, as noted in chapter 6. These conflicts correspond in part to what one analyst sees as the components of national security:

> Military security concerns the two-level interplay of the armed offensive and defensive capabilities of states, and states' perceptions of each other's intentions. Political security concerns the organizational stability of states, systems of government and the ideologies that give them legitimacy. Economic security concerns access to the resources, finance and markets necessary to sustain acceptable levels of welfare and state power. Societal security concerns the sustainability, within acceptable conditions for evolution, of traditional patterns of language, culture and religious and national identity and custom. Environmental security concerns the

5. It may be hard for some steeped in the American liberal tradition to appreciate that there are alternatives to strict economic liberalization and multiparty democracy as strategies for development. The Asian model of developmental dictatorship refutes the necessity for rigid economic and political liberalization as keys to economic growth. Whether the Asian model is appropriate or desirable for Southern Africa is a different question. We have grave doubts about its applicability in Africa, which we discuss later in the chapter.

maintenance of the local and planetary biosphere as the essential support system on which all other human enterprises depend.[6]

The failure of Southern Africa's countries to resolve various domestic conflicts places each of these dimensions of security at risk.

As argued earlier, domestic conflict resolution in Southern Africa generally occurs on an *ad hoc* basis, in response to crises. Southern Africa's countries, with the exception of Botswana, lack the basic institutions for resolving conflict steadily and preventing conflict from turning violent. A basic prerequisite for national security, then, is an environment that supports the ability of individuals, groups, society writ large, and government to resolve conflicts without recourse to violence.

Conflicts cannot be resolved unless people learn to create mutual interests through inquiry and debate, tools with the power to change positions and volitions. In the words of Charles Lindblom,

> There exist countless social problems for which no adequate solutions come into sight unless and until people reconsider the positions they have taken and consequently alter them. Short of that, the state lacks the capacity to act. . . . A critic might argue [that] solutions have to be found—and often imposed by appropriate authorities . . . [because] often they [parties to the conflict] cannot or will not alter [their positions]. But that sorry fact does not necessarily make authoritative imposed solutions possible. Instead it promises inaction, stalemate. Resistance to change in disposition and position taken often explains why problems like ethnic discrimination, inflation, threat of war, civil disorder, urban decay and congestion, and poverty persist indefinitely. The choice for a society often comes down to making a new inquiry into attitude and belief, difficult as that may be, or finding no adequate solution at all.[7]

Problem solving through inquiry and debate will not provide a solution "reached wholly by examining its merits."[8] Nor will problem solving bring about total agreement among disputants; "some exercise of

6. Barry Buzan and others, *People, States and Fear*, 2d ed. (Boulder, Colo.: Lynne Rienner Publishers, 1991), pp. 19–20.

7. Charles E. Lindblom, *Inquiry and Change: The Troubled Attempt to Understand and Shape Society* (Yale University Press, 1990), pp. 6–7.

8. Lindblom, *Inquiry and Change*, p. 46.

power will always be required in order to proceed over objections from those who do not agree."[9]

Southern Africa demonstrates the potential and limitations of problem solving. Economic policymaking in Botswana is a good example of the intermix between "inquiry and the impositions of power" leading to effective problem solving.[10] When important economic decisions are taken in Botswana, consultation occurs between foreign and domestic economists, between those economists and the bureaucrats who formulate policy, between those bureaucrats and the politicians (both ruling and in opposition) who are accountable for policy and have their own interests, and between those politicians and their constituencies, who ultimately must live with the consequences of government policy.[11] Consultation and debate may never attain consensus, but they do lead to better policies: economists learn the constraints upon politicians; politicians learn about economic options, strategies, and realities; both learn what citizens can live with; and, if people must sacrifice, they have the opportunity to learn why. Important to this process is the attitude that a sense of mutual interest must be created. Ultimately, of course, it is still the government that decides the course of action. But if the society is an open one, policy results are monitored and present opportunities for challenge.

Botswana's greatest policy mistakes have occurred when the government has forgone inquiry and failed to engage all relevant constituencies in debate. For example, one policy failure concerned government plans to dredge the Okavango delta to provide water for farmers and mines outside the delta. The decision was made after consulting only those groups that stood to gain from the water diversion; other concerned citizens and environmental groups were bypassed. To

9. Lindblom, *Inquiry and Change*, p. 46. Lindblom's point is supported by democratic theorists who note that elections are devices to impose one person's will on another after debate, deliberation, and reason have been taken. See Adam Przeworski, *Democracy and the Market: Political and Economic Reforms in Eastern Europe and Latin America* (Cambridge University Press, 1991), pp. 18–19.

10. Lindblom, *Inquiry and Change*, p. 47.

11. This account is derived from Stephen R. Lewis, Jr., "Policymaking and Economic Performance: Botswana in Comparative Perspective," in Stephen John Stedman, ed., *Botswana: The Political Economy of Democratic Development* (Boulder, Colo.: Lynne Rienner Publishers, 1993), pp. 11–26.

Botswana's credit, the government did not in the end impose its policy decision. Criticism was open and loud, and it eventually prompted the government to reconsider and change its course.[12]

A greater flow of information, greater interaction among peoples, and greater competition of ideas enable better problem solving.[13] South Africa provides vivid evidence on this score. Only four years ago the African National Congress and the National Party, as well as big business and labor, held gross stereotypes of their adversaries and advocated slogans as solutions to the vexing problems of their country. As a solution to the complexities of creating a new constitution, different sides demanded "group rights and power sharing" or "one person, one vote." On the difficult issue of devising an economic policy that could lead to growth yet satisfy the demands of the majority for a larger share of economic rewards, the debate started at the level of "nationalization" versus "the free market."

But four years of interaction, shared information, and, often, heated debate have yielded progress. The amount of intellectual energy and debate spent on competing constitutional ideas and economic strategies far exceeds that expended in the American constitutional convention of 1787. Some may dismiss the South African fascination for economic scenario-building and constitutional engineering, but the four-year period of problem solving has bridged the gap between former enemies so that they are willing and able to work together. The results of that interaction are obvious: bases of compromise and workable programs have begun to emerge in South Africa. Those compromises could have come only through inquiry, debate, and interaction.

A different South African example, however, raises a key point about the ability of a society to engage in sustained problem solving. Debate and exchange require protection. People will not participate and express opinions or challenge powerful groups, even the state itself, unless they know that they can do so without retaliation. Some minimum amount of confidence, morale, and security is needed to be partisan and

---

12. "A Second Look Saves a Great Delta," *Washington Post*, June 18, 1992, p. A28. No such change of policy has taken place regarding another controversial policy taken secretively, the construction of the new Botswana Defence Force air base.

13. Lindblom, *Inquiry and Change*, passim.

oppose other volitions.[14] Likewise, protection is needed to be able to reach out and even agree with an adversary. In the killing fields of Natal in South Africa, some communities have been able to make peace by bringing together representatives of Inkatha and the ANC to lead community rebuilding programs. Unfortunately, many of those representatives on both sides have been assassinated, often with police involvement. Without adequate protection from violence, conflict resolution in South Africa is a risky, deadly endeavor.

Inquiry, debate, and interaction thrive best in an atmosphere of predictable and frequent exchange.[15] What economists have suggested about markets—that uncertainty limits investment—is true of politics: uncertainty limits the willingness of antagonists to interact, to share information that might prove useful to them both, and to trust that information sharing or the attempt to create mutual interests will not be turned against them in the future. The incredible amount of political uncertainty in Angola, Mozambique, Malawi, and South Africa exacerbates those countries' myriad conflicts.

THE ROLE OF STATES AND SOCIETIES IN PROBLEM SOLVING

States can promote conflict resolution in society and hence help achieve national security by creating an atmosphere conducive to problem solving. To produce that atmosphere, states must facilitate debate and exchange of goods; promote interaction among peoples and access to information; provide protection; and implement solutions. But there is a catch in carrying out these tasks: by making demands on a population, even in the hope of improving conflict resolution, states themselves generate conflicts.[16] Problems arise from (1) possible contradictions among the tasks; (2) the fact that states must implement policies

14. E. E. Schattschneider, *The Semisovereign People: A Realist's View of Democracy in America* (Holt, Rinehart & Winston), p. 17.

15. Donald Rothchild, "Structuring State-Society Relations in African States: Toward an Enabling Political Environment," paper presented at the Colloquium on the Economics of Political Liberalization in Africa, Harvard University, March 6–7, 1992, p. 1.

16. Lindblom, *Inquiry and Change*, p. 49.

that are unpopular among certain groups or individuals, since problem solving rarely engenders unanimity about solutions; (3) the actions states take to gain the capabilities for fulfilling their tasks; and (4) the use of state capabilities to further the interests of those who manage the state, at the expense of the people.

First, the tasks states must undertake to advance effective problem solving are not necessarily complementary. The greatest tension is between the need to create rules for facilitating exchange of goods in a society and the need to provide protection for citizens. Protection involves more than safety from direct physical violence. It also implies protection against unregulated exchange and the by-products, or lack, of market competition. Exchange and protection often involve trade-offs, for instance, when the demands for environmental security require regulation for pollution control and protection for species biodiversity. Economic security often means that the demands of producers for unfettered exchange must be weighed against the need to protect consumers from faulty or harmful merchandise. Economic security may also call for antitrust legislation to protect consumers from monopoly capital. Protection in the form of "safety nets" is needed to provide basic security for the poor and unemployed who suffer most when markets fail. Labor laws have to counterpose business demands for unfettered exchange with the need to protect workers from harsh, exploitative working conditions. No state in the world has resolved the contradiction between these competing necessities; a delicate balance can and must be struck, however. States that ignore protection risk the revolt of those harmed by unregulated exchange, and states that provide too much protection shackle exchange.

Second, as stated earlier, the best that problem solving can do is change enough positions and dispositions to enable solutions. States must then implement solutions, which may not be accepted by all individuals in society. If inquiry and debate flourish, the implementation of policy does not end controversy; rather, it lays the groundwork for conflict to continue under new circumstances. Difficulties could arise if a government misjudged how much support it had for imposing solutions, if it imposed solutions without adequate debate and inquiry, or if it refused to impose solutions because a small minority was intransigent. The dilemma is evident in South Africa today, where no new constitution will gain the approval of all. The parties who agree on new institutions will have to impose solutions in conjunction with the state.

The big question is whether agreements that meet the demands of the major players—the ANC and the National Party—will have to meet the demands of parties such as Inkatha and the Afrikaner Volksfront, which represent relatively few South Africans yet could spoil any agreement that ignores them.

Third, states need resources and capabilities to carry out the tasks described above. Four capabilities—penetration, extraction, regulation, and appropriation of resources—are essential to strong states.[17] Strong states penetrate society in order to extract resources; doing so enables the state to purchase skills, training, technology, and resources necessary for its other tasks. Penetration of society also enables the state to regulate the activities of groups and individuals, as well as to protect groups and individuals in society. This regulation and protection then enable freer debate and predictable exchange relationships. Finally, strong states have the capability of appropriation—using resources in a purposive manner—which lets them implement solutions to problems.

While the endpoint—a strong state that establishes an atmosphere for problem solving—may lessen overall violence and conflict in society, the process of state building is an inherently conflict-producing process. By asserting central state authority at the expense of local and regional authority, states create conflict. By seeking to wring economic surplus out of its population in order to expand its economic base, states create conflict. By putting forward national symbols and insisting on national identity, where before only local identities existed, states create conflict.

State making in Southern Africa has been made more difficult by the circumstances of the states' creation. Colonial patchwork borders produced states without nations, often encompassing multiple ethnic and language divisions within a single territory while splitting coherent ethnic and language groups into different countries. The fact that borders have not corresponded to nations has contributed to the prevalence of internal conflict in the region. The economic legacy of colonialism is a weak, vulnerable economic base for the new states. Colonialism's neglect of its subjects deprived the new states of crucial human capital. And, finally, the newly independent states of Southern Africa gained their freedom in a regional war. The battle to maintain

17. This set of capabilities is suggested by Joel S. Migdal, *Strong Societies and Weak States: State-Society Relations and State Capabilities in the Third World* (Princeton University Press, 1988), p. 4.

settler states and colonialism created a hostile atmosphere unconducive to basic political trust among groups and leaders within the new states; moreover, South Africa exacerbated internal conflicts through its use of sabotage.

The leaders of the new states recognized that they had to strengthen state capabilities to achieve national security, but, not surprisingly, the actions and choices that they took to strengthen their states produced more conflict and insecurity. In Zimbabwe, for example, the need to extend control over all of its territory brought the state into sharp confrontation with rivals in Matabeleland, who were reluctant to accept central authority. Similarly, in Angola and Mozambique the need to defeat externally supported challengers led both states to coerce their own citizens. In Mozambique the need to extract resources from its population made the state force local communities to abandon traditional forms of agriculture and authority. Zambia, desperate to satisfy its burgeoning urban population, systematically intervened in the rural economy to cut agricultural prices so that it could feed the urban masses.

Fourth, Southern Africa's experience shows that strong state capabilities are not enough to provide national security and a problem-solving environment. Indeed, the presence of strong capabilities centered in a single large organization provides a tempting target for individuals, groups, or parties to capture and use for predatory purposes. In some countries, for example, Malawi, Swaziland, Lesotho, and South Africa, the state itself has proved to be the greatest threat to individual security. In Tanzania, Zimbabwe, and Zambia before 1991, internal sovereignty was established, but state resources were captured by one-party regimes that have little accountability.

This does not imply, as some suggest, that conflict resolution would be furthered in Africa by weakening state capabilities. In countries like Angola and Mozambique, the absence of a functioning state sentences populations to a Hobbesian nightmare. Clearly, the formation of a strong state is necessary—but not sufficient—for individual security. "Without strong states, there will be no security, national or otherwise."[18]

---

18. Buzan and others, *People, States and Fear*, p. 106.

State strength needs to be redefined to include *norms* as well as capability. Capability has already been discussed. Norms refer to a set of roles, preferences, and conceptions of the public good, as perceived by officials within the state. As Eric Nordlinger argues, for the state to be an independent actor, its agenda of preferences must be its own.[19] The state must minimize what he calls malleability, so that officials within it have an understanding of state interest that does not collapse to the interest of the leader or political party in power or to particular societal, class, or ethnic interests. Obviously, the interests of these other bodies may coincide with the interest of the state at any given time or even over long periods. But if a state is to pursue its own interest, officials must distinguish that interest from other, competing interests.[20] For instance, Botswana's bureaucracy formulates policies that sometimes conflict with the interests of the ruling party. In Zimbabwe the judicial arm of the state has often stood opposed to the demands of Robert Mugabe and ZANU-PF.

Capability and norms must exist hand in hand; one without the other cannot produce a strong state. Without institutional norms of the public good and state interest, the machinery of the state is corrupt, captured by societal interests, or subservient to the power lust of individual leaders or political parties. For example, one ethnic group in South Africa captured the state and built up an impressive coercive capability to regulate relationships, extract resources, and redistribute resources. The state provided security and rewards to Afrikaners at the expense of most South Africans. Yet without institutional capabilities, a state with admirable norms of the public good is impotent to carry out policies, a fate that befell Mozambique. In both cases the weaknesses on one side of the equation eventually eroded state strengths on the other. In South Africa the resistance against the Afrikaner capture of the state severely constrained the ability of that state to regulate social relationships; by the late 1980s "dual sovereignty" was the rule in many black townships. In Mozambique the continual frustration of state attempts to meet obligations induced some bureaucrats to abandon the public good for personal gain.

19. Eric Nordlinger, "The Return to the State," *American Political Science Review*, vol. 82 (September 1988), p. 881.
20. "Other, competing interests" include self-interest, defined in terms of corruption, self-aggrandizement, and personal power.

While bureaucratic norms of autonomy and national interest are key components of state strength, it helps if there is a strong civil society that demands bureaucratic accountability. When the state is strong and society weak, erosion of state norms and bureaucratic stagnation, corruption, and conflict are common.[21] Widespread bad governance has persuaded many international analysts to dismiss the role of the state altogether in providing security and development; instead, they think, civil society is the answer to Southern Africa's problems. But when society is strong and states are weak, courts, police, security forces, and ministries are captured by well-organized societal groups; chaos and conflict often result. A weak state and strong civil society is as dangerous as a strong state without a strong, autonomous society.

Civil society's role in conflict resolution also depends on capability and norms. Capability in civil society refers to the presence of thriving autonomous social organizations that can aggregate and communicate the preferences of individuals. But civil society, if it is to facilitate conflict resolution, also requires norms of tolerance and concern for the greater good. The lack of these norms breeds violent competition among multiple autonomous organizations, excessive demands on the state, and a zero-sum struggle for resources and rewards; South Africa may have to deal with this problem in the future. And the organizations that do embrace tolerance and civic concern need to be strong, or they will be subject to the whim of the corrupt and powerful, as political watchdog groups and trade unions have found in Zimbabwe.

The relationship between state and civil society will always be filled with tension. Botswana, for instance, hosts two nascent political cultures, one based on governance and bureaucratic authority, the other on democratic accountability. The first, deeply rooted in the state, takes pride in its exceptional performance and professionalism and sees democratic control as impinging on its ability to govern. The second fears that bureaucratic autonomy will lead to bureaucratic corruption and tyranny. The two cultures of accountability and autonomy can never be completely reconciled.[22] But in Botswana, where the state is strong and

21. Recent cases of corruption in Botswana have raised fears that unless civil society becomes more powerful and keeps attention focused on bureaucratic performance in Botswana, state performance will decline quickly.

22. This well-known tension is explored by Robert Dahl in *Autonomy and Control: Dilemmas of Participatory Democracy* (Yale University Press, 1982).

the civil society growing, the tension is healthy because it is based on rights and obligations, legitimacy, communication and bargaining, and nonviolent conflict resolution.

SOUTHERN AFRICA'S STATE-BUILDING EXPERIENCE IN HISTORICAL PERSPECTIVE

Southern Africa's brief history of state building must be placed in historical perspective. High, perhaps unrealistic, expectations have been held for many states in the third world in general and for Southern Africa in particular. Those expectations, Mohammed Ayoob argues, stem from applying Western standards of state responsiveness to countries with little ethnolinguistic unity and few economic resources, states that from independence suffer from a deficit of legitimacy—in short, states that are not nations.[23] And those standards of responsiveness set for the third world were attained only recently by the Western industrialized states themselves, a point often overlooked by critics.[24] State building in the West was a lethal process.

European states reached their high levels of domestic consensus on issues such as social and political organization only after lengthy instability and upheaval. State building in Western Europe was intimately linked to wars against external enemies and coercion of domestic groups.[25] Responsive politics and distributional economics rose from drawn-out bargaining during which states learned to make accommodations with their peoples in order to survive in a world of warring states.[26]

23. Mohammed Ayoob, "The Security Predicament of the Third World State: Reflections on State Making in a Comparative Perspective," in Brian Job, ed., *The Insecurity Dilemma: National Security of Third World States* (Boulder, Colo.: Lynne Rienner Publishers, 1992), p. 78.

24. See, for example, Charles Tilly, *Coercion, Capital, and European States, AD 990–1992,* rev. ed. (Cambridge, Mass.: Blackwell, 1992).

25. Tilly, *Coercion, Capital, and European States;* Charles Tilly, ed., *The Formation of National States in Western Europe* (Princeton University Press, 1975); Anthony Giddens, *The Nation-State and Violence* (University of California Press, 1987); and Basil Davidson, *The Black Man's Burden* (London: James Currey, 1992).

26. Tilly, *Coercion, Capital, and European States,* pp. 114–26.

The state formation process in Sweden, for example, began in the eleventh century, but universal suffrage was not introduced until 1921. In the United States, the most important issues of national identity and political legitimacy were forged over a century. It took fifty years to consolidate a competitive party system; the separation of the state from gross political patronage took over one hundred years.

And state making in the West was not accomplished bloodlessly. The very idea that the United States would be one nation was enforced by a devastating civil war that cost the lives of 650,000 soldiers and untold more civilians. National reconciliation was then achieved at the expense of the systematic deprivation of the rights of African-Americans.[27] And the triumph of one nation meant the systematic eradication of tens of others, achieved by campaigns of extermination against Native Americans.[28] The point is not that coercion and violence should be condoned for the states of Southern Africa because the West used those methods. The point is that expectations and demands placed on African states should be realistic. Conditions in Southern Africa are far less favorable to the development of strong states and democratic politics than those that existed when the West undertook state making and nation building. The challenge today is for the countries of Southern Africa to build strong states without unreasonable recourse to violence—"to turn the immense power of national states away from war and toward the creation of justice, personal security, and democracy."[29]

DEMOCRACY AND CONFLICT RESOLUTION

Foreign governments and international lending institutions hold certain expectations for Southern African countries, as expressed by the various conditionalities they place on aid and assistance. The combination of these external pressures and internal demands for political participation have led many of the countries in the region to install multiparty democratic regimes. Will democracy meet the conditions

27. Eric Foner, *Reconstruction: America's Unfinished Revolution, 1863–1877* (Harper and Row, 1988).

28. Robert M. Utley, *The Indian Frontier of the American West, 1846–1890* (University of New Mexico Press, 1984).

29. Tilly, *Coercion, Capital, and European States*, p. 227.

described above for national security and domestic conflict resolution? If so, is democracy achievable in the short run in Southern Africa?

Democracy is a system of participation and contestation for power. Its rules bound competition between elites, supplying an intertemporal perspective for competitors.[30] Power is contested through elections and held temporarily by the winners, who must hold elections within some set time to compete to keep power. Winners must not use their power to eliminate their rivals, who must be free to organize opposition to the regime in anticipation of contesting for power in the future. In exchange for the right to organize and to contest in the future for power, the loser agrees to keep its opposition legal.

Some argue that multiparty democracy is not a particularly efficacious method for resolving conflict in divided countries.[31] They allege that democracy creates or exacerbates conflict.[32] This issue needs to be put to rest immediately. Democracy does bring conflict into the open and does amplify it, but that does not mean democracy *causes* the conflict.[33] Every society, democracy or not, has conflicts over participation, identity, legitimacy, and distribution.[34] Every society has opposition to ruling parties, whether that opposition is legal or illegal, organized or unorganized.[35]

In fact, democracy's major virtue as a conflict resolution system is that it brings conflict into the open. When conflict is public, the parties

30. Przeworski, *Democracy and the Market*, p. 19.

31. Alvin Rabushka and Kenneth A. Shepsle, *Politics in Plural Societies: A Theory of Democratic Instability* (Charles E. Merrill, 1972); and, more recently, Charles Williams Maynes, "Containing Ethnic Conflict," *Foreign Policy*, no. 90 (Spring 1993), pp. 11–15.

32. Sidney Verba, "A Research Perspective," in Commission on Behavioral and Social Sciences and Education of the National Research Council, *The Transition to Democracy: Proceedings of a Workshop* (Washington, D.C.: National Academy Press, 1991), p. 77.

33. Schattschneider, *Semisovereign People*, pp. 13, 16–18.

34. Stephen John Stedman, "Conflict and Conflict Resolution in Africa: A Conceptual Framework," in Francis Deng and I. William Zartman, eds., *Conflict Resolution in Africa* (Brookings, 1991), pp. 373–77. The chapter draws from the work of Leonard Binder and others, *Crises and Sequences in Political Development* (Princeton University Press, 1971).

35. See Edward Shils, "Opposition in the New States of Asia and Africa," *Government and Opposition*, vol. 1 (February 1966), pp. 175–204.

concerned have the opportunity to organize to defend their interests, access to information about their options and the effects of their actions, and access to competing ideas about resolving conflicts. Airing conflict also increases the chances that some people will change their minds on issues. As Lindblom states, problem solving, debate, and inquiry "often make the difference between a collection of people and a society."[36] And evidence from group decision making shows that partisanship produces better solutions to problems than a quest for unity.[37]

Democracy has its own problems that hinder social inquiry, but flows of information, competition of ideas, and interactions among peoples are greater than under authoritarian regimes.[38] Increased information, competition of ideas, and increased interaction, however, mean little unless the regime can provide protection. Widespread societal intimidation and violence constrain—and sometimes block entirely—rights to public debate, free speech, and a free press. Democracies vary greatly in their ability to provide protection against such upheaval, but it is unclear that authoritarian regimes do better. They often replace threats from societal intimidation and violence with state intimidation and violence.

PREREQUISITES FOR DEMOCRACY IN SOUTHERN AFRICA

If democracy has value as a system for conflict resolution, then what is needed to create and sustain it in Southern Africa? Can social and political engineering produce the prerequisites of democracy?

Some theorists think democracy can thrive only in societies that have reached a high level of socioeconomic development and enjoy a broad societal consensus and an absence of ethnic cleavages. If these are preconditions, then we can reject democracy as a system of conflict resolution for Southern Africa until such time as countries there "take off" economically or become true nation-states. All of the countries

36. Lindblom, *Inquiry and Change*, p. 48.
37. Lindblom, *Inquiry and Change*, p. 53.
38. Henry Bienen and Jeffrey Herbst, "Authoritarianism and Democracy in Africa," in Dankwart A. Rustow and Kenneth Paul Erickson, eds., *Comparative Political Dynamics: Global Research Perspectives* (New York: Harper Collins, 1991).

suffer from poverty; they lack thriving middle classes (which histori-cally have been a force for democracy); many are emerging from civil violence; and some possess deep ethnic cleavages.

Evidence—including one case from the region, Botswana—shows that lack of economic development need not be an impermeable barrier to political democracy, however. Likewise, some ethnically divided societies possess stable democracies. And transitions to democracy often take place during periods of violence and civil unrest.[39] In the long run the consolidation of democracy may depend on economic growth, tolerance, and social consensus, but in the short run these conditions should be seen as facilitators of democracy rather than strict prerequi-sites for it.[40]

In the absence of shared values, democracy can promote societal inquiry to help produce them. In fact, democracy is needed precisely where cleavages are intense. For example, UNITA and MPLA support-ers cooperated extensively before and during the 1992 elections in An-gola, which few who are familiar with the severe ethnic and political divisions in that country might have expected. They learned through working together in operating the elections that they could work to-gether on other issues. What frustrated many international observers of the elections was not that democracy was doomed to failure by divi-sions in Angolan society, but that Jonas Savimbi prevented the oppor-tunity for democracy to work to bring divided peoples together when he rejected the election results.

The Savimbi example opens a window to a different approach to prerequisites for democracy, one that marries political and economic conditions to the calculations of leaders in democratic competition.[41] Democracy works when parties believe that it will persist. According to

39. Terry Lynn Karl, "A Research Perspective," in National Research Council, *Transition to Democracy*, p. 32; and René Lemarchand, "Africa's Troubled Tran-sitions," *Journal of Democracy*, vol. 3 (October 1992), pp. 98–109.

40. Larry Diamond, "Economic Development and Democracy Reconsidered," *American Behavioral Scientist*, vol. 35 (March–June 1992), pp. 450–99. For a dis-cussion of narrow transition and consolidation of democracy in South Africa, see Stephen John Stedman, "South Africa: Transition and Transformation," in Stephen John Stedman, ed., *South Africa: The Political Economy of Transformation* (Boulder, Colo.: Lynne Rienner Publishers, 1994), pp. 7–27.

41. This discussion draws heavily from Przeworski, *Democracy and the Market*.

game theorists, an election has to be perceived as one play for temporary power in a game that will be repeated regularly and indefinitely in
the future, not as a one-shot game for permanent power. How do
parties come to believe that there is a long "shadow of the future?"[42]
And if they do not believe, why would they obey the rules?

To a certain extent the answer is uncertainty about outcomes. If
competitors for power believe they can win an election, they are more
willing to play by democratic rules. That belief induced warring parties
in Zimbabwe in 1980 and in Angola in 1992 to agree to elections. In
competitive elections, however, only one party will win. What is to stop
an actor like Jonas Savimbi in Angola from abandoning a supposed
commitment to democracy if he loses?

For one thing, there is the possibility of winning in the future, so long
as there is reasonable confidence that there will be a next election. There
could still be incentives for remaining committed to democratic politics,
even if future elections were certain to be lost. The benefits of obeying
the rules (which include safety, possible side payments from the winning party, or overall gains that accrue from a stable democratic political system) would have to be weighed against the costs and probability
of overthrowing the regime and the benefits that would accrue from
winning a civil war.

The September 1992 elections in Angola proved that UNITA and
Savimbi had much less support than the leader had presumed. The
numbers were close enough, however, to allow Savimbi to believe he
might win power in future elections. Given the gargantuan task of
reconstructing the Angolan economy, the MPLA and dos Santos were
bound to lose some support in the future. Thus the explanation for
Savimbi's refusal to abide by the results of the elections lies elsewhere.
Since the UNITA army remained intact during the cease-fire while the
MPLA army withered, Savimbi probably assumed that his army could
win total power by going back to war. He probably also believed that
the United States would not actively oppose his return to war and that
allies in South Africa would continue to back him, beliefs that turned
out to be accurate.

---

42. Robert Axelrod and Robert O. Keohane, "Achieving Cooperation under
Anarchy: Strategies and Institutions," in Kenneth A. Oye, ed., *Cooperation under
Anarchy* (Princeton University Press, 1986), p. 232.

No democratic institution can ensure that a loser (or winner) will remain committed to democratic politics. Nonetheless, if the Angolan constitution had offered the losing party a share of power, and if a unified army had been established well before the election, odds for a successful transition to democracy would have been bettered. As it stands now, however, the Savimbi example shows the dangers of attempting a democratic solution to civil war when leaders define the conflict in all-or-nothing terms.[43]

Botswana illustrates two points concerning the commitment of losers to democratic rules. First, unlike other democratic experiments in Africa, Botswana has a thriving system of local and city government. When the foremost opposition party, the Botswana People's Party, loses a national election, it usually keeps its local base of support and power. Second, Botswana reveals why economic development is so often associated with sustainability of democratic politics. A thriving overall economy reduces the stakes of political competition. The greater the opportunities for resources away from the state, the greater the likelihood of opposition accepting the loss of an election.

To turn the question around, what is to keep an elected leader from using a temporary position of power to assume a presidency for life, and then to try to eliminate the opposition? A winner will most likely stay committed to democracy if the cost of usurping authority is higher than the benefits of continuing to obey the rules. Such a determination depends on the probability of eliminating the opposition, the costs of doing so, and the benefits that would accrue from having no opposition, weighed against the benefits of tolerating opposition. Zimbabwe is instructive. Upon taking power in 1980, Robert Mugabe announced his intention of eliminating democratic politics and establishing a de jure one-party state when the Lancaster House constitution expired. By gradually pressuring ZAPU into merging with ZANU-PF and restricting rights of opposition, voice, and organization, Mugabe established a de facto one-party state. The gains from formally banning political competition were then minimal and the costs of doing so would have

43. Stephen Stedman has explored the issue of elections, leader perceptions of conflict, and resolution of civil war in "United Nations Intervention in Civil War: Imperatives of Choice and Strategy," paper presented at the conference "Beyond Traditional Peacekeeping," Naval War College, Newport, Rhode Island, February 23–24, 1994.

been high. Foreign lending governments would have punished the move and there would have been vocal, albeit ineffectual, protest within the country. Mugabe seemed intent on destroying Zimbabwe's teetering multiparty democracy, but he eventually caved in to party members who thought the external costs of a de jure one-party state would be too high.

In Botswana, the dominant party feels no real threat from opposition and knows that any moves to eliminate opposition would incur extremely severe penalties from the international community. As one analyst suggests, democracy has been one of Botswana's most successful export products, and it has brought millions of dollars of aid and assistance to the country.[44]

SUSTAINING DEMOCRACY IN SOUTHERN AFRICA

Three factors—strong states, vibrant competition among political parties, and learning—can help create and sustain the sense of uncertainty that drives democracy as an institution, and can raise the costs and decrease the likelihood of reneging on democratic commitment.

A Strong State

A strong state, *defined by both capabilities and norms*, is necessary to sustain democracy in Southern Africa for several reasons. First, a strong state aids democracy by assuring losing political parties that they will not suffer discrimination. Moreover, a strong state can provide rights, protection, and an environment conducive to inquiry and debate so that defeated parties can continue to offer opposition and engage the ruling party in problem solving.[45] Second, a strong state raises the cost of abrogating the rules of democratic competition. This is especially important in Southern Africa, where elections often are tied to the resolution of violent conflict. The presence of an independent bureaucracy,

44. Patrick P. Molutsi, "International Influences on Botswana's Democracy," in Stedman, ed., *Botswana*, pp. 51–61.

45. Dietrich Rueshsmeyer, Evelyne Huber Stephens, and John D. Stephens, *Capitalist Development and Democracy* (University of Chicago Press, 1992), p. 275.

military, police, and judiciary—characteristic of only strong states—can restrain political parties from breaking the rules.[46] Third, a strong state checks the financial irresponsibility that can accompany democracy and limits the feeding-frenzy aspects of patronage after an election.[47] In the absence of strong states with norms of bureaucratic autonomy, multiparty democracy seems to ensure corrupt, clientelist politics in which political parties pillage the state and enjoy the spoils of victory. In the rest of the world countries have been able to climb out of this trap only when political parties reach a balance of power and agree to provide the state with needed autonomy.[48] Fourth, a strong state enables democratic governments to implement policy and impose solutions.[49]

Southern Africa lacks states that combine capability and norms of public interest. The simple answer—strengthen civil societies—is a programmatic one that can lead to disastrous results if universally applied. In Mozambique and Zambia, for example, where state capabilities are weak, the strengthening of civil society may lead to increased demands that the state cannot meet and result in the further collapse of central

---

46. As Lindblom observes in *Inquiry and Change*, p. 289: "If one asks, then, why people outvoted in a democratic election do not mount an insurrection but instead accept their defeat without disturbance to social stability or the continuation of democracy, one finds an answer in the many external controls exercised over them rather than only in those internalized controls represented by their convergences in thought. Whatever their internalized norms, many people will not turn in defeat to insurrection, sabotage, terrorism, or street violence because they fear, among many external influences that bear on them, the law, the possibility of their own deaths in resulting violence, or their social isolation from their friends."

47. Joseph A. Schumpeter, one of the founders of the theory of competitive democracy, argues that a strong state is a prerequisite for democracy: "It is not enough that the bureaucracy should be efficient in current administration and competent to give advice. It must also be strong enough to guide and, if need be, to instruct the politicians who head the ministries. In order to be able to do this it must be in a position to evolve principles of its own and sufficiently independent to assert them. It must be a power in its own right." *Capitalism, Socialism and Democracy*, 3d ed. (Harper and Row, 1950), p. 293.

48. Barbara Geddes, "A Game Theoretic Model of Reform in Latin American Democracies," *American Political Science Review*, vol. 85 (June 1991), pp. 371–92.

49. Claude Ake, "Rethinking African Democracy," *Journal of Democracy*, Winter 1991, pp. 32–44.

authority. Even assistance aimed at helping communities help themselves, without recourse to the state, substitutes foreign aid for state capability and sentences those countries to perpetual dependence. Foreign assistance must attempt to build the state and civil society simultaneously.

In Zimbabwe, where the state has strong capabilities but weak norms, a different approach may be needed. Focusing on the development of civil society there could produce a reduction of ZANU-PF control over the state and an increase in autonomy for civil society, which would be a balanced, desirable outcome.

Vibrant Competition among Parties

All things being equal, the more competitive the party system in a country, the more uncertainty introduced into democratic politics and the greater the likelihood of lasting democracy. The presence of more than one effective party with broad appeal creates a perception that no single party has a lock on political power. Moreover, according to the theory of competitive democracy, competition among parties results in better policies and increased consultation between politicians and the masses.

Democratic politics in Africa lacks vibrant competition. Bandwagon politics—not balancing politics—is the norm. Opposition tends to vanish in the aftermath of elections, in part because weak states are easily plundered by elected politicians, which gives incentives to a losing party to defect to the winning side. The price of principled opposition is to remain outside the spoils system. As organized opposition dissipates, incentives grow for the winning party to declare a de jure one-party state.

Zambia illustrates this point. In 1991 Frederick Chiluba and his Mass Movement for Democracy (MMD) party defeated Kenneth Kaunda and the United National Independence Party (UNIP) by an overwhelming majority, winning 125 of 150 parliamentary seats. The opposition disappeared. Rather than try to maintain autonomy and counter the MMD in the future, many long-time UNIP members turned to MMD to get a piece of the political pie.[50] The lack of strong opposition contributed to Chiluba declaring the short-lived state of emergency in March 1993.

50. Michael Bratton, "Zambia Starts Over," *Journal of Democracy*, vol. 3 (April 1992), p. 93: "The losers have embarked on mass conversions to MMD, presumably motivated by the opportunistic assessment that it no longer 'pays to belong to UNIP.' "

So how do the countries of Southern Africa go about building strong competitive party systems? What cleavages within Southern African societies can produce balanced party competition? In the West the history of balanced parties reflects the division of societies into those who benefited from unregulated markets and those who sought protection from the market. The market creates profits, capital, classes, and winners and losers. It destroys the mechanisms people had developed to cope with scarcity. Those who benefit from the market demand "efficiency," and those who do not benefit scream for protection. In the course of Western history, parties organized and demanded participation in politics as a way to gain protection; they pushed governments to regulate markets and redistribute resources to compensate for the market's ill effects. In some cases those who sought protection did so while embracing the need for capitalism; in other cases they rejected the market imperative.[51]

In Southern Africa, the low level of economic development and the legacies of colonialism have produced only a small constituency for a party of efficiency; nearly everyone wants protection against the deleterious effects of the market economy.[52] This leaves regional and ethnic cleavages as prime candidates for party mobilization. These cleavages, however, militate against uncertainty in electoral competition, which is an essential component of democratic politics. Donald Horowitz, for instance, notes that uncertainty about electoral outcomes disappears in deeply divided ethnic societies in which parties mobilize along ethnic lines. In his words, an election becomes a census, and participants know the results beforehand.[53] Lack of uncertainty in a state without bureaucratic autonomy results in a one-time feeding frenzy. Democracy then fails to provide an intertemporal perspective.

51. Adam Przeworski and John Sprague, *Paper Stones: A History of Electoral Socialism* (University of Chicago Press, 1986).

52. Even in South Africa, the most industrialized country in the region, the only party for market efficiency, the Democratic Party, received less than 2 percent of the vote in 1994. The National Party has been an interventionist force in markets and used extensive state powers to protect Afrikaner interests. Whether it will transform itself into a party for market efficiency remains to be seen.

53. Donald Horowitz, *Ethnic Groups in Conflict* (University of California Press, 1985), p. 86.

What cleavages, then, will maintain some uncertainty in party loyalty and provide competitive balance? For two reasons the urban-rural split in Southern African societies may be the most promising cleavage for the sustenance of democracy. First, rural and urban dwellers have different, competing needs, but ruling parties have for the most part favored the urban population at the expense of the rural agricultural producers. This urban bias has perverse consequences. The burden on peasants to produce food cheaply, without adequate resources and infrastructure from the state, has led many rural dwellers to gradually disengage from the state. On the other hand, the result of urban bias "has not been to create an appropriately grateful and state-supporting population of city dwellers, so much as to encourage the immigration to towns of people who, swamping the available facilities and employment opportunities, became alienated in their turn."[54] Rural neglect leads to a massive legitimacy crisis, as it did in Zambia.

Moreover, demographers estimate that by the year 2020 nearly 72 percent of Southern Africa's population will be urban, if current migration trends continue.[55] The carrying capacities of cities such as Lusaka, Maputo, Luanda, and Johannesburg are already stretched to the breaking point. Unless the practical concerns of rural dwellers are met and basic trust in government is established, the region will face major urban breakdown soon.

Botswana, the only Southern African country in which multiparty democracy has thrived, again illustrates the point. Interestingly enough, the ruling party, the Botswana Democratic Party, is best described as a rural party that promotes the interests of cattle and land owners and peasants. The BDP's strong identification with rural interests has ensured that the state remains legitimate in the eyes of most of the population. The rural orientation of the BDP also enables Botswana's opposition parties to make gains among the urban population.

But Botswana is the exception. Regionwide, the development of parties that identify with the rural population and promote policies that benefit them is constrained by the legacy of land maldistribution.

54. Christopher Clapham, "The African State," in Douglas Rimmer, ed., *Africa 30 Years On* (London: James Currey, 1991), p. 99.

55. Allan G. Hill, "African Demographic Regimes, Past and Present," in Rimmer, ed., *Africa 30 Years On*, p. 57.

Zimbabwe, Namibia, and South Africa (after April 1994 elections) are limited in how far they can correct gross inequalities in land distribution, so they cannot fully address the needs of the largest rural constituency, the rural poor. In those cases, the legacy of the resolution of the participation conflict—at the expense of nonresolution of the distribution conflict—may stand in the way of developing a party that could contribute to sustained multiparty democracy.[56]

Learning

A necessary condition for the sustenance of democracy is learning. During transitions to democracy and in their immediate aftermath, elites must come to believe in "the relative effectiveness of democratic institutions for the fulfillment of group goals."[57] Elites must learn the costs of the authoritarian option; how to achieve their goals through bargaining and persuasion; and the consequences of violating democratic rules. In the process of consolidating democracy, leaders must constantly evaluate and improve institutions. During democratic transitions followers must learn the practice and limitations of democracy, what it can and cannot deliver.[58] Consolidation of democracy depends on followers learning to appreciate democracy as a way to have their needs and concerns considered, even when their party is not the ruling one. Most important, leaders and followers must learn to value and practice tolerance.

56. And indeed it may lead the rural poor to support extraparliamentary opposition aimed at undermining the state.

57. Nancy Bermeo, "Democracy and the Lessons of Dictatorship," *Comparative Politics*, vol. 24 (April 1992), p. 274.

58. This includes learning "the importance of voting and being informed; the need to temper partisanship with respect for opposing parties and viewpoints; the means through which grievances and needs can be brought before elected officials, both directly and through the mass media; the techniques by which communities can organize themselves to achieve common ends; and the details of how their own electoral system, legislature, bureaucracy, local government, and legal system work." Larry Diamond, "Introduction: Civil Society and the Struggle for Democracy," in Larry Diamond, ed., *The Democratic Revolution: Struggles for Freedom and Pluralism in the Developing World* (New York: Freedom House, 1992), p. 17.

CONFLICT RESOLUTION AND THE CRISIS
OF ECONOMIC PRODUCTIVITY

Are the institutions that will assist the countries of Southern Africa in resolving their domestic conflicts at odds with the institutions and policies that will help alleviate their crushing crises of economic productivity? The international financial institutions insist that structural adjustment is the only policy that can breathe life into the economies of the countries of the region. As Thomas Callaghy and John Ravenhill observe, structural adjustment "is an attempt to take African countries back to the 1960s. . . . On the economic side, it means rehabilitating primary product export economies and making them work properly, without the pernicious effects of countervailing political logics and weak capabilities."[59] Structural adjustment requires that states deregulate their markets, devalue their currency, decrease their spending, and privatize state companies. According to the theory behind the program, in the short run unemployment and prices will increase, but in the long run inflation will be brought under control and new private investment will create jobs.

Some structural adjustment is simple economic sense: no economy can grow by clinging to distortions like overvalued exchange rates, unprofitable state enterprises, and overregulation of markets. Other aspects of adjustment have proven more controversial. The mandate to aggressively and indiscriminately cut back state involvement in the economy stems more from liberal ideology than from empirical cases of successful development or logic.[60] As practiced now, structural adjustment sentences African economies to be permanent exporters of primary goods.[61] User fees levied on populations for health care and

59. Thomas M. Callaghy and John Ravenhill, "How Hemmed In? Lessons and Prospects of Africa's Responses to Decline," in Thomas M. Callaghy and John Ravenhill, eds., *Hemmed In: Responses to Africa's Economic Decline* (Columbia University Press, 1994), pp. 524–25.

60. Callaghy and Ravenhill, "How Hemmed In?" pp. 556–58; and Thomas J. Biersteker, "Reducing the Role of the State in the Economy: A Conceptual Exploration of IMF and World Bank Prescriptions," *International Studies Quarterly*, vol. 34 (December 1990), pp. 477–92.

61. Roger Riddell, "The Future of the Manufacturing Sector in Sub-Saharan Africa," in Callaghy and Ravenhill, eds., *Hemmed In*, pp. 215–47.

schooling have fallen disproportionately on the poor.[62] Beyond quarrels with the content of adjustment programs, many African regimes have bridled at the heavy-handedness of the World Bank and International Monetary Fund and their rigid, formulaic approach to economic problems.

The results of a decade of structural adjustment in Africa have been mixed. Indeed, they have been difficult to calculate because of gross variations in African compliance with the programs.[63] A consensus has developed, however, over four points. First, the tacit bargain behind structural adjustment has not been fulfilled. It was originally believed that if African countries followed the dictates of the Bank and the Fund, foreign capital would return. But as Callaghy points out, foreign investors have not come through.[64] Second, the World Bank has grudgingly acknowledged that structural adjustment does indeed impose serious short-term costs on societies.[65] Third, Africa lacks the basic social and political institutions conducive to economic growth.[66] Fourth, there is no alternative to structural adjustment in Africa. Although Africans have argued convincingly that alleviating poverty and building capacity must be part of any economic program, they have not put forward any coherent alternative to adjustment that is likely to lead to sustained economic growth. Africa simply lacks the basic capabilities and resources to attempt the Asian model of state-driven economic development.[67]

One of the biggest problems with structural adjustment programs is that they generate intense conflict yet lack mechanisms for conflict resolution. Structural adjustment impedes the development of security in several ways in Southern Africa. In the case of a fledgling democracy,

62. Reginald Herbold Green, "The IMF and the World Bank in Africa: How Much Learning?" in Callaghy and Ravenhill, eds., *Hemmed In*, pp. 61–62.

63. World Bank, *Adjustment in Africa: Reforms, Results, and the Road Ahead* (Oxford University Press, 1994).

64. Callaghy, "Africa and the World Economy," p. 40.

65. John Ravenhill, "A Second Decade of Adjustment: Greater Complexity, Greater Uncertainty," in Callaghy and Ravenhill, eds., *Hemmed In*, pp. 35–37.

66. Callaghy and Ravenhill, "How Hemmed In?" pp. 559–60.

67. Callaghy, "Africa and the World Economy"; Green, "The IMF and the World Bank"; Callaghy and Ravenhill, "How Hemmed In?"; and Tony Hawkins, "Industrialization in Africa," in Rimmer, ed., *Africa 30 Years On*, pp. 130–53.

such as Zambia, economic liberalization promises to overwhelm it from the start. Dramatic increases in the costs of staple foods and basic provisions, layoffs of tens of thousands of workers, and inadequate safety nets have produced riots in Lusaka. In the case of Mozambique, undertaking structural adjustment during the civil war proved ludicrous; the state was forced to reduce its state expenditure and involvement in the economy while fighting a war to provide basic security for its peoples. In Zimbabwe, economic liberalization has led to increased disease and food insecurity at a time of reduced state spending on health and medicine. Few adjustment programs contain adequate protection for those people hurt by the market.

Two approaches to alleviate the conflict potential of structural adjustment seem possible. The first is to use democratic practice to encourage debate, discussion, and learning between states and societies in the adjustment process. The state could explain the basis of economic policies and the international pressures for them; the society could describe its limits and pain threshold. The result would almost certainly mean slower implementation of adjustment, with a risk that some measures would have to be rescinded if popular objection were convincing enough. Structural adjustment would proceed to the degree that a social contract could be developed between rulers and ruled. This method of conflict resolution would be assisted if the international community helped fund safety-net programs to alleviate the short-term costs of adjustment. So far, however, such programs have not materialized.

Alternatively, states could resolve conflict by imposing their will. The authoritarian solution would use violence and the threat of violence to mute or at least postpone conflict over participation and distribution of goods. Those who support this approach reason that authoritarian regimes are more likely to be able to withstand societal pressures to abandon costly economic policies. Some argue that Africa's economic crisis is so severe that the risks of the democratic solution are too high and may fatally delay the imposition of needed reforms. Others justify authoritarianism by insisting that democracy will be a temporary phenomenon in Africa in any case, because it lacks facilitating conditions.

The stakes in this debate are extraordinarily high. The inability of Southern Africa to address its economic decline will exacerbate every conflict discussed in chapter 6. Some might think that the risks of the democratic approach and the odds against democratic consolidation point to the authoritarian choice, yet the authoritarian solution assumes what is problematic in both strategies: a strong state in terms of capabilities and norms of autonomy and public interest. If authoritarianism by itself led to economic development, African economies would be booming. *Both* those in favor of the democratic solution and those in favor of the authoritarian solution have to address the question of how to attain strong, normatively responsible states in Southern Africa. At least those in favor of the democratic solution have an answer to the problem of accountability and responsiveness of states, which is to build up civil society. But unless civil society is strengthened concurrently with the development of state capabilities, the result will more likely be anarchy than all good things.

CONCLUSION

Africa's economic and political problems defy easy solutions. The countries of Southern Africa need to be able to resolve outstanding and new conflicts without undue recourse to violence. National security will depend on states that can create an environment in which problem solving can succeed. Such an environment will foster inquiry, debate, and exchange, but also provide protection for peoples. Here the recommendations of the World Bank for "good governance" are half right.[68] States must establish stable property rights, honor the rule of law, practice fiscal responsibility, and create responsible accounting procedures. The World Bank's emphasis on transparency and accountability can help strengthen norms of state interest. But for states in Southern Africa to be agents of conflict resolution, good governance will have to mean more than supplying market efficiency. States will still need to protect parts of their population against market forces, regulate markets, and safeguard labor and consumers. They will need to alleviate poverty. Capabilities will need to be strengthened substantially: bureaucracies will need to tax peoples, budget wisely, protect their citizens from internal and external threats, regulate relationships, and provide basic services.

68. The World Bank, "Managing Development: The Governance Dimension," Discussion Paper, August 29, 1991.

Multiparty democracy can be an effective system for conflict resolution in Southern Africa, but strong states and strong competitive party systems are prerequisites for democracy to take hold. Change has to take place at the state level, at the societal level, and at the organizational level—the party—which bridges state and society. A crucial part of the process of making democracy work in Southern Africa will be the rediscovery of rural interests and local government. Without substantial learning on the part of both elites and masses, democracy will not take root.

Can the countries of Southern Africa develop strong states and democratic politics while undergoing economic liberalization and structural adjustment? We believe it is possible, if expectations are lowered and persistence applied. The attainment of "all good things together" will depend on flexibility in the timing and sequencing of economic reforms, public discussion, and education of key groups about economic options and their likely effects.[69] If the countries of Southern Africa take the democratic route to economic reform, international donors and financial institutions will have to radically alter the way they interact with the governments and peoples of the region. In essence, international aid and lending organizations will have to create their own capacity for conflict resolution, a point we return to in the concluding chapter.

69. "All good things together" refers to an element of American development doctrine of the 1960s. See Robert A. Packenham, *Liberal America and the Third World: Political Development Ideas in Foreign Aid and Social Science* (Princeton University Press, 1973). For explorations of how timing and sequencing of reform can better the chances for sustaining democracy, see Thomas J. Biersteker, "The Relationship between Economic and Political Reforms: Structural Adjustment and the Political Transition in Nigeria," unpublished paper, August 1990; and Larry Diamond, "Economic Liberalization and Democracy," unpublished paper, June 21, 1993.

PART 3

The Regional Question

Chapter 8

Conflict and Its Resolution in Postapartheid Southern Africa

Whether Southern Africa can attain security for all its peoples depends now on completing unfinished business: ending Angola's civil war, consolidating the peace in Mozambique, and transforming societies to support transitions to multiparty democracy in South Africa and elsewhere in the region. As it strives to accomplish these difficult tasks, the region will also face new interstate conflicts stemming from four sources: the potential for conflicts within countries in Southern Africa to diffuse and spill over borders; territorial disputes; basic issues of interdependency; and the enormous asymmetry of economic and military power in the region.

There are competing visions of how Southern Africa should cope with these conflicts. At one end of the spectrum are those who advocate that South Africa ignore the region and focus on its relations with Europe, the United States, and Asia. At the other end are those who desire an ambitious, rapid creation of a fully economically and politically integrated Southern Africa. Both solutions would produce disastrous consequences. All of the countries of Southern Africa stand to benefit from new regionwide economic and security cooperation, but that cooperation must transcend narrowly construed national interests yet shun overreaching, quixotic, unattainable goals. The challenge will be to create through multilateral negotiation a framework that links cooperation in economics and security; focuses on specific, limited issues and projects; provides immediate, tangible benefits to all member states; and sets out a clear vision of regional development and equity, while accepting that these goals must be attained slowly and pragmatically.

SPILLOVER CONFLICT IN A NEW SOUTHERN AFRICA

Security in Southern Africa is linked inextricably to the domestic security of the area's component states. But the central unit of analysis in international relations—the state—cannot be taken for granted in Southern Africa, and without strong states, domestic conflicts cannot be contained within borders.

Internal violence continues to spill over borders in Southern Africa. Refugees fleeing the renewed civil war in Angola stretch the weak carrying capacity of rural Zambia and Namibia and add to the urban migration problem in South Africa. Border conflicts flare between UNITA and the Zambian and Namibian armies.[1] Regionwide skepticism that the South African Defence Force (SADF) will abandon its destabilizing role is heightened by reports of SADF complicity in supplying UNITA. Anti-ZANU-PF Zimbabweans who fought with RENAMO continue to operate in the Mozambican province of Manica; they have reportedly tried to recruit Mozambicans to fight in Zimbabwe.[2] As late as July 1993, Zimbabwean officials complained that violence in South Africa adversely affected Zimbabwe.[3]

Even resolution of violent conflict can have negative spillover effects on regional security. During the cease-fires in Angola in 1992 and in Mozambique in 1993, weapons of those wars were resold in South Africa. A large cross-border trade in AK-47s, from Mozambique into

1. In May 1993, UNITA warned the Zambian government against stationing troops along the Angolan-Zambian border and accused the Namibian government of providing support to an Angolan government offensive against UNITA on the Namibian border; see "Angolan Rebels Warn Zambia," *Weekend Argus*, May 29–30, 1993, p. 5. The Zambian troops had been placed on the border to deal with the waves of refugees fleeing into Zambia, whom the Zambian defense minister, Ben Mwila, described as "a security risk." See "Zambia Fears Unita Attack," *Cape Times*, May 27, 1993.

2. "Zimbabwean 'Dissidents' in Manica," *SouthScan*, vol. 8 (March 26, 1993), p. 95.

3. "SA Crime 'Spilling' into Zim," *Cape Times*, July 19, 1993. One month later the Zimbabwean defense minister, Moven Mahachi, warned that continued fighting in South Africa could push refugees into Botswana and Zimbabwe. He noted that "a disorganized neighbor is a liability." "Zimbabwe Fears SA Violence," *Argus*, August 13, 1993, p. 3.

South Africa, fuels violence in Natal and the townships around Johannesburg.[4] In Swaziland, which has become a center for the illegal arms trade, AK-47s can be purchased for as little as six dollars.[5] The illegal arms trade has also spurred violent crime rates in Zimbabwe and South Africa.[6]

Countries of the region try to combat the spillover effects of domestic violence, of course.[7] Their ability to do so successfully will be hampered, however, by the intense domestic conflicts many of them will confront in coming years over participation, distribution, and identity.

TERRITORIAL CONFLICTS

Southern Africa has been remarkably free of territorial conflicts, with only a few exceptions. Angola has clashed with Zaire because Zaire supported UNITA and Cabindan rebels who demanded secession from Angola, but those conflicts stem from Angola's struggle for internal sovereignty, not from disputes over territory with Zaire. In Namibia, the troubling issue of sovereignty over Walvis Bay was resolved peacefully by the Multiparty Negotiating Forum in South Africa in 1993. Malawi, under Banda, has been the only state in the region to claim a greater historical destiny that would carve territory from neighbors (in this case, Mozambique); the Tanzanian government dissuaded Banda from pursuing such ambitions, however.

Nor has national irredentism been a problem in Southern Africa. One ethnic group, the Tswana, overlaps Botswana and the homeland of Bophuthatswana in South Africa, but Botswana has never expressed a desire for a greater Tswana nation and the homeland will be part of a

4. Greg Mills, "AK-47 is Still a Grave Threat to Stability in SA," *Cape Times*, February 16, 1993, p. 10.

5. Tendai Msengezi, "Illegal Arms Trade: An Ingredient for Crime," in Southern African Research and Documentation Centre, *Southern Africa News Features* (Harare, Zimbabwe, June 11, 1993), p. 2.

6. Msengezi, "Illegal Arms Trade," p. 1.

7. For instance, knowing that the arms problem could be arrested only through international cooperation, the governments of South Africa, Mozambique, and Swaziland agreed in June 1993 to establish a "Trilateral Crime, Security and Border Co-ordination Monitoring Committee." See "SA-Maputo Deal Aims to Stem Arms Flow," *Argus*, June 15, 1993.

new South Africa. The Ndau people, who straddle the border between Zimbabwe and Mozambique, have never made a claim for an Ndau nation.

The strong norm within the region of border stability could still be undermined, however. One current territorial dispute is between Namibia and Botswana. In 1992 skirmishes broke out over an island that sits between those two countries. Namibia and Botswana agreed to let world court arbitration decide sovereignty of the island, but the dispute has sparked regional speculation that such conflicts may become more common.[8]

Moreover, white extremists in South Africa demand an Afrikaner homeland and the Zulu-based Inkatha Freedom Party threatens civil war and secession in Natal. Jonas Savimbi and UNITA, some fear, may reorient their strategy to pursue a territorial dismemberment of Angola and an Ovimbundu state in central Angola. Likewise, many in Tanzania feel that Zanzibar might attempt to secede. Other ethnically based movements in the region would only be encouraged if any of these separatist goals were to reach fruition.

INTERDEPENDENCY CONFLICTS

Growing numbers of issues in Southern Africa know no borders. In addition to the arms trade mentioned above, refugee movements, migrant labor, water supply, drought relief, environmental degradation, and AIDS and other diseases are all issues that need a coordinated regional response. Unless they are handled with skill and tact, they could lead to severe conflicts among the nations of Southern Africa.

Refugees

There are more than two million external refugees in Southern Africa. While the international community views such individuals as a humanitarian problem, host countries see them as a security problem and a substantial economic burden. Refugee camps have been an important

8. For example, see Peter Vale, "Reconstructing Regional Dignity: South Africa and Southern Africa," in Stephen John Stedman, ed., *South Africa: The Political Economy of Transformation* (Boulder, Colo.: Lynne Rienner Publishers, 1994), p. 157.

recruitment base for those who want to use the refugees as weapons against their country of origin. Refugee camps are also fertile grounds for the spread of dangerous diseases such as AIDS, tuberculosis, and cholera.

In general, refugee camps are volatile social entities made up of individuals who have been forced to abandon their homes and culture. The refugees are cut off from the normal instruments of social communication and they have limited access to information; thus they are easily manipulated. Because of the general distribution conflict that characterizes all the countries in Southern Africa, refugees often become a target for the anger of the host country population. For example, in August 1993 residents of Soweto in South Africa accused refugees from Mozambique of "aggravating almost every problem faced by township dwellers: unemployment, adverse living conditions, official corruption, and violence," and demanded that they return to their own country. As one township resident complained, "They should go back to where they belong. We have our own unemployment problems and with them around the situation is becoming worse."[9]

Cross-Border Migration and Migrant Labor

Migrant labor has always been a central building block in the Southern African economy. War, drought, and poverty, however, have lately led more and more Southern Africans to cross national borders in search of a better life. Often that migration is to the largest cities in the region, where jobs can sometimes be found. But more often than not, urban areas become centers for masses of people without the means of subsistence.

The cities of South Africa, in particular, are potentially explosive because they are swelling so rapidly from the urban migration of black South Africans and of others from outside South Africa. Political instability, financial exhaustion, environmental degradation, and local conflict over scarce resources follow in the wake of this urbanization. Foreigners become easy scapegoats for the frustrations of long-time residents. As one Johannesburg resident complained, "These people do

9. "Soweto's New Second-Class Citizens," *Weekly Mail and Guardian*, August 6–12, 1993, p. 15.

not share 40 years of oppression with the local populations—there is no solidarity."[10]

Cross-border migration has led to a thriving regional informal market, which, although it boosts local economic activity, also fosters smuggling in drugs and weapons. Migration and the new regional informal economy have even redefined the region. As Paul Runge of the South African Foreign Trade Organization observes, "Shaba Province (in Zaire) is definitely part of Southern Africa."[11] One apartment complex in Johannesburg, the fifty-four–story Ponte City, is now known as Little Zaire.

Brain drain from the rest of the region to South Africa adds another dimension to the migration problem. Semiskilled, skilled, and professional people throng increasingly to South Africa, which generally offers higher salaries and better chances for advancement than their home countries can. Losing these people to South Africa could be economically disastrous to the home economies of neighboring countries and could become a potential conflict issue between those countries and South Africa.[12]

Water Supply and Drought Relief

Given that Southern Africa suffers periodic debilitating droughts, water is the most precious natural resource in the region. Since the region's rivers traverse national boundaries, one country's attempts to utilize a river's resources can have immense implications for neighbors. This basic interdependence prompted Botswana's deputy permanent secretary of mineral resources and water affairs, Moremi Sekwale, to

10. "A Shining Beacon in the Darkness," *Sunday Times*, June 6, 1993. The article places the number of illegal immigrants in South Africa in the "hundreds of thousands," and states that in 1992, 61,200 Mozambicans were deported for illegal residence in South Africa.

11. "Hawkers Do It Informally," *Africa South&East*, July 1993, p. 10.

12. Zimbabwe is among the Southern African countries most affected by the regional brain drain. The Zimbabwean educational system has produced highly skilled professionals, but they have been leaving for Namibia, Botswana, and South Africa. For example, in 1991 alone, 200 doctors left Zimbabwe for Botswana and South Africa. See "Slowly Bleeding to Death," *Africa South&East*, July 1993, p. 24.

caution: "If there is anything we are likely to go to war over in Southern Africa, it is water."[13]

The particular issue that raised Sekwale's warning is a Zimbabwean project to construct a 450-kilometer pipeline to supply water from the Zambezi river to the province of Matabeleland and its largest city Bulawayo, an area devastated by Southern Africa's most recent drought. The issue is a highly emotional one in Zimbabwe; many Matabeleland politicians have proclaimed that the pipeline project will signal whether Zimbabwe's ruling party is serious in its attempts to heal the wounds of its military attacks on the region in the mid-1980s. Fervor for the plan grew with a report that estimated the project would create 500,000 jobs.[14]

Other nations in the region, including Botswana and South Africa, have also developed projects to tap the Zambezi river. As already noted, Botswana objects to the Matabeleland pipeline; Zambia has raised a protest over a different Zimbabwean plan to build a hydroelectric plant along the Zambezi. In response to the proliferation of river development plans and the conflicts they have engendered, the nations of Southern Africa have prepared a protocol spelling out how the river will be shared. The proposed protocol has not yet been formally adopted, but it has, for the time being, kept conflicts in check.

Environmental Protection

The example of water resource use points to a larger set of interdependencies that could lead to interstate conflict: How shall the nations of the region cope with environmental degradation? Air and water pollution and the maintenance of biodiversity are problems of natural ecosystems that extend beyond the artificial borders of states. Some environmental problems, such as deforestation, link directly to the migration of refugees. As with the Zambezi river, the region acknowledges the potential for conflict to arise out of environmental interdependency. In June 1993 government officials and representatives of nongovernmental organizations convened a regional conference and

13. "Botswana Raises Obstacles to Zimbabwe Water Plan," *Southern Africa Monthly Research Bulletin*, March 1993, p. 11.
14. "Half Million Jobs in Matabeleland Project," *Southern Africa Monthly Research Bulletin*, April 1993, p. 5.

agreed on a set of guidelines to direct policy on land and water use, pollution, recycling, soil degradation, deforestation, and protection of wildlife habitats.

AIDS

Southern Africa faces an AIDS epidemic of crisis proportions. Between 1988 and 1992, 57,133 cases of AIDS were reported in the region.[15] This official number almost certainly understates the prevalence of the disease.[16] From 15 percent to 20 percent of the sexually active population of five countries in the region (Angola, Malawi, Tanzania, Zambia, and Zimbabwe) were estimated in 1992 to be HIV-positive. One model predicts that South Africa, which currently has a much smaller percentage of HIV-positive individuals than other countries in the region, will lose 2.5 million people to AIDS by the year 2005. The spread of AIDS in Southern Africa is exacerbated by many problems: the flight of refugees, cross-border migration, rural-urban migration, and migrant labor, among others. The AIDS epidemic, like those issues, defies national solution. It demands a regional response.

ASYMMETRY CONFLICTS IN SOUTHERN AFRICA

The fourth main source of insecurity in Southern Africa stems from regional asymmetry in economic and military power. Asymmetry conflicts are not at the foreground of present conflict resolution concerns. They are latent, however, and may ultimately decide the outcome for democracy, economic reconstruction, stability, and security in Southern Africa.

15. All figures in this paragraph are taken from Alan Whiteside, "At Special Risk: AIDS in Southern Africa," *Indicator*, vol. 10 (Summer 1992), pp. 67–68.

16. Incorrect diagnosis, inefficient medical reporting, and inadequate data collection cause thousands of AIDS cases to be missed in the official tally. In May 1993, the head of Botswana's national AIDS control program reported that Botswana alone had 60,000 patients with AIDS. See "Botswana Hit Hard by AIDS," *Cape Times*, May 31, 1993. Until mid-1992 only 277 total cases of AIDS had been reported there. See Whiteside, "At Special Risk," p. 67.

Economic Asymmetry

South Africa dwarfs the region economically, and will continue to do so even when the ANC leads the government. The region—except for Angola and Tanzania—is dependent on South Africa for its economic livelihood.

Table 8-1 illustrates the absolute economic hegemony that South Africa commands. With approximately 40 percent of the region's total population and only 20 percent of its total area, South Africa has a gross domestic product over three times that of the member states of the South African Development Community (SADC) combined, and a per capita gross national product about four times the SADC average.

Economic asymmetry undoubtedly produces tension between the countries of Southern Africa and South Africa. But that asymmetry does not have to lead to continued economic domination by South Africa. Creative possibilities for equitable regional growth and development can be pursued if business leaders and politicians so choose. The failure of such cooperative projects will leave the region open to deep, profound conflict between the haves and the have-nots.

An ANC-led government will not automatically pursue equitable regional development. ANC rhetoric proclaims the need for equitable regional economic cooperation after apartheid.[17] The ability of the ANC to match policy to rhetoric may be constrained, however, by the nature of the transitional bargain, South Africa's domestic economic crisis, and the need to work with South African business leaders, who will have their own ideas about regional economic matters.[18]

17. For a statement of ANC regional policy, see Nelson Mandela, "South Africa's Future Foreign Policy," *Foreign Affairs*, vol. 72 (November–December 1993), pp. 90–93.

18. See the ambivalent remarks of ANC economic chief Trevor Manuel in Chris Louw, "Manuel Warns of Apartheid 'Web,'" *Die Suid-Afrikaan*, October–November 1992, pp. 2–28. On the one hand Manuel promises that ANC economic policy is firmly behind the goal of regional economic cooperation "that will correct existing imbalances and promote non-exploitative relationships." On the other hand, he warns, "there can be no guarantees" that an ANC-led government will not dominate the region. He quotes, approvingly, Walter Sisulu: "Given that we shall have been left an appalling legacy of apartheid, our contribution in the economic life of the subregion is likely to be limited—at least initially."

TABLE 8–1. *Basic Economic Indicators, 1991*

Country	Area (thousands of square kilometers)	Population	Gross domestic product (millions of dollars)	Per capita gross national product (dollars)
Angola	1,247	9,700,000	7.72	610
Botswana	582	1,300,000	3.64	1,600
Lesotho	30	1,800,000	0.58	470
Malawi	118	8,800,000	1.99	180
Mozambique	802	16,100,000	1.22	80
Namibia	824	1,500,000	1.96	1,030
Swaziland	20	800,000	0.80	900
Tanzania	945	25,200,000	2.22	130
Zambia	753	8,300,000	3.83	390
Zimbabwe	391	10,100,000	5.54	650
Total SADC	5,712	83,600,000	29.50	604[a]
South Africa	1,221	38,900,000	91.17	2,560

Source: World Bank, *World Development Report, 1993.*
a. Average of the per capita figures for the ten SADC countries.

Military Asymmetry

Achieving security in Southern Africa depends on much more than redressing the economic asymmetry between South Africa and its neighbors. Also to be tackled is the basic military asymmetry between South Africa and the region (see table 8-2). These data need to be interpreted with the following cautions in mind: the reliability and validity of military data is often suspect because of the secrecy, disinformation, and lack of transparency surrounding the subject; and military capability on paper is often, for various qualitative reasons, a weak indication of actual warfighting capabilities.

Moreover, warfighting capabilities depend largely on infantry weapons and communications equipment available to an army, the training and motivation of the soldiers, the quality of intelligence gathering, and so on. We cannot assess those crucial variables here. Of particular interest in the data we do present is the level of mechanization in the armies or, put differently, the degree of protection, mobility, flexibility, and firepower of the infantry. The best indicator of mechanization is simply to divide the estimated personnel strength of the army with the

TABLE 8–2. *Quantitative Balance of Military Power in Southern Africa, by Selected Force Levels Related to Offensive Capabilities, Early 1990s*

Country	Regular troops (thousands)	Paramilitary and reserves (thousands)	Tanks[a]	Other armored vehicles[b]	Artillery[c]	Jet combat aircraft[d]	Helicopters[e]	Major warships[f]
Angola	100.0[g]	50.0	550[h]	455[h]	575	154[h]	140[h]	0
Botswana	4.5	1.0	0	20	10	8	5	0
Lesotho	2.0	0	0	10	0	0	5	0
Malawi	7.0	1.0	0	34	12	0	4	0
Mozambique	72.0[i]	5.0	100[h]	260[h]	230	40[h]	20[h]	0
Namibia	5.0	8.0	0	0	0	0	0	0
Swaziland	0.4	0.8	0	0	0	0	0	0
Tanzania	46.8	11.4	126	95	445	22	15	0
Zambia	16.2	1.2	60	100	148	51	37	0
Zimbabwe	54.6	20.0	43	218	70	64	26	0
Total SADCC	308.5	98.4	879	1,192	1,490	339	252	0
South Africa	77.4	670.0	250	4,600	420	305	163	12

Source: International Institute for Strategic Studies, *IISS Military Balance, 1991–1992* (London: IISS, 1991).

a. Heavy, medium, and light tanks. b. All types.

c. Guns and howitzers with caliber equal to or greater than 75 millimeters, and multiple rocket launchers.

d. All types of armed fighters and trainers. e. All types.

f. Ships with displacement equal to or greater than 400 tons.

g. Excludes about 50,000 UNITA regulars. The 1991 Bicesse Peace Accord stipulates the formation of a unified 50,000-strong defense force.

h. Unknown number grounded or mothballed due to lack of spare parts or maintenance.

i. Excludes about 20,000 RENAMO regulars. The 1992 Rome Peace Accord stipulates the formation of a unified 30,000-strong defense force.

estimated number of available armored fighting vehicles and personnel carriers. Thus, the lower the resulting figure, the higher the level of mechanization.

Computation along these lines yields dramatic results: ratios are 219 (to 1) for Angola, 276 for Mozambique, 492 for Tanzania, 162 for Zambia, 250 for Zimbabwe, and only 17 for South Africa. Hence, judging from quantitative data alone, the SADF soldier is vastly more protected and mobile than regional counterparts and has a substantial edge in firepower.

Assumptions about qualitative aspects of regional military capabilities also underline deficiencies in the armed forces of South Africa's neighbors and give the edge to the South African Defence Force. They include the following:

—SADF soldiers receive training superior to that given soldiers in the armed forces of neighboring countries. They are also better fed, better clothed, and, at least in the recent past, better motivated.

—Despite the mandatory U.N. arms embargo in force since 1977, the average age of the SADF arsenal is markedly lower than that of neighboring countries. The technology incorporated in South Africa's major weapon systems is newer than that of SADC member states.

—South Africa has, in contrast to all of its neighbors, a sizable and sophisticated arms industry.

—The capacity of SADC states to maintain, upgrade, and modernize weaponry is low compared to the capacity of South Africa. The situation is particularly difficult for Angola and Mozambique.

—Spare parts for, and training in, weapons supplied to the SADC states are in short supply. Consequently, large portions of the military inventories—sometimes over 60 percent—either malfunction or get put in storage. Readiness levels are therefore low. This problem is especially serious in Mozambique. Even under the arms embargo, South Africa does not have such problems on a similar scale.

The correlation of qualitative and quantitative military asymmetries to the outbreak of interstate armed conflict is doubtful, even though weaker states may feel threatened by obvious imbalances and even though the very number of weapons by itself constitutes a general threat to security. But military asymmetries may generate interstate conflict more indirectly. More powerful states may seek military solutions to political conflicts in the weaker states. For example, if the barely nascent democratization process in the three small, militarily weak countries of Lesotho, Malawi, and Swaziland leads to domestic violence and repressive measures by intransigent regimes—conflict that might spill over borders, as described earlier—then militarily stronger neighbors might intervene promptly.[19]

Also, the share of government spending devoted to security in the region is high, particularly in relation to prevailing levels of economic development and the socioeconomic needs of populations.[20] The opportunity cost of security spending is therefore exceptionally high. If perceptions of threat caused by militarily superior neighbors lead to even more spending to build up the armed and other elements of the security forces, opportunity costs rise even higher. Domestic insecurity and violence may result from dearth of social investment. Then the domestic violence may spread over national borders, precipitating interstate conflict, with predictable, unfortunate results.

TOWARD REGIONAL CONFLICT RESOLUTION: EXISTING NORMS AND INSTITUTIONS

Southern Africa lacks the kinds of security institutions that might counteract interstate conflict. First, there are no formal crisis prevention, crisis management, or conflict resolution mechanisms or institutions at the regional level. Second, there are no formal regional confidence-building measures in the military arena. Third, no process exists by

19. Thus during instability in Lesotho in 1994, Zimbabwe put forward a proposal to send regional troops into the country to enforce peace.

20. Zambia, Zimbabwe, and Botswana have all come under criticism for high defense spending. Between 1985 and 1990 the Zambian government spent on average "at least 100 percent more on the military than on education and 200 percent more than on transport and energy"; "Money in the Wrong Pockets," *Southern African Economist*, March 1993, p. 13. The World Bank and International Monetary Fund have suggested that Zimbabwe and Zambia reduce military spending as part of their economic adjustment programs. While Zimbabwe has agreed to a 40 percent cut in the size of its army, Zambia has criticized such advice as interference in security matters. See "40% Military Cut Planned under IMF Pressure," *Southern Africa Monthly Research Bulletin*, April 1993, p. 5. Botswana, as described in chapter 6, has provoked questions over its decision to build a new air force base, estimated to cost $300–$500 million.

which force levels, military arsenals, and military expenditure might be substantially reduced. On the economic side, competing institutions for managing regional cooperation proliferate, with the net effect of creating confusion and dissipating unity and focus over appropriate ways to address regional interdependencies and asymmetries.

The task of developing new institutions to grapple with the regional conflicts of the future will depend as much on the actions of the region as a whole as on the actions of a new South African regime. To the extent that the various states in the region choose a regional norm of friendship over enmity and limited national self-interest, the greater the possibility of avoiding violence and mitigating conflict arising from South Africa's preponderant economic and military position.

Security Cooperation

Security cooperation that has taken place to date in Southern Africa has been in the context of the regionwide, central conflict between white minority rule and African liberation. Forged in the 1970s, the Front Line States (FLS) of Zambia, Botswana, Tanzania, and Mozambique provided training, bases, and arms for the independence movements in the rest of the region. After Zimbabwean independence in 1980, the Front Line States cooperated to counter South African destabilization by sharing military information, consulting frequently over threats and ideas for resolving ongoing conflicts, and occasionally supplying military troops and equipment to assist one another. Military intervention by Zimbabwe and Tanzania in Mozambique at the request of the FRELIMO government saved that regime from collapse in the 1980s.

Although the presence of a common enemy often led to impressive sacrifice and unity, important differences existed between the leaders of the FLS and the liberation movements in Angola and Rhodesia (and the Angolan and Zimbabwean governments, when independence came). Solidarity among all these states declined in the late 1980s and early 1990s as new leaders came to power—leaders whose perspectives were shaped at least as much by postindependence experiences and recent events as by colonialism and the struggle of the 1960s and 1970s.

For example, while Zimbabwe and Tanzania contributed much to enable Mozambique's survival, the alliance grew strained as the price of maintaining FRELIMO grew. By the late 1980s FRELIMO's leadership was making many key decisions concerning its internal conflict without consulting its allies. Tanzania withdrew its troops from Mozambique in 1989, in part out of pique at Mozambican president Chissano's diplomacy with South Africa. When FRELIMO signed a preliminary cease-fire with RENAMO in December 1990, Zimbabwean authorities were told by fax that their troops should be withdrawn from Mozambique.[21]

The settlement of the civil war in Mozambique and the legitimacy it has conferred on RENAMO prompted Zimbabwe to rethink its ideological heritage with FRELIMO and pursue a narrow, realist foreign policy. As Edison Zvobgo, then Zimbabwean minister of public services and member of the ZANU-PF politburo, described in 1991, "It matters little to us whether the ultimate survivor in that conflict is Frelimo or Renamo. We just want a peaceful neighbor in Mozambique. We know that if it was Renamo, we would have to develop relations with them because of the imperatives of economics."[22]

The rise of multiparty democracy in Southern Africa has already proved a mixed bag for regional cooperation. On the one hand, the spread of democracy has forged new alliances between some countries and weakened other alliances. Frederick Chiluba's victory in the 1991 presidential elections in Zambia produced a sharp change in Zambia's relations with South Africa, as Zambia rushed to promote bilateral ties with its wealthy neighbor.[23] In 1993 Chiluba angered supporters of the ANC, PAC, and AZAPO in South Africa by entertaining F. W. de Klerk on an official state visit. Zambian relations with Tanzania and Zimbabwe have been chilly, too, because Chiluba has been vocal in supporting opposition groups in both countries.

21. Fadzai Gwaradzimba, "The Southern African Development Coordination Conference (SADCC): Search for Autonomy and Regional Security in Southern Africa, 1980–1990," Ph.D. dissertation, Johns Hopkins University, 1992, pp. 192–95.

22. Quoted in Gwaradzimba, "Southern African Development Coordination Conference," pp. 195–96.

23. For a discussion of Chiluba's election and the effects on regional cooperation, see Gilbert Khadiagala, "Southern Africa's Transitions: Prospects for Regional Security," in Stedman, ed., *South Africa*, pp. 171–75; and Stephen Chan, "Democracy in Southern Africa: The 1990 Elections in Zimbabwe and the 1991 Elections in Zambia," *The Round Table*, vol. 322 (April 1992), pp. 183–201.

On the other hand, the rise of multipartyism in the region has reinforced the legacy of pragmatism among Southern Africa's leaders. In the search for regional peace, both Robert Mugabe and Sam Nujoma have shown a willingness to engage leaders such as Dhlakama of RENAMO and Buthelezi of Inkatha, who traditionally have been enemies of Zimbabwean and Namibian allies in Mozambique and South Africa.

Some have suggested that there is little need for confidence or security building in Southern Africa now that National Party rule is over in South Africa. Since South Africa under apartheid was the sole source of interstate insecurity in the region, they argue, an ANC government will assure regional security.[24]

Such arguments are shortsighted and also fundamentally misunderstand the nature of the South African transition. First, as we stated earlier in this chapter, even with a new government in power in South Africa there will be no shortage of interstate conflict issues in Southern Africa. Second, regional security confidence among South Africa's neighbors has been decreasing, not increasing.[25] Third, South Africa's protracted transition will not result in a revolutionary overhaul of the South African bureaucracy and defense forces. Many of those who participated in South Africa's war against the region will remain in office, in most cases for at least five years. To attain security, military personnel and diplomats in the region must gain confidence in former enemies in South Africa.

Moreover, this argument assumes that an ANC government will pursue policies that will engender regional security. Yet there exist

24. See, for example, Herman C. Lupogo, "Southern Africa: Confidence- and Security-Building in the Military Area," in United Nations, Department of Political Affairs, *Disarmament: Topical Papers 14, Confidence- and Security-Building Measures in Southern Africa* (New York, 1993), pp. 112–13. To be fair, General Lupogo's views on the topic may have changed, since he is now one of the leading proponents of regional security-building with South Africa and an advocate of functional cooperation on a number of projects to build regional confidence.

25. Thus at regional conferences on military cooperation, discussion has been acrimonious over Botswana's military expansion and construction of a new air base and over Zimbabwe's training exercises with American special forces. These issues per se have not provoked anger among the region's militaries; instead, the lack of transparency concerning Botswana's and Zimbabwe's motives raises ire.

important differences within the ANC over the desirability of decreasing the size of the military and converting the weapons industry to nonmilitary purposes; there is no unanimity even over what likely threats South Africa will face in the future. Within the ANC's military wing, Jacklyn Cock observes, there is a "militarist tendency that is eager to maintain a powerful defense capability and not to erode the technological capacity South Africa's arms manufacturers have developed."[26]

In favor of the possibility that the region will be able to create new, durable security arrangements are two facts. First, as mentioned earlier, Southern Africa is free from irredentist movements and nationally based enmities. Second, Southern African leaders acknowledge the need for security cooperation. Every state in the region has experienced the pain of war, either directly or indirectly. With only a few exceptions, the peoples of Southern Africa and their leaders share one norm: the need for peace. The new buzzwords in Southern African regional relations are collective and common security, good neighborliness, peaceful resolution of interstate conflicts, cooperation, and integration. Political leaders know that "the combined effects of political insecurity (for example, emanating from ethnic divisions), economic insecurity (e.g., reduced economic aid to Third World countries, low productivity, etc.), social insecurity (migration in large numbers across borders, language and cultural conflicts) and environmental insecurity (droughts and desertification) may well increase general insecurity in Southern Africa as a regional security complex."[27] As one writer put it, there has been

26. Jacklyn Cock, "The Dynamics of Transforming South Africa's Defense Forces," in Stedman, ed., *South Africa*, p. 140. See also the quote by Bernie Fanaroff, a leading trade unionist in South Africa, in Peter Vale, "Southern African Security: Some Old Issues, Many New Questions," in United Nations, Department of Political Affairs, *Disarmament*, p. 45: "There is a strong argument for retaining the [arms] industry in a modified form because it represents a very large public investment in what is virtually the only major resource of technology, high level skills and sophisticated plant. It can thus play a decisive role in upgrading South Africa's manufacturing sector."

27. Pierre Steyn, "Challenges and Prospects for the SA Defence Industry Equipping the Armed Forces for the Future," *South African Defence Review*, no. 11 (1993), p. 3. These are the words of a lieutenant-general of the South African Defence Force.

extensive cross-national learning on security affairs in Southern Africa.[28]

Economic Cooperation

Southern Africa's experience with economic cooperation provides a mixed legacy for the postapartheid era. Regional institutions to address economic issues do exist, unlike institutions for security issues. But the three institutions for economic cooperation in Southern Africa offer different programs and visions of economic integration.

SACU (the Southern African Customs Union), consisting of South Africa, Botswana, Lesotho, Swaziland, and Namibia, "is the only institution in the region which meets the textbook definition of economic integration. It provides for the duty-free movement of goods and services between member countries and also for a common external tariff against the rest of the world."[29] SACU also mandates that South Africa compensate its smaller partners in order to share revenue more equitably.

The future of SACU is in doubt. Negotiations in 1969 and 1976 between the smaller countries of the union and South Africa resulted in a marked increase in revenue for the smaller countries over the last twenty years. For example, in 1990–91, South Africa received about 75 percent of the receipts, down from about 96 percent in 1970–71. In 1976 South Africa's partners demanded a stabilization procedure to assure them a rate of revenue between 17 percent and 23 percent.[30] South Africa's dwindling percentage of returns has prompted some within the country to call for an end to the union. Rumors circulated in 1993 that Finance Minister Derek Keys had decided to withdraw South Africa from the union but was dissuaded by officials from the Department of Foreign Affairs.[31]

28. Gilbert M. Khadiagala, "Security in Southern Africa: Cross-National Learning," *Jerusalem Journal of International Relations*, vol. 14 (1992), pp. 82–97.

29. Gavin Maasdorp, "The Advantages and Disadvantages of Current Regional Institutions for Integration," in Pauline H. Baker, Alex Boraine, and Warren Krafchik, eds., *South Africa and the World Economy in the 1990s* (Brookings, 1993), p. 239.

30. Maasdorp, "Advantages and Disadvantages," p. 240.

31. Ciaron Ryan, "State Moves to Stem Flow from Customs Union," *Sunday Times*, February 7, 1993, p.4.

Officials in South Africa's Department of Trade and Industry have signaled to their SACU counterparts that an alternative scheme for revenue sharing must be negotiated. Those countries also desire renegotiation of union terms because it now takes two years for them to receive compensation from South Africa. One commentator maintains that the new South African government probably will not upset the status quo on SACU in the short run, but that domestic economic difficulties may prompt the ANC to disband it in the future.[32]

SACU competes with another regional organization that aims to foster economic integration through increased trade: COMESA (Common Market for Eastern and Southern Africa), formerly the PTA (Preferential Trade Area for Eastern and Southern Africa). Originally founded to reduce tariffs among member states and provide a clearing house for member trade, the organization changed its name in late 1993 to reflect new goals—a common market for Eastern and Southern Africa by the year 2000, including a single currency and a stock market.

Given the limited accomplishments of the PTA, its renaming and declaration of greater ambitions seem bizarre. By 1993 the PTA had been in operation for nine years and had nineteen member states. Over those nine years, intra-PTA trade increased by only about 5 percent of members' total trade. As Gavin Maasdorp points out, "Six member countries—Sudan, Djibouti, Ethiopia, Somalia, Mozambique and Angola—do not have the economic capacity to play any role in the Clearing House. Some other countries do not have the political will to implement PTA protocols on trade and transport."[33] Nonpayment by member states created acute financial problems for the PTA secretariat in 1993.[34]

Two problems prevent COMESA from being an effective agent for economic cooperation. First, COMESA lumps together countries of diverse capabilities over two regions where there "are hardly any trade

32. Jan Isaksen, "Prospects for SACU after Apartheid," in Bertil Odén, ed., *Southern Africa after Apartheid: Regional Integration and External Resources* (Uppsala: Scandinavian Institute of African Studies, 1993), p. 193.

33. Maasdorp, "Advantages and Disadvantages," p. 243.

34. Alfred Taban, "COMESA Finance Ministers Meet in Sudan, *African Business*, Feburary 1994, p. 9.

links or even the basic infrastructural basis for such links."[35] Second, the PTA had no developmental component and hence little capacity or strategy to link trade with expansion of transportation and communications capabilities and industrial complementarity. To the extent that COMESA attempts to create such a component, it duplicates and competes with the newly named SADC, or Southern African Development Community.

SADC is the successor of SADCC (the Southern African Development Coordination Conference). Originally established to minimize Southern African dependence on South Africa, the organization sought to avoid pitfalls that had affected regional integration schemes throughout the third world. It aimed to coordinate development priorities among its member states and attract foreign funding for interstate projects, without pitting national interest against regional interest. Member states aligned themselves with SADCC decisions, projects, and objectives if—and only if—SADCC programs converged with their own short-term national priorities. It is therefore not surprising that SADCC found success in the areas of transportation, communications, and food security. SADCC did not provide for effective cooperation in industry and economic policy, however; conflicts emerged when Zimbabwe pursued economic policies that cost its neighbors—Zambia, Tanzania, and Botswana—revenue, jobs, and resources.

Clearly SADCC failed to create regional interests that take priority over national ones. Ibbo Mandaza, for one, suggests that SADCC furthered member-states' vertical integration with the more developed countries of the North over horizontal integration with one another.[36] In anticipation of a new South Africa, SADCC has tried to redefine itself to play a stronger, more powerful role in the region. In August 1992, SADCC was transformed into SADC, which can make treaties and seeks ambitious formal economic and political integration.

But such an ambitious program for regional cooperation can go only so far as political will can take it. There will be powerful incentives for leaders to choose national solutions over regional solutions. National

---

35. Arve Ofstad, "Will PTA be Relevant in the Post-Apartheid Era?" in Odén, ed., *Southern Africa after Apartheid*, p. 201.

36. See Ibbo Mandaza, "Southern Africa in the 1990s: Resolving the South African (National) Question," *Southern Africa Political and Economic Monthly*, vol. 4 (May 1991), pp. 10–12.

economic reform packages developed by the World Bank and the International Monetary Fund increase the likelihood of "beggar your neighbor" policies over regional economic initiatives. States may eschew cooperation and attempt to quickly forge bilateral trade relations with the new South Africa, a pattern already evident with Zambia and Mozambique.[37]

In other words, SADC may hold forth a promising vision of a future Southern Africa, but the behavior of its member states in the recent past and the enormous incentives for those states to respond nationally to the economic and political challenges ahead raise skepticism. Political will among SADC members may not be strong enough to bring the vision into being.

South African Perspectives on the Regional Economy

South Africans have three different perspectives on the proper extent of regional cooperation and the basis on which it should be structured. The first approach sees little future in regional cooperation and advocates benign neglect toward South Africa's weaker neighbors. Its proponents see South Africa's economic future tied to Europe or the Indian Ocean Rim rather than to the rest of Southern Africa. This approach is exemplified by the Nedcor/Old Mutual economic program described in chapter 5. Considered from a domestic perspective, the program is impressive—it outlines a comprehensive strategy for growth and redistribution in South Africa. The program report makes slight reference to the larger region, however. It notes that South Africa will make a "one-time gain" when trade relations with Southern Africa are normalized. Moreover, it observes that South Africa cannot be an oasis amid regional poverty; that would invite unwanted cross-border migration to its cities. But the report also contends that the low- or zero-growth rates predicted for sub-Saharan Africa, combined with "the incidence of meningitis, TB, hepatitis, and AIDS, as well as other tropical dis-

37. See the comments of Ronald Penza, Zambia's minister of commerce, trade, and industry, and Jacinto Veloso, Mozambique's minister of cooperation, in Chris Louw, "We Just Want to Get Back to Business," *Die Suid-Afrikaan*, October–November 1992, pp. 31–33. Both ministers state that their countries' national interest in working bilaterally with South Africa takes precedence over SADC and regional interests.

eases," will turn the region into a "plague area" in the 1990s. The real challenge to South Africa, therefore, is whether it will "manage to be different."[38]

David Graham, general manager of the international division of the South African Foreign Trade Organization, argues that the best target market for South African exporters is the Indian Ocean Rim. Graham cites myriad problems of trade with African countries—lack of cohesion of languages and laws, inadequate transport and telecommunications, and economies characterized by recession and chronic payment problems—and points to various regions of the Indian Ocean as South Africa's best opportunity for economic growth.[39] Officials in South Africa's Trade and Industry Department go even further: they promote an "Indian Ocean Rim trade bloc."[40]

The second approach to South Africa's economic policy acknowledges that the region can boost South African economic growth. It emphasizes quantitative expansion of existing relations and assumes that *any* expansion in trade between South Africa and the region will be mutually beneficial. This approach holds that trade liberalization and the removal of barriers to capital flows should be the main pillars on which to build regional cooperation.

South African acceptance of Namibian independence and political changes inside South Africa since February 1990 have already created a new context for increased economic interaction between South Africa and the rest of the continent. Although complete statistics are still not available, some indicators point to an appreciable increase in trade. South African exports to other African countries reportedly rose by 40 percent in 1989, with a further 22 percent increase in 1990, 26 percent in

38. Bob Tucker and Bruce R. Scott, eds., *South Africa: Prospects for a Successful Transition: Nedcor–Old Mutual Scenarios* (Kenwyn, South Africa: Juta, 1992), pp. 45–47. The report describes a future economic relationship between South Africa and the region: "Southern Africa also constitutes a sort of 'hinterland' for South Africa. Neighboring countries could well use our capabilities in engineering, construction, and contract management services as well as our manufactures. Their successful growth would enlarge our market." (P. 46).

39. David Graham, "The Indian Ocean Rim—Oppurtunities for Exporters," *South Africa Foundation Review*, March 1993, p. 8.

40. Edward West, "Indian Ocean Trade Bloc Mooted by SA," *Business Day*, July 29, 1993, p. 1.

1991, and 39 percent in the first six months of 1992.[41] Sales to Africa increased as a proportion of total exports from 6.5 percent in 1984 to around 10 percent in 1990.[42] In early 1990 the total value of trade with the rest of the continent was estimated officially at R 7 billion, R 5 billion in exports and R 2 billion in imports.[43] A year later officials put this figure at R 10 billion.[44] Some increase in investment by South African companies also is reported, with nonbank investments in the region at about R 4 billion in early 1991.[45]

The partial but progressive amelioration of South Africa's international pariah status created new opportunities for state officials and corporate leaders to gain greater access to regional decision makers and to emerge as increasingly active proponents of various plans and projects for long-term regional economic cooperation. Senior South African corporate executives have promoted the idea of a Southern African common market; managers of parastatal corporations—notably, Transnet, Portnet, Eskom, and the Development Bank of Southern Africa—have been prominent proponents of plans for cooperation in their sectors.[46]

Although these actors have not presented a monolithic front, the processes they promote have strengthened the influence of the "cooperation without transformation" approach. Indeed, André du Pisani writes that part of the National Party's strategy between 1990 and 1993

41. "SA's Trade with Africa Shows Signs of Flagging," *Southern Africa Monthly Regional Bulletin*, April 1993, p. 13.

42. Kevin Davie, "SA Firms in Major Drive into Africa," *Business Day*, March 6, 1991, pp. 1–2, quoting Paul Runge, head of the African Business Development Group of the South African Foreign Trade Organisation; and "Opening up Africa," *Financial Mail*, January 5, 1990, p. 38.

43. Michael Chester, "Trade with Africa is Booming," *Star*, February 28, 1990, p. 4, quoting Glenn Babb, a nominated member of parliament, formerly with the department of foreign affairs.

44. Marcia Klein, "Trade with Africa Now Worth R 10bn and Growing Fast," *Business Day*, March 15, 1991, p. 3, quoting Rusty Evans of the department of foreign affairs.

45. Klein, "Trade with Africa," p. 3.

46. See, for example, Michael Hastnack, "Zim Support for Shared Electricity," *Cape Times*, November 13, 1990, p. 5; "Call for Regional Airline," *Cape Times*, March 16, 1991; and Chris Freimond, "Grid and Track," *The Watershed Years: A Leadership Publication, 1991* (Johannesburg: Leadership Publications, 1991), pp. 156–57.

was "to shape the domestic, regional and international environment under which any future post-apartheid government would have to operate, thereby ensuring that its room for manoeuvre would be inherently limited." An integral part of the strategy was "to ensure and strengthen the country's hegemonic position in the region."[47]

Critics argue that expanded relations without transformation will increase the region's reliance on South Africa and intensify dependence on South African financial, investment, and commodity markets as well as transportation and communications services. A precise replication of all features of previous patterns of regional relations would be unlikely, however. Among other things, the flow of officially contracted migrant labor to South Africa, which has been on the wane since the mid-1970s, probably will not be stepped up significantly.[48]

Although a rapid expansion of existing relations may yield short-term benefits to postapartheid South Africa, critics argue that such an outcome would not be in the longer-term interests of a democratic, nonracial South Africa. A situation in which the wealthiest country in the region visibly benefited most from the new order would not be conducive to a peace-based, development-oriented approach to building security in Southern Africa. A more balanced pattern of development would be in South Africa's long-term economic interests also: without concomitant growth among South Africa's neighbors, the region's potential market will remain limited. In February 1993 statistics revealed a 12-percent drop in South African exports to Africa; some see that precipitous decline as evidence that the region has reached its hard-cash capacity to buy South African goods.[49] Indeed, a failure to promote development in other regional states could adversely affect

47. André du Pisani, "Ventures into the Interior: Continuity and Change in South Africa's Regional Policy, 1948–1991," in A. Van Nieuwkerk and G. Van Staden, eds., *Southern Africa at the Crossroads: Prospects for the Political Economy of the Region* (Johannesburg: South African Institute of International Affairs, 1991), p. 219.

48. These points are further developed in Robert Davies and William G. Martin, "Regional Prospects and Projects: What Futures for Southern Africa?" in Sérgio Vieira, William G. Martin, and Immanuel Wallerstein, eds., *How Fast the Wind? Southern Africa, 1975–2000* (Trenton, N.J.: Africa World Press, 1991), pp. 350–52.

49. "SA's Trade with Africa Shows Signs of Flagging," p. 13.

South Africa's own development efforts. Already there is a significant clandestine emigration to South Africa, a trend that could accelerate in the years ahead if existing imbalances grow.

The third approach to regional policy advocates expanding and simultaneously restructuring economic relations toward more equitable, balanced development. It stresses the need for future cooperation between South Africa and the rest of the region, based on a qualitative transformation of existing economic patterns. According to this perspective, a regional cooperation program should aim explicitly to promote equity, mutual benefit, and interdependency; it must also address extant problems created by hegemony and dependency. The pace and form of economic integration would be determined by willingness to address these issues and success at doing so.

Proponents of this approach can be found within the ranks of the new government. The ANC in 1992 officially endorsed its "Discussion Document on Economic Policy," which had been released in September 1990. The paper advocates promotion of "greater regional economic interaction along new lines which would not be exploitative." That policy would necessitate "prioritising the interests of the most deprived of our neighbours in certain areas, according to basic principles of affirmative action."[50] But as one observer notes, before the ANC can reconstruct regional dignity, it will, at a minimum, have to thoroughly transform South Africa's diplomacy.[51]

WHAT IS TO BE DONE?

All of the countries of Southern Africa stand to benefit from new regionwide economic and security cooperation, but that cooperation will have to overcome narrowly construed national interests. The challenge is to identify an institutional framework in which every state gains.

50. African National Congress, Department of Economic Policy, *Policy Guidelines for a Democratic South Africa*, Johannesburg, May 1992, p. 20. For a more recent formulation of ANC regional intentions, see Mandela, "South Africa's Future Foreign Policy," and Tripartite Alliance, *Reconstruction and Development Program, Draft Six*, released in February 1994, pp. 31–32.
51. Vale, "Reconstructing Regional Dignity," pp. 161–65.

A workable institutional framework for Southern Africa would have to address regional interaction in a multidimensional way, including politics, economics, and military security. It would also have to consider the linkages between subnational, national, and regional levels. The Organization for African Unity (OAU) advocates such an approach, as do some groups such as the Africa Leadership Forum and the Global Coalition for Africa. For instance, in 1991 a call for a "Conference on Security, Stability, Development and Cooperation in Africa" went out in the so-called Kampala Document; since early 1992, the proposal has been on the OAU agenda.[52]

Southern Africa has begun a dialogue on building a regional framework along the lines of the Conference for Security and Cooperation in Europe (CSCE), but the security concerns of Europe and Southern Africa differ in some respects.[53] In many areas, the CSCE is far too elaborate for Southern African needs. Moreover, many problems in Southern Africa are alien to the European scene. Nonetheless, a process grounded in regional norms regarding transparency of military establishments and force levels, exchange of information, confidence building, and mutual trust has tremendous appeal.

The idea of having different "baskets" (or "calabashes") to deal with economic as well as military and nonmilitary aspects of security is also attractive. The European CSCE operates with four broad baskets, thus allowing bargaining space within and among baskets. For Southern Africa, other baskets would have to be constructed. The 1992 SADC treaty posits seven areas of cooperation, which by and large translate into just such a set of baskets.[54]

52. "Kampala Document for a Proposed Conference on Security, Stability, Development and Cooperation in Africa," unpublished report, Kampala, May 1991.

53. See, for example, Peter Vale, "Points of Re-Entry: Prospects for a Post-Apartheid Foreign Policy," *South Africa International*, vol. 21 (April 1991), pp. 214–30; and Laurie Nathan, "Towards a Conference on Security, Stability, Development and Co-operation in Africa," *Southern African Perspectives*, no. 13 (May 1992). The prospects and limitations of such a framework were explored in detail at a U.N. seminar on confidence- and security-building measures in Southern Africa held in Windhoek, Namibia, February 24–26, 1993.

54. The areas are food security, land, and agriculture; infrastructure and services; industry, trade, investment, and finance; human resources development and science and technology; natural resources and environment; social

Any new regional framework for cooperation should emerge from a process of multilateral negotiation. Immediately such negotiation must confront the question posed earlier in this book: How can the powerful be convinced that it is in their interests to create institutions to militate against asymmetry in resources? Everyone agrees, even those who advise South African benign neglect toward neighbors, that South Africa cannot be an island of prosperity amid grinding poverty and violent conflict. But unlike those who preach regional avoidance, we contend that South Africa can benefit from increased trade with Southern Africa. And unlike those who argue for any expansion of trade, we believe that only a developing region can sustain expanded trade.

An alternative to market-based integration would encourage equity-based regional exchange and integration over a wide range of issues: security, trade, energy, mineral development, transportation, food security, migrant labor, and industrial policy. Linking trade-offs on diverse issues can compensate for some of the region's military and economic weakness vis-à-vis South Africa. By combining diverse sectors under one framework, progress in one functional area can positively affect other areas. For instance, to the extent that the region succeeds in building military confidence and common norms of security, more resources will be available for tackling economic issues. Conversely, if progress is made in the nonmilitary arena, then threat perceptions will be reduced, which should lead to quicker reassessments and redefinitions of national security needs.

Such a framework demands that political will—not only market forces—play an important role in structuring economic cooperation. Unlike ambitious, overreaching programs of economic integration that call for huge bureaucracies and set unreasonable goals, however, a successful framework for sectoral cooperation identifies specific projects for mutual gain. By providing a vision of long-term regional cooperation, the framework ensures that specific, short-term policies and even bilateral cooperation contribute incremental progress to regional security and development.

---

welfare, information, and culture; and politics, diplomacy, international relations, peace, and security.

Key Sectoral Issues

All nations of the region stand to benefit from working together on issues of security, trade, energy, transportation, mineral development, food security, migrant labor, and industrial policy. In some sectors certain countries stand to benefit disproportionately. The role of an overarching institutional framework is to open creative possibilities for trade-offs among issues.

SECURITY. Regional cooperation could confer several important benefits in the military security arena. First, it could build confidence and increase transparency with respect to armed forces, the quality and quantity of military arsenals, actual and perceived threats, and threat projections. One activist has suggested that as a first step the states of the region should share their national threat assessments in order to start debate on formulating a regional threat assessment.[55] Second, the region stands to gain from coordinated responses toward crisis prevention, conflict management, and conflict resolution. Third, regional cooperation could facilitate an orderly, coordinated, and mutually agreed regional disarmament process, involving reduced military expenditures, force level and hardware reductions, and, where relevant, military-civilian conversion projects.

TRADE. Postapartheid South Africa could benefit directly from greater trade with the region and the wider continent. African markets can be of particular importance for South Africa's future as an exporter of manufactured goods. While trade with non-SACU members accounts for only about a tenth of total trade, it makes up 32 percent of South Africa's manufactured exports.[56] A study of the period 1970–79 found that although the combined gross domestic product of Botswana, Lesotho, and Swaziland was only 3 percent that of South Africa, the increase in South African exports to those countries was responsible for

---

55. Laurie Nathan of the Centre for Intergroup Studies in Cape Town has been at the forefront of creating a regional discussion on the concept of regionally based threat perceptions and projections. See his unpublished paper, "Towards a Post-Apartheid Threat Analysis," prepared for a seminar of the Military Research Group, March 23, 1993.

56. Michael Chester, "Trade with Africa is Booming," *Star*, Johannesburg, February 28, 1990, p. 4, quoting Minister for Trade, Industry, and Tourism Kent Durr.

27 percent of new value added and around 67,000 jobs in South Africa's manufacturing sector.[57] In 1985, South Africa's export sales to non-SACU countries constituted 28.2 percent of total exports of chemical products, 45.8 percent of plastic products, 44.7 percent of footwear and millinery, 35.9 percent of machinery, and 26.6 percent of vehicles and transport equipment.[58] These percentages would have been higher had published statistics been available for South African trade with all African countries, including other SACU members.

Although South Africa apparently traded with almost all OAU members, apartheid posed a barrier to the full development of trade relations. In some instances, the trade was conducted clandestinely, presumably on less favorable terms. Only within the South African Customs Union did South African goods receive preference over those from outside the continent. Majority rule promises both to open up prospects for a major expansion of trade between South Africa and the rest of the continent and to improve the terms of this trade for South Africa.

However, if regional and continental markets were opened *indiscriminately* to accommodate postapartheid South Africa, problems could ensue. Existing imbalances might be enhanced, industrial development in other countries might be impeded, and trade among SADC member states might be swamped. If such consequences are to be avoided, trade agreements that address potential trouble spots will have to be concluded. Such agreements might give preferential treatment to South African suppliers over those from outside the continent, but they must also take account of the need to protect local industries and facilitate increased trade among regional states. Trade with South Africa should not be at the expense of intraregional trade or the development of local industries in SADC countries.

Trade restructuring after apartheid also has to address South Africa's advantaged position in the trade deficit. The imbalance could be offset in part if South Africa made greater use of services from the region—

57. Earl McFarland, Jr., "Benefits to the RSA of Her Exports to BLS Countries," in M. A. Oommen, ed., *Botswana's Economy since Independence* (New Delhi: Tata McGraw Hill, 1983).

58. See David Muirhead, "Trade and Trade Promotion," in Erich Leistner and Pieter Esterhuysen, eds., *South Africa in Southern Africa: Economic Interaction* (Pretoria: Africa Institute of South Africa, 1988), p. 102, table 5.

transportion, electricity, water. South Africa could also increase its visible imports from the region, along with expanding the base of imported goods. Those imports now consist largely of agricultural products and raw materials, plus a small quantity of manufactured goods from Zimbabwe. Any trade restructuring would have to investigate ways in which South Africa could increase its purchases not only of agricultural commodities and raw materials but also of certain manufactured goods. Indeed, there will be a need for South Africa to work with its neighbors to enlarge the market and create new possibilities for industrial development.

ENERGY. Cooperation with South Africa on water and electricity projects could generate significant additional revenue for regional states. Although at present the region imports power from South Africa, the situation may reverse as South Africa's consumption of electricity increases dramatically and the region develops its abundant hydroelectric resources. Some major projects for neighboring countries to supply South Africa with water resources and/or hydropower are already under way and others are planned.

In June 1993 concrete was poured for the Katse Dam, a part of the Lesotho Highlands Water Project.[59] The first phase of the project, scheduled for completion in October 1996, will supply 18.2 cubic meters of water per second to the greater Johannesburg region. Ultimately, in the year 2020, the project will supply 70 cubic meters of water per second to the Witwatersrand.[60] The treaty has come under strong criticism in Lesotho, however, because its terms were set in 1986 by South Africa and the then-military government of Lesotho, viewed by many as a South African puppet. The newly elected government in Lesotho has asked to review the agreement with Pretoria to ensure that compensation is adequate and local employment is generated by the construction of the dam.[61]

The Cahora Bassa power project in Mozambique was completed in the mid-1970s, but it has been out of action since 1985, with a third of

59. *Cape Times,* June 30, 1993.

60. Robert Davies, "Economic Growth in a Post-Apartheid South Africa: Its Significance for Relations with Other African Countries," *Journal of Contemporary African Studies,* 1993, p. 57.

61. "New Government to Review Highlands Water Scheme Agreement with Pretoria," *SouthScan,* vol. 8 (July 23, 1993), p. 223.

the pylons along the 3,000-kilometer powerlines sabotaged. Mozambique, South Africa, and Portugal signed an agreement in September 1988 to cooperate on the repair of the lines, but the agreement has not been implemented. A major wave of sabotage in the two months following the signing of the agreement more than doubled the estimated costs of repair, bringing work to a halt.[62] With an end to the war in Mozambique, however, Cahora Bassa could supply up to 8 percent of South Africa's electricity. Eskom officials have spoken of the longer-term possibility that South Africa could draw hydropower from other sources, even as far away as Zaire.[63] Chief Executive Ian McRae advocates establishing a regional electricity grid embracing South Africa and eventually all COMESA member states. McRae claims that six of these countries—Lesotho, Botswana, Swaziland, Mozambique, Malawi, and Namibia—have demonstrated a "positive approach" to the proposal. Zaire, he says, is also interested.[64]

A regional power grid does indeed hold out a number of potential advantages for both South Africa and the region. As McRae argues, greater use of regional hydropower could extend the life of South African coal reserves and reduce the environmental pollution caused by thermal stations. Supplying the larger Southern African grid would also provide revenue for neighboring states. Some marginal projects could become economically viable.[65]

But other factors also need to be taken into account. Under SADC auspices, the power grids of six member states—Botswana, Malawi, Mozambique, Tanzania, Zambia, and Zimbabwe—have been interlinked. In addition, sixty-one SADC-sponsored projects in the electricity sector are under way or are being planned.[66] The *raison d'être* of many of these projects is to reduce dependence on the South African grid. Cooperation in the electricity sphere between postapartheid South

62. See Tim Cohen, "Renamo Pledges to Halt Attacks on Eskom's Cahora Bassa Plant," *Business Day*, October 30, 1990, p. 3, for a report of a speech by Eskom's chief executive on prospects for reestablishing power supplies "within the next few years."

63. See interview with Ian McRae in "Grid and Track," p. 157.

64. "Grid and Track," p. 157.

65. "Grid and Track," p. 157.

66. *SADCC Annual Progress Report, 1991–1992*, Maputo, Republic of Mozambique, January 29–31, 1992, pp. 99–102.

Africa and the rest of Southern Africa should not lead to marginalization or sidelining of these projects. Their importance for local development and a more balanced pattern of regional development needs to be upheld when reducing ties with South Africa ceases to be a political imperative. Important also is that a regional power grid be controlled and administered by the *region*, not exclusively by South Africa.

MINERAL DEVELOPMENT. Minerals policy is another potential area for future cooperation. SADC member countries produce significant quantities of the following mineral products: oil, copper, diamonds, gold, nickel, ferrochrome, cobalt, steel, asbestos, coal, chromite, zinc, tin, iron ore, silver, and lead. The most valuable are oil (Angola); diamonds (Botswana, Namibia, and Angola); copper (Zambia, Zimbabwe, and Botswana); gold (Zimbabwe); nickel (Zimbabwe and Botswana); ferrochrome (Zimbabwe); and cobalt (as a by-product of copper production in Zambia, Zimbabwe, and Botswana). In some cases the SADC members produce significant proportions of world output: 15 percent of cobalt, 18.7 percent (excluding Namibia) of diamonds, 7.2 percent of ferrochrome, 4.6 percent of chromite, 4.8 percent of asbestos, and 4.0 percent of nickel.[67]

The extent of South Africa's mineral wealth is well known. It has 44 percent of the world's known gold reserves, 82 percent of manganese, 78 percent of platinum, 56 percent of chrome ore, 47 percent of vanadium, 24 percent of diamonds, 14 percent of zirconium, 11 percent of titanium, 37 percent of aluminosilicate ore, and 10 percent of known coal reserves. In terms of current output, South Africa produces about one-third of the world's gold and about two-thirds of the world's platinum; for other minerals, figures are 36.2 percent for chromite, 16.8 percent for manganese ore, 10.6 percent for uranium, and 43.9 percent for vanadium. South Africa also accounts for about 5.2 percent of world coal exports.[68]

Future cooperation in mineral production would call for SADC members to supply South Africa with mineral products, including Angolan oil. In turn, South Africa might supply its neighbors with both minerals and—more important—mining technology. Beyond this reciprocal

67. Philip Paul Jourdan, *Provisional Implications for the SADCC Mining Sector of a Post-Apartheid South Africa*, report prepared for the SADCC Mining Sector Coordinating Unit, Johannesburg, March 1992, p. 53.
68. Jourdan, *Provisional Implications*, pp. 30–31.

trade, the entire region might work together to develop a strategy for mineral marketing and raw materials processing.

TRANSPORTATION. There are two dimensions to regional transport relations. The most important concerns regional use of ports and railways in South Africa as opposed to those in the SADC states. The second is the decline in South African use of facilities in other regional states, particularly Mozambique.

Pretoria's destabilization policies largely shaped both dimensions. As an integral part of "total strategy," South Africa sought to secure a monopoly over regional traffic. Pretoria had a critical strategic interest in securing additional leverage over regional states. In pursuit of this objective, South Africa in the 1970s and 1980s attempted—often successfully—to divert traffic that might otherwise have passed through the ports and railways of SADC states. Alternative routes, particularly those through Mozambique and Angola, were regularly sabotaged by South African–backed armed bandits; special contract rates, with discounts of up to 50 percent of the normal fee, were offered in an effort to lure traffic away from alternative routes.[69]

The combined effect was that by 1984–85 regional traffic passing through South African ports had increased to one and one-half times the 1981–82 level. Diversion of traffic to and from Malawi and Swaziland accounted for much of the increase. Substantial tonnages of cargo from Zaire, Zambia, and Zimbabwe, which normally would have passed through Mozambican and Angolan ports, were also rerouted through South Africa.[70] At the same time, South African traffic using the port of Maputo declined sharply, from 6.8 million cargo tons in 1973 to 420,000 tons in 1988.[71]

SADC was not passive in the face of these trends and developments. The organization placed priority on the rehabilitation of transport

69. See Jeanne Stephens, "A Baixa de Preços e a Preservação da Dependência: A Resposta Sul Africana às Iniciativas do Sector de Transportes em Moçambique e na SADCC," *Estudos Mocambicanos*, no. 5–6, 1986.

70. *Financial Mail*, August 15, 1986.

71. The 1973 figure is from Republica Popular de Moçambique, Commisão Nacional do Plano, *Informação Estatistica*, complemento A, Maputo, May 1984, p. 102; the 1988 figure is from *Estatistica dos Transportes e Communicacoes, 1989* (Maputo: Comissão Nacional do Plano Direccao, Nacional de Estatistica, 1989), p. 25.

routes both to reduce vulnerability to Pretoria's pressures and to promote trade among its members. In 1992 SADC counted 216 transport-related projects in various stages of planning and implementation. Foreign finance worth $2,875 million was secured to support these projects, and a further $3,191 million is currently under negotiation.[72] Although these SADC projects did not fundamentally alter the trend toward increased dependence on the South African transport system, they achieved significant results. The Beira Corridor Programme (BCP), begun in 1986, led to a modest increase in traffic using the port (transit traffic, plus Mozambican exports and imports), from 1.33 metric tons in 1986 to 1.83 metric tons in 1990.[73] SADC investments in the transport sector will yield full returns only after the next few years, however, and the outlay will not be recouped until several years after that. The still-unfinished "core projects" of the BCP will afford Beira an annual capacity of 5 million tons.

Restructuring regional transport relations in the postapartheid era will have to start with these points in mind:

—The concentration of regional traffic through the ports of South Africa is abnormal—a product, in part, of South African economic and military aggression. Restructuring will therefore have to aim at rectifying existing distortions and imbalances.

—Several SADC countries must be acknowledged as the natural hinterland for ports in Mozambique and Angola—not South Africa.

—SADC should be entitled to recoup and benefit from investments it made in transport facilities as part of the struggle against apartheid.

South African transport authorities will have to stop "poaching" cargo from SADC ports. Tariffs should be structured so that the shorter distances to Mozambican ports from several SADC countries reflect real savings for customers. Technical support should also be provided by South Africa to regional transport authorities on reasonable terms, and the successor to Safmarine (South Africa's shipping parastatal) should ensure that regional ports have adequate shipping services. In addition, South Africa and Mozambique will have to come to a mutually accept-

72. *SADCC Annual Progress Report, 1991–1992*, p. 38.
73. Figures are from the statistical annex to "Review of Nordic Technical Assistance to the Beira Corridor Authority," a report prepared by the Institute for Transport Economics under commission from NORAD (Transport-Økonomisk Institut), Oslo, 1991.

able agreement over the use of Maputo harbor by South African concerns. Ideally, the agreement would specify fixed tonnages and provide for a reasonable mix of high-rated as well as bulk cargo.

FOOD SECURITY. SADC currently has 125 ongoing or planned projects in the area of food security, agriculture, and natural resources. Some $141.62 million in external funding has been secured to support these projects and $230.75 million more is under negotiation. The projects comprise agricultural research and training, livestock production support, fisheries, forestry and wildlife, and soil and water conservation.[74] They also seek to ensure regional food security by setting up an early warning system to identify potential food deficits and establishing a regional food reserve. A democratic South Africa could make a significant contribution to such programs since it has a strong technical and resource base, and it could also benefit from the experience of ongoing regional projects.

MIGRANT LABOR. One of the thorniest questions of regional relations concerns migrant labor. As indicated earlier, the recent past has seen considerable fluctuations and manipulations of migrant labor flow. In the mid-1970s the South African Chamber of Mines began a program of "internalization" to increase the percentage of South Africans in the mine labor force. "Foreign" workers made up over 80 percent of the force in 1973; by the end of the 1980s, that figure was 40 percent, with the absolute number declining from 336,000 in 1973 to 159,253 in 1991.[75] There has also been some attempt to differentiate between external states supplying commuter labor and those supplying only ad hoc or emergency labor needs. In addition, migrant labor flows have been subject to political manipulation. In October 1986 Pretoria banned the recruitment of Mozambican novices and prevented in-service Mozambican workers in the less-skilled job categories from renewing their contracts. When the ban was lifted in November 1988, the Chamber of Mines estimated that the total number of Mozambican mine workers had fallen from about 60,000 to 47,000.[76] If the South African mining industry continues to experience difficulties, significant layoffs and

74. *SADCC Annual Progress Report, 1991–1992*, p. 36.

75. The 1973 figures are from Jonathan Crush, Alan Jeeves, and David Yudelman, *South Africa's Labour Empire: A History of Black Migrancy to the Gold Mines* (Cape Town: David Phillip, 1991), p. 101. The 1991 figures are from Chamber of Mines of South Africa, *Annual Report*, 1991, p. 60.

76. *Business Day*, November 16, 1988.

perhaps even closings of marginal mines will result. Migrant workers from neighboring states are likely to be hurt by these developments.

South Africa's migrant labor policy has produced important repercussions for the economies of supplier states. The overall reduction in recruitment has been at a rate and pace determined by mining capital, not by the interests of supplier states. It has proceeded more rapidly than the capacity of these states to productively absorb former migrants has grown. The result is that the unemployment inherent in the process of mechanization—which underlies the internalization program—has been exported to the supplier countries, whose rural economies have been forced to to bear the economic and social costs. Moreover, this "exported unemployment" has been spread unevenly among supplier states: Mozambique has suffered most, and Botswana has been more affected than either Lesotho or Malawi.

A broader regional approach to migrant labor will have to recognize that supplier states cannot, without considerable economic and social disruption, immediately withdraw from the system. Their capacity to extricate themselves from what is ultimately an exploitative relationship depends on the generation of domestic employment, and particularly on the transformation of labor reserve areas. Supplier states need stability of both earnings and employment from migrant labor while programs of economic regeneration are implemented. Any new cooperative approach to this question during the postapartheid era therefore would have to involve both short-term measures and a long-term program of reconstruction. In the short term, new agreements on the supply of migrant labor will have to tilt the balance of advantage toward supplier states, with the following considerations in mind:

—The contribution of foreign migrant workers to the creation of wealth in the South African mining industry needs to be recognized. Migrant workers should be granted rights identical to those of South African workers regarding wages, security of employment, opportunities for promotion, benefits, trade union membership, and so on. Such workers should not be penalized for their "foreignness"; indeed, certain categories of long-serving foreign migrants must be granted the same rights to settle in the industrial areas of South Africa as will presumably be accorded South African workers (including those from the Bantustans) in a liberated South Africa.

—The ability of mining managers to manipulate the flow of migrants at will has to be constrained by the broader interests at stake. The importance to supplier states of stability of employment and earnings from migrants during an interim period, at least, will have to be acknowledged. Binding agreements on numbers—taking account of supplier states' interests—will have to be negotiated.

—The whole system of benefit and compensation payments for migrant workers will have to be reexamined. Bureaucratic delays in payment processing are one problem; also, the health services of supplier states often bear the hidden costs of diseases contracted in South African mines.

INDUSTRIAL POLICY. The most direct way for the region to address the problems of asymmetrical trade and migration would be to develop a common industrial policy. If South Africa and the other countries of the region can work out a cooperative policy on the attraction and location of industry, then the stage would be set for regionwide equitable development. As John Ravenhill points out, however, the location of industry is the largest problem that faces regional development: "Not surprisingly, they [third world states] see little benefit in facilitating their neighbors' industrialization if it comes at the expense of their own. Disputes over the distribution of gains from cooperation have been the principal factor causing the breakup of regional schemes among developing countries."[77]

South Africa dominates the region in industrial capacity. Some corporations that located outside South Africa because of sanctions have expressed interest in moving back to South Africa, which would exacerbate asymmetries in the region. A key problem in gaining South Africa's participation in a regionwide industrial cooperative scheme is the failure of SADC to confront the issue over the last ten years.

Future Regional Cooperation

Southern Africa will face no shortage of conflicts in the future. But if the region can draw on its legacy of pragmatism and revive and adapt its history of regional solidarity for a new era with different challenges, Southern Africa can establish durable, flexible institutions to manage those conflicts and build the foundation for long-term regional cooperation. The mere fact of enormous asymmetry between South Africa and its

77. John Ravenhill, "Reversing Africa's Economic Decline: No Easy Answers," *World Policy Journal*, vol. 7 (Fall 1990), pp. 724–25.

neighbors does not preclude the creation of a peaceful, secure region. Indeed, in one of the first and most important studies of regional security, Karl Deutsch concluded that the presence of a regional giant can be a positive force for building regional peace.[78] The notion that South Africa—the region's giant—will be too inwardly focused to take the lead in creating an equitable region mistakenly assumes that such a task would impede resolution of its domestic crisis. In fact, a growing, developing Southern Africa can help meet the needs of South Africa's people.

78. Karl W. Deutsch and others, *Political Community and the North Atlantic Area: International Organization in the Light of Historical Experience* (Princeton University Press, 1957), pp. 137–39.

Chapter 9

A New Southern Africa?

In 1993 parts of Southern Africa were headed in different directions. In February Angola's renewed civil war took more than 16,000 lives.[1] Pictures of the war were few, but one brave camera crew from Portugal managed to get to Huambo, where fierce street battles between UNITA and MPLA troops had killed 6,000 people.[2] The crew filmed MPLA soldiers carrying corpses into a building where harried nurses recorded the names of the dead. What the narrator of the film did not mention was that the building had a history: it was first a classroom, and then in September 1992 it was a polling place that one of us had visited as an observer to Angola's first national election. Now, five months later, it was a morgue.

In February, as Angola achieved the dubious distinction of hosting the world's deadliest war, two events took place that portended the beginning of a new era for the region. In South Africa the National Party and the African National Congress announced that they had reached agreement on the substance of and mechanisms for a transition to democracy. Later that month, generals and diplomats of every country in Southern Africa—including unofficial representatives of the de Klerk government—met in Windhoek, Namibia, under U.N. auspices to discuss the creation of new institutions for regional security.

Will South Africa and Mozambique follow the progression of polling place to morgue? Or will the elections of April 1994 in South Africa and those scheduled for Mozambique in October 1994 prove that Angola's return to civil war is an anomaly in a region where peace and pragmatism have become the norm?

---

1. Victoria Brittain, "The Worst is Yet to Come in Angola," *Weekly Mail*, February 5–11, 1993, p. 15.
2. "6,000 Dead in Huambo Battle," *Cape Times*, February 15, 1993.

This book has described the dying of an old order, but as the title insists, a new Southern Africa is not yet born. Apartheid and settler colonialism and the fight to overcome them leave behind legacies that stand in the way of a secure region. To overcome those legacies requires the domestic consolidation of Southern African countries through strong states, thriving civil societies, and functioning markets. Southern African leaders must also create regional institutions to address conflicts of interdependency and asymmetries of economic and military power.

The future path of the region will be decided mostly by its peoples and leaders, but the international community can help those who want to pursue peace. It is customary to rally support for aid and assistance by invoking the nightmarish consequences of failure. Such a strategy, however, ignores the remarkable achievements of the region. The birth of a new Southern Africa deserves international help because the region can succeed and provide the continent with an important motor for change.

REAPING THE WHIRLWIND: CUMULATIVE LEGACIES

The creation of a new Southern Africa must face constraints set by the distant and immediate past. Racist doctrines developed in the 1800s continue to reverberate today. Political freedom has yet to translate into social and economic equality in the region. Divide-and-rule colonial strategies continue to plague nation building in the region. The resumption of civil war in Angola, the recalcitrance of Mangosuthu Buthelezi in South Africa, and the need to transform RENAMO from a killing machine into a political party in Mozambique all stem in part from the attempts by white settlers to sow disunity and set African against African. Leaders in Angola and Mozambique—states in name only—must still transcend the effects of Portuguese colonialism. Regional economic patterns established in the early 1900s persist: almost all roads (and train tracks) lead to South Africa. National economic patterns that centralized white landholding and wealth created an enduring economic inequality in Southern Africa. The conjoining of capitalism and racism in the region for hundreds of years persuaded some Africans that the two are inextricably linked.

More recent influences of the past—states with extremely diverse populations; new countries without human and social capital; a model of nation building in which the state is perceived to be in a zero-sum conflict with society; a liberation struggle supported by the socialist East, not the capitalist West—compounded early legacies. Additional, specific legacies derive from apartheid and regional destabilization, the enormous costs that these policies have exacted, and the use of violence to seek justice. Together these legacies produced a region rife with enduring conflicts, pregnant with new conflicts waiting to emerge, and devoid of the capacity to resolve them.

The central conflict in the region—the attempt by white South Africans to maintain racial domination at home and in the region—leaves tremendous socioeconomic destruction and human costs. Different sources estimate that between 1.2 and 1.9 million people were killed in Angola and Mozambique during 1980–88 as a result of the wars there. At least 850,000 of these were children under the age of five. The resumption of war in Angola in 1992 and casualties in political violence in South Africa between 1984 and 1993 adds another 120,000 deaths to the total. Millions of land mines placed during the regionwide war will continue to maim and kill. In Angola and Mozambique, close to 7.5 million people—almost half the rural population in the two countries—were forced from their homes and land. The majority were displaced inside their own country, while another 1.5–2 million were forced to flee to neighboring countries, thus imposing a heavy burden on their countries of refuge. One study covering the period 1980–88 put the loss at $60.5 billion, which is more than three times the total foreign debt of all the SADC member states, or some four times the value of all development assistance received by these countries in the same period.[3]

The war also exacted a terrible toll on Southern Africa's wildlife and ecology. One hundred thousand elephants were slaughtered in southern Angola in the 1980s, mainly by UNITA forces who used the ivory to pay South Africa for its support. Similarly, Mozambique's loss is about 50,000 elephants, or 90 percent of the country's elephant population at the time of independence in 1975.[4] Deforestation and soil erosion have

---

3. UNICEF, *Children on the Frontline: The Impact of Apartheid, Destabilization and Warfare on Children in Southern and South Africa* (New York, 1989), annex A, pp. 35–38.

4. Phyllis Johnson and David Martin, *Apartheid Terrorism: The Destabilization Report*, report prepared for the Committee of Commonwealth Foreign Ministers on Southern Africa (London: James Currey, 1989), pp. 11, 44.

followed in the wake of the movement of refugees and displaced persons. An area extending 100 kilometers around Maputo, Mozambique, is now barren of trees; half of Mozambique's 9,700-kilometer coastal mangrove forest has been cut down.[5]

Finally, there are costs that cannot be measured. How can one tabulate the cost of hundreds of thousands of children and young people traumatized for life by war experiences? In Angola and Mozambique, where war has been under way since the early 1960s, life expectancy is about forty years, and half of the populations are under twenty; war is the normal state of affairs for most. In South Africa a substantial number of black youths see violence as an integral part of their identity. How much does it cost to mend the torn social fabric of such societies?

PARTIAL TRIUMPHS OF CONFLICT RESOLUTION

Given the ferocity of fighting, depth of conflict, and intensity of passions, one would not have predicted that Southern Africa would be the site of remarkable efforts to make peace. Yet in the last fifteen years civil wars in Zimbabwe and Namibia and an interstate war between Angola and South Africa have ended through negotiation. South Africa has, against all odds, found a way out of the dead end of apartheid and white domination. In Mozambique a precarious peace continues to hold.

But even the resolution of conflicts leaves mixed legacies. In almost all cases resolution was partial and failed to address key aspects of the conflict. Indeed, the pattern of conflict resolution in Southern Africa has been to resolve conflicts of political participation at the expense of not resolving intense conflicts over the unequal distribution of wealth. In Angola, Mozambique, Namibia, South Africa, and Zimbabwe, conflict resolution came only after the dispossessed used violence to impress upon the powerful the costs of continued oppression. Although the region has been fortunate to possess leaders and peoples who were pragmatic enough to make peace, the legacies of violence—mental and physical—still abound.

5. Mutizwa Mukute, "Environment: Another Victim of War," *Southern Africa News Features*, February 1993, pp. 1–2.

Unfinished business plagues Southern Africa. A new South Africa must still overcome recalcitrant parties tied to the old apartheid order, which use terror to fight change. The new government must begin to meet the expectations of followers who want security and prosperity. Civil war continues in Angola; Mozambique could easily return to the carnage of two years ago. The region's peoples and leaders must draw from two positive legacies of the recent past—enormous pragmatism and regional cooperation—to end the ongoing violence.

REQUISITES FOR REGIONAL SECURITY

The ending of apartheid in South Africa does not mean that the people of Southern Africa will achieve dignity, justice, and basic human rights. The ending of violence in Angola and Mozambique will not by itself confer security on the peoples of those countries. Instead, they are first steps. Regional security will depend on domestic consolidation—the strengthening of states and civil societies to provide an environment conducive to conflict resolution—and a regional institutional framework that can help states cooperate to avoid violent conflicts over interdependence and asymmetries of power.

In Southern Africa conflict between weak states and embattled societies has spilled over borders and endangered the whole region's security. Even as old conflicts expire, new ones arise. A complex of issues concerning participation, distribution, and identity could lead to violence in almost every country in the region. Such conflicts will most likely be intensified if Southern Africa cannot overcome its crisis of economic productivity. Unfortunately, with the exception of Botswana, the countries of the region lack the capabilities to resolve their pressing conflicts and gnawing crises.

Multiparty democracy offers the best set of arrangements for conflict resolution and problem solving, but establishing it hinges on strong states, vibrant party systems, and learning. Open conflict between eviscerated states, free markets, and threatened civil societies has to be replaced by a healthy and creative tension between states that can govern and societies that are autonomous and organized to defend their interests. Several changes at the national level in perception and function can help create an environment in which problem solving can flourish:

—States and societies need to stop regarding each other as adversaries in a zero-sum battle wherein one gains and the other loses.

—States need to be strengthened so that they have the capacity to regulate conflict, social relations, and economic activity within their borders, thus engendering both individual welfare and national growth and development.

—Societies need to be strengthened so that they can hold states accountable and can facilitate market-based, socioeconomic development.

The development of stronger states and societies in Southern Africa is a necessary condition for security, but it is not sufficient. The countries of the region are tied together through economic and social interdependencies that pose challenges and opportunities. The challenges are twofold. First, some of the interdependencies—the prevalence of AIDS and environmental destruction, for example—defy national solutions; only regional cooperation can address such crises. Second, some of the interdependencies—cross-border migration, use of natural resources, and migrant labor—are issues with the potential for explosive conflict. The opportunities are also twofold. First, the existence of so many interconnections among the nations of the region means that the smaller countries have bargaining leverage with a new South Africa, which can moderate the conflict potential of asymmetries of economic and military power. Second, if Southern Africa can cooperate to solve its conflicts of interdependencies and asymmetries, it will lay the foundation for deeper economic integration, which will strengthen the region's position in the world economy.

We caution, however, against overambitious, rapid programs of regional integration. Purely market-led integration in Southern Africa would exacerbate inequalities between South Africa and its neighbors. Political plans to create a Southern African economic community lack the requisite will from national leaders. Instead, regional cooperation should stem from an integrated set of negotiated agreements covering at least security, environmental protection and natural resource use, mineral development, migrant labor, and AIDS prevention. The region should work toward an eventual policy on industrial location.

Gradual change, careful pacing and sequencing of measures, and establishment of mechanisms to address regional imbalances will require the full attention of political executives. Along the road to a fully integrated economic and political community, countries will find that functional cooperation, sometimes involving only bilateral partnerships, can be a big step forward.

THE NEED FOR INTERNATIONAL ACTION

Writing in *Foreign Affairs* in 1993, Nelson Mandela argued that the major challenge to the post–cold war world concerned diversity in a world of increasing interdependence. Those countries that make diversity and tolerance strengths will prosper in the post–cold war world, he contended, while those that cannot accommodate diversity will implode like Bosnia or many of the countries of the former Soviet Union.[6] The implications of his warning are clear for South Africa: its extraordinary mix of peoples, races, and ethnicities will either create a country that will be a positive force for development and stability in the region, or those differences will destroy the country and its violence will be exported to all of Southern Africa.

The international community has a stake in a successful South Africa. First, a world marred by ethnic hatred and genocidal impulses desperately needs to see diverse peoples coexisting within borders and cooperating to achieve political and economic goals. Second, South Africa, with the continent's largest economy and best infrastructure, can contribute to Africa's recovery. Third, South Africa, like Namibia, Zimbabwe, and possibly Mozambique, can show the world that peoples long at war can make peace.

The international community can help those in Southern Africa who desire a more secure region, but too much emphasis has been placed on dollar amounts of aid and assistance. Obviously, more financial aid could help the region, especially aid in the form of a fund for reconstruction to help rehabilitate war-torn societies. More important than increased aid, however, are measures to establish an international environment that will maximize Southern Africa's chances for sustainable security, economic growth, and political democracy. Such measures require that the international community bring more coherence to peacemaking efforts and more humility to development efforts.

6. Nelson Mandela, "South Africa's Future Foreign Policy," *Foreign Affairs*, vol. 72 (November–December 1993), pp. 86–97.

The current conflicts in Angola and Mozambique require that the United Nations and its member states develop a strategy for peacebuilding and intervention in civil war. Rules need to be established to punish domestic parties, such as UNITA, that fail to uphold a commitment to negotiated settlement and democratic elections. We do not advocate U.N. military intervention to defeat recalcitrant parties,[7] but there are a host of alternatives short of active combat that could help isolate obdurate leaders. One step would be to make such leaders responsible for the effects of their actions by indicting them for war crimes, and to obligate any U.N. member to arrest them for international trial. Another step would be for the international community to police international supply lines to warmongering parties. Another possibility would be to put an international diplomatic embargo on such parties and thus curtail their ability to represent themselves in the international community.

In Mozambique the United Nations should prepare for the possibility that RENAMO, like UNITA in Angola, might renege on its commitment to democratic elections. The international community tacitly assumed that everyone in Angola would honor the terms of agreement; when UNITA backed out, the United Nations had no well-thought-out response. In the case of Mozambique, too much faith is being placed in the demobilization process in the belief that RENAMO will not return to war if it has no guns. That logic might hold if the United Nations had the will to enforce demobilization strictly. But as of April 1994 demobilization still had not succeeded in Mozambique, and the United Nations had restated its commitment to elections in October 1994. The United Nations is not at fault for failing to impose demobilization—such action could stray into peace enforcement. Nor should elections be delayed if demobilization does not take place—that would give a recalcitrant party a veto over the peace process. But the United Nations can, and should, work to deny international support to any party that violates an agreement after an election, and thus minimize the likelihood of its return to war.

In addition to improving its implementation of peace agreements, the United Nations should make it a priority to stay engaged in those

7. For a discussion of the dangers inherent in such interventions, see Stephen John Stedman, "The New Interventionists," *Foreign Affairs*, vol. 72 (Special issue, 1993), pp. 1–16.

countries just emerging from years of civil war. The United Nations cannot get involved in all of the conflicts around the world; it should therefore give preference to those countries whose leaders commit themselves to peace. The U.N. commitment to cases like Mozambique or Namibia should go beyond the narrow confines of getting to the first election; programs for the integration of former combatants into society, the rehabilitation of those physically and psychologically scarred by violence, and the reconstruction of the economy are all essential to stable peace. Another compelling need is for programs to slash the enormous number of guns in countries like Mozambique.

The United Nations should also work to improve early warnings of violent domestic conflict and act in concert with neighboring countries to minimize the spillover of such violence. At least two new possibilities loom for diffusion of violence in Southern Africa. Elections in Malawi might fail to resolve that country's participation conflict; if civil war breaks out there, ramifications will be immediate for Mozambique, where violence could easily spread as refugees cross borders and armed groups seek easy sanctuary. In the case of South Africa, armed adherents of Buthelezi and Inkatha may seek bases and sanctuary in Lesotho, Swaziland, and southern Mozambique.

Even beyond peacekeeping and peacebuilding, the international community can contribute to conflict resolution by helping countries build stronger states and vibrant civil societies. If in the past aid and assistance donors have focused too much on the state and ignored the development of an autonomous civil society, the new fashion of aiding civil society at the expense of the state threatens to tilt the balance in the other, also unhealthy, direction. If development is to succeed in Southern Africa, it will demand both autonomous civil societies and strong, responsive states. Security will not arise out of the one-sided glorification of civil society.

The international community should encourage the countries of Southern Africa to continue with their processes of political liberalization and democratization. But as we pointed out in chapter 7, the simultaneity of democratization and structural adjustment places a huge burden on the region. The crisis of economic productivity is so vast and compelling that it is impossible to counsel against the structural adjustment programs of the international financial institutions. It is therefore incumbent on the donor nations of the world, as well as on the World Bank and the International Monetary Fund, to take bold steps to maximize the chances for sustainability of simultaneous political and economic liberalization.

A first step would be to ease the debt burdens of the nascent democratic governments in Southern Africa. With the exception of Botswana, Namibia, and South Africa, the countries of the region reel from debt distress. Large levels of debt compared to gross domestic product produce two negative consequences for sustained economic growth: first, capital from exports goes toward debt repayment rather than investment; second, large levels of debt deter investor confidence.[8] The individual donor nations of the world have recognized the deleterious effects of African debt, and many have written off or reduced bilateral loans.[9] A substantial part of African debt is carried by the international financial institutions, however. Neither the International Monetary Fund nor the World Bank has shown an inclination to reduce debt, even though both of those institutions realize that a substantial amount of African debt will never be collected. As Jeffrey Herbst recommends, the U.S. government should take the lead in persuading the international financial institutions to construct creative debt reduction programs that will reward those countries in Africa that are reforming their economies.[10]

A second step would be to bolster the ability of Southern African countries to participate in the international economy. Thomas Callaghy and John Ravenhill argue that the international community should work to facilitate market access for African exports and improve prices for commodities. Developed countries could set up, for an extended period, special tariff exclusions to promote export opportunities for African goods. The international community could help African countries establish commodity agreements to improve their collective bargaining ability.[11]

---

8. Jeffrey Herbst, *U.S. Economic Policy toward Africa* (N.Y.: Council on Foreign Relations, 1993), pp. 53–54; and Thomas Callaghy and John Ravenhill, "How Hemmed In? Lessons and Prospects of Africa's Responses to Decline," in Callaghy and Ravenhill, eds., *Hemmed In: Responses to Africa's Economic Decline* (Columbia University Press, 1994), p. 552.

9. David F. Gordon, "Debt, Conditionality, and Reform: The International Relations of Economic Restructuring in Sub-Saharan Africa," in Callaghy and Ravenhill, eds., *Hemmed In*, p. 100.

10. Herbst, *U.S. Economic Policy*, pp. 55–59.

A third step would be for the international financial institutions to seek "social contracts" with the states of Southern Africa. Southern Africa's domestic economic and political problems deny simplistic, formulaic solutions; policy advice developed by the financial institutions must take into account the political constraints and human limits of the countries involved. Solutions that are imposed upon these countries will not be sustained, which means that the international aid and donor organizations should commit themselves to a lengthy process of dialogue, debate, and learning with societal and state leaders in Southern Africa. Here Botswana's example is compelling: that country has been aided immensely by international economists who have been willing to educate and learn from politicians and economists in Botswana. From the beginning the international experts set as their benchmarks not only short-term, quality economic decisions but also the ability of Botswana's politicians and economists to make good policy decisions on their own. For Botswana to succeed, its leaders had to learn the economic criteria of good policy decisions; the international economists had to learn the political concerns of Botswana's leaders.[12] While mutual education may sound naive, many experts now acknowledge that such learning is indispensable if structural adjustment is to work in Africa.[13] And if countries are implementing democracy, such learning will have to include important groups within society.[14]

11. For these and other proposals to strengthen African exports, see Callaghy and Ravenhill, "How Hemmed In?" pp. 553–55.

12. Stephen R. Lewis, Jr., "Policymaking and Economic Performance: Botswana in Comparative Perspective," in Stephen John Stedman, ed., *Botswana: The Political Economy of Democratic Development* (Boulder, Colo.: Lynne Rienner Publishers, 1993), pp. 11–25. At a conference on South Africa's economy, Lewis emphasized that "when I hear economists and economic advisers say that the government won't do what the economists think is 'right' because of what they call 'political constraints,' I know the policy process has failed." See Stephen R. Lewis, Jr., "Conclusion: Conference Highlights," in Pauline H. Baker, Alex Boraine, and Warren Krafchik, eds., *South Africa and the World Economy in the 1990s* (Brookings, 1993), p. 251.

13. See, for instance, Callaghy and Ravenhill, eds., *Hemmed In*, passim.

14. Too often Western economists assume that groups in civil society, such as trade unions, will obstruct economic reform. Yet at a meeting in Harare, Zimbabwe, in May 1993, African trade unionists accepted the need for structural adjustment, but demanded "more direct involvement in the design and

These few recommendations could, if taken together, provide power-ful support for the creation of a new Southern Africa. But perspective is vital: the countries of the region are attempting to do in years what took centuries in Western Europe and the United States. There will be set-backs. Building strong responsive states, democracy, and market econ-omies will demand patience, consistency, and engagement from inter-national actors, and continued pragmatism and creativity from Southern Africans. Expecting all of these attributes to mesh properly at all times would be absurd; not aiming for them to come together at all at some point would be tragic. The old is dying, and the new need not be stillborn.

---

implementation of the painful economic measures." Andrew Meldrum, "Unions Want More Say in IMF Reforms," *Weekly Mail*, April 30–May 6, 1993, p. 26.

Guide to the Countries of Southern Africa

Angola (People's Republic of Angola)
Formerly under Portugal; independence: November 11, 1975
Botswana (Republic of Botswana)
Formerly Bechuanaland, under Great Britain; independence:
September 30, 1966
Lesotho (Kingdom of Lesotho)
Formerly Basutoland, under Great Britain; independence:
October 4, 1966
Malawi (Republic of Malawi)
Formerly Nyasaland, under Great Britain; independence:
July 6, 1964
Mozambique (Republic of Mozambique)
Formerly under Portugal; independence: June 25, 1975
Namibia (Republic of Namibia)
Formerly South West Africa, under Germany and South Africa;
independence: March 21, 1990
South Africa (Republic of South Africa)
Formerly Union of South Africa, under Great Britain;
independence: May 31, 1910
Swaziland (Kingdom of Swaziland)
Formerly under Great Britain; independence: September 6, 1968
Tanzania (United Republic of Tanzania)
Formerly Tanganyika and Zanzibar (merged on April 26, 1964),
under Germany and Great Britain; independence: December 9, 1961
(Tanganyika); December 9, 1963 (Zanzibar)
Zambia (Republic of Zambia)
Formerly Northern Rhodesia, under Great Britain; independence:
October 24, 1964
Zimbabwe (Republic of Zimbabwe)
Formerly Southern Rhodesia, under Great Britain; independence:
April 18, 1980

Index